This is the autob... ...y of the world's most well-known fan club president, Todd Slaughter, not through celebrity but because of his unforgettable name. His encounters with the rich and famous occurred - not that anyone wanted to meet him, but everyone wanted to talk about Elvis.

Conceived on the battlefields of Flanders (coastal Belgium) during WWII, adopted into poverty by loving parents, and growing up in the cosmopolitan East Midlands city of Leicester, this is the story of one man's determination to promote and preserve the legacy of Elvis Presley.

Todd's passion for Elvis is unquestionable. His achievements for Elvis, for the Official Elvis Presley Fan Club of Great Britain and its members are remarkable. His involvement with entertainment industry moguls is unbelievable.

Despite bad luck, bad health and bad people, Todd has survived to tell a remarkable story.

ELVIS AND MORE: THE SPOILS OF WAR

Published by Todd Slaughter

Jacket Artwork Jon Aldersea (Goldphone), and layout Neil Pickering (NA&C Consultants Ltd.)

ISBN – 9798550953389

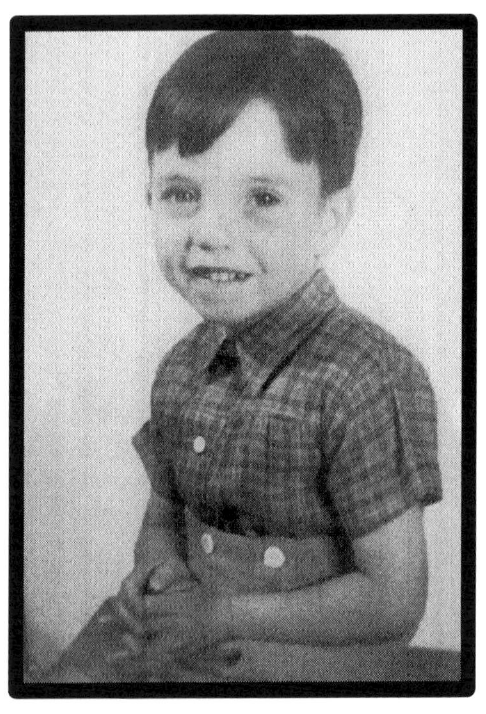

ELVIS AND MORE: THE SPOILS OF WAR

An Autobiography by Todd Slaughter

INTRODUCTION

I am proud to admit that Elvis Presley has dominated my life, but, having said that, not exclusively. I have other interests, fair-weather fads and fascinations. I have missed opportunities like most people, and as the years roll by the opportunity to revisit past hopes and dreams diminish. I hate my age.

Through my respect for Elvis Presley I have been able to do things most people can only dream about. I have been able to peep through from the outside into a world that is both magical and challenging. It is also a prohibitive environment where lack of talent is instantly visible. There is no room for a great pretender or a charlatan.

There had never been an artist like Elvis Presley. He was sculpted to perfection. His frame, his torso, his face, his gait, and his hands were flawless. Added to this mix of magnificence was his voice. Not any ordinary voice but a choral variety of human sounds that transmitted warmth, passion, spirit, soul and sexual gratification. A style to be admired, exalted, emulated, but never equalled. Copied by many, impersonated by thousands, but none ever coming close to Elvis' consummation of excellence. Yes, Elvis has dominated my life, and I am pleased that I have contributed to the preservation of his heritage in some small way.

For more than sixty years every pop star has stolen either a big chunk or a little inflection from Elvis and many are proud to admit capturing some of his wizardry. Yes, Elvis cast a spell on everyone who has a love for musical entertainment.

I never ever considered myself worthy of investing in a pair of blue suede shoes and a skin-tight leather outfit. My allegiance was to look, admire and watch with amazement as we all crawled towards his altar of perfection.

For me there was, and still is, life outside of my Elvis bubble. Throughout this autobiography, I tell you about my life, my family and my failures, at least some of them. I share my adventures, trials and tales as a nobody who attempts to make a difference. I have stumbled through bad luck, bad health and bad people to celebrate the rare successes and my love of life, despite those who dislike me. I cherish those who have cared for, loved and helped me

Todd Slaughter

Dedicated to: Ada and John Slaughter, Vikki, Gregory and Joanne, Geoff, Paula and Sophie, Juliet, Jennifer, Tom and Charlotte, Matt, Sally, Charlie and Margaret, together with my new found family the Gitshams, headed by my Auntie Sheila Lapthorn, Jenny and John McKay, Sue and Paul Marks with Gordon and Brenda Wilkinson and my birth mother Betty Doreen Gitsham.

Chapter One – My Emotions

It is the first time I have met anyone famous. Well, not quite.

I had a major crush on Brenda Lee, and she was a friend of Elvis Presley. Brenda was appearing on stage at the Birmingham Town Hall on 10th April 1962. I had to meet her, I just had to, so I wrote to promoter Don Arden (Sharon Osborne's father) who agreed to my request. Just before the end of her act, Don scooped me out of my seat and I watched her encore from the wings. As my beloved walked off stage, she fainted and I never realised my dream.

It is now August 1963 and I am backstage at the Aquarium Theatre in Great Yarmouth, talking with Helen Shapiro, little me, talking to Helen – not my Brenda, but chart-topping Helen Shapiro for heaven's sake!!! The compere I have come to meet is still on stage.

This outrageous radio DJ escorted me to his dressing room. In one corner was a "minder" someone not the full quid, in the other two Leicester girls known as "The Animals", and he, the star, dropped his trousers. No under-crackers! He washed his bollocks in the sink then put on a different pair of strides. So, this is show business!

In later years I have been in theatre dressing rooms when singers and dancers have disrobed for costume changes, but in 1963 I was only 17 years old and was not expecting the sight of his ginger nuts.

I was born on 3rd December 1945. My mum and dad were Ada and John Slaughter and we lived on the outskirts of Leicester. When I was a pre-school kid my mum would have home work delivered to our two-up two-down end terrace house. She painted dolls' faces. The smell of the paint was gorgeous, but, combined with the smoke from our coal fire, it stimulated my asthma. The only "reliever" in them-there-days was for me to find a recently creosoted telegraph pole and to inhale the vapours. Apparently, such madness can cause asthma and kidney failure, but for me it did the trick, however do not try this at home. When I was no longer an infant, I would dose up on ephedrine hydrochloride which I was able to buy across the counter from the local chemist.

My dad was a brickie, and immensely proud of his craft. He would often acknowledge that Churchill was a member of the Amalgamated Union of Bricklayers and that Winston was forever building walls around the garden of his Chartwell home in Kent. Dad would go to work on his pushbike in his overalls wearing a sports coat, shirt and tie. He was a humble gentleman, always laughing and singing but we were poor. As a child I wasn't aware of our poverty. It was only when I passed the 11-plus and went to a grammar school that I realised just how impoverished our family unit was in comparison with my scholarly pals.

My mum put me in nursery school in an attempt to get a proper job in a box making factory, but like the character Violet Elizabeth Bott, played by Bonnie Langford in the TV series *Just William,* I screamed and screamed and screamed. So, box making went out of the window, and in through the door came more dolls' faces.

I was a sickly, weedy child, often ill and always having asthma attacks. The highlight of my therapy was to go to the Leicester Isolation Hospital on Anstey Lane once a week and sit naked alongside other boys and girls in front of what appeared to be a former anti-aircraft searchlight. This practice was known as “sun ray treatment.” We all wore goggles then afterwards were immersed in a communal ice-cold bath of what could only be described as sheep dip. It tasted very salty – hardly Radox – no doubt a primitive muscle relaxant.

The winter of 1947 was one of Arctic proportions. The snow fell in January and didn’t thaw until March. Power stations failed to generate electricity, and coal couldn’t be delivered to keep the home fires burning. Manny Shinwell, the Minister of Fuel and Power, received death threats and had an around the clock military and police escort. People could not travel to work and as for bricklaying, carving out frozen cubes of snow to build an igloo was more the order of the day. For three months without pay or state aid we were starving, we were skint, we were sitting on the bones of our arses. Our little home in Leicester was a housing association property, so mum and dad had to sell their shares choosing to pay rent in the future in exchange for a few quid to be able to feed us. We lived next to a railway embankment so my dad would yomp through the snow-covered slopes to the railway track and glean the lumps of coal which had fallen from the firebox of the iconic “Master Cutler” steam train where it passed on its way to Sheffield. At weekends, being a “handy” flyweight, Dad would fight in boxing tournaments at the Belgrave Liberal Working Men’s Club for half a crown (12½p) hoping to win the prize purse of ten bob (50p).

When I was five, I started school at Stocking Farm Infants, which was a ten-minute walk from my home on Thurcaston Road via Belgrave Boulevard then up Halifax Drive. At the top of the hill was a field that led to Stocking Farm, a newly built council estate with a shop, a pub, a church and an infant and primary school. In the scorched earth field were remnants of a German Junker 88, a WWII bomber that had been shot down by anti-aircraft guns positioned to protect the City of Leicester. I walked to school every day with my next-door neighbour, Pat Cook, who was my age, her big sister, Janice, and Lesley Marris, a girl from a couple of doors away. The class numbered about 50 kids and we had an adorable teacher, Miss Mary Miller. She looked after year one from 9.00 until 4.00 every day. Each lunchtime we had school dinners cooked on the premises and they were "top-drawer". The following year it was the turn of Peter Scutt, a good-looking dude who I warmed too, that is until he married Mary Miller. Once a month throughout term time there was the obligatory testing of our air-raid siren when we all had to evacuate onto the playground and scan the skies for non-existent aircraft.

Although we had nowt, Christmas was magical, and this was the only time the family on my mum's side got together. (Dad's family lived in Norwich, so we saw them every summer when we holidayed in Great Yarmouth.) My Aunty Hilda, mum's sister, lived around the corner in Halifax Drive. Her husband Albert was a concert pianist who played at the Working Men's Club on Checketts Road and he would play Christmas Carols for the family. He was also competent on the trumpet and when Hilda had a "cob on", which was most of the time, he would pound the keyboard and blow a bugle with all his might. Happy times. The first time I ever saw jiving was at school Christmas parties. The teachers were young and it was certainly stockings and suspenders time as they jitterbugged around the classroom to *Rock Around the Clock.*

Like most families we didn't have a television until a couple of months before the coronation of Queen Elizabeth II. Prior to that, entertainment was delivered through the speaker of our battered Bakelite Bush radio. When I was very young it was *Listen with Mother*, two nursery rhymes and a story from Daphne Oxenford "Are you sitting comfortably? Then I'll begin." She went on to have big parts in *Coronation Street*, *To the Manor Born* and a handful of TV serial dramas. In the evening it was somewhat bland on the BBC so my dad used to tune in to the American Forces Network, and when we could get a good signal, Radio Luxembourg – at the time this was not a music station; it had more variety, quizzes and talent competitions. When commercial TV started in the mid-50s many of the team of 208 game show presenters took their ideas to ITV.

I was seven when Princess Elizabeth was crowned as Queen at Westminster Abbey. On BBC TV for the kids there was *Watch With Mother, Muffin the Mule, Andy Pandy* and *The Flower Pot Men*. Adult viewing in 1953 included *The Appleyards* (the first home-grown "soap"), *Panorama, The Quatermass Experiment, Animal Vegetable or Mineral*, a bit of tennis, and *BBC Television Newsreel.* It was very tame in comparison to what would be on offer a couple of years down the line when ITV beamed into our living room.

I was a bit of a clever clogs in junior school despite absences due to my poor health. My teacher, Peter Staniford, went that extra mile to ensure that I caught up on missed lessons. I had such a happy time at junior school, and it was no surprise that I passed the 11-plus examination enabling me to go to grammar school.

Next to my junior school stood St Luke's Church. Father Henry was the minister and this newly built C of E house of worship was outstanding in both design and the luxury of its internal pinewood finishings. The exterior was dominated by a dramatic statue of Jesus Christ. Although christened but not confirmed, I was anxious to join the church and become a chorister in the newly formed choir. I was unsure about my devotion to the Lord, but Father Henry welcomed me into the congregation and onto his team. I was fitted out with cassock, surplice and ruff and was happy singing at Sunday Morning Prayer, Holy Communion and Evensong for many months. We got thruppence for a funeral, and a tanner for a wedding, but best of all, after morning prayers, we enjoyed a parish breakfast in the vicarage served by his beautiful wife Ruth.

All was heavenly until one day during a parish fete the verger asked me to help carry a table into one of the tents. He exposed himself, and indecently assaulted me. I never returned to the church, and since that time I have no faith. Father Henry, bless him, came to see my dad asking why I was no longer attending services. My dad, knowing what had happened, but not wanting to upset the vicar, kept his council, and answered

"Brian is about to go to grammar school and will get loads of homework so he won't have time to continue in the choir". When he left, my dad sobbed. I missed the church and at times of need have ventured occasionally into a random holy house but left feeling empty.

"Brian" is about to go to grammar school. Yep, my given name is Brian, but I am known as Todd. Norman Carter Slaughter was an actor best known for playing over-the-top maniacs in macabre plays and films. *Maria Marten & The Red Barn Murders,* and *Sweeney Todd: The Demon Barber of Fleet Street* were two of the most well-known melodramas starring Norman Slaughter. In 1925, possibly due to the adopted persona of Sweeney Todd, his audience would call him Todd so he changed his name, boasting that he was the only actor on stage committing fifteen murders every day, and thirty when there was also a matinee performance. All my teachers at Alderman Newton's Boys School in Leicester were of an age that they were aware of the actor Tod Slaughter. Where every scholar was called by their surname by lecturers, I was addressed as "Todd" especially when I was being told to stop pissing about in class.

Alderman Newton's Boys' School in Leicester City Centre dates back to 1784, thanks to money bequeathed by a former Lord Mayor of Leicester, Gabriel Newton. Land at Greyfriars, acquired by the school in 1863, later proved to be the site of the friary church that contained the unmarked grave of King Richard III. As the school was next to Leicester Cathedral, when any dignitary or member of the Royal Family visited our city, selected pupils were expected to dress in stinky 18th century green-coated uniforms. Notable former pupils include author and scientist CP Snow, his younger brother test cricketer Philip Snow, who became the Governor of Fiji, and another sibling historian Eric Snow. Oh, and let's not forget Trevor Storer, the founder of Pukka Pies.

Our school was in competition with Wyggeston Grammar which also has its share of illustrious "old boys". Under the tutelage of their father Frederick, principle of University College in Leicester, his three sons have excelled in their careers; John Attenborough (head of Alfa Romeo UK), Lord Richard Attenborough (actor and producer), and Sir David Attenborough (naturalist, broadcaster, and former head of BBC2 television). Further down the pecking order, but still top of their game, are Tim Piggott-Smith (actor), Andrew Bailey (Governor of the Bank of England), Professor Brian Edward Carpenter (internet pioneer), Geoffrey Owen (head of BBC Radio and founder of BBC Radios One and Two), plus dozens of other luminaries. Still, they didn't have the baker who founded Pukka Pies, or a playground that for over 700 years concealed the mutilated remains of King Richard the Third.

Grammar School holds mixed emotions for me. I was terrified of some of the staff who were brutal both verbally and physically. Most teachers would carry a slipper in their brief cases to inflict pain for even the most minor of misdemeanours. A couple of masters had a piece of wood, or a broken chair-leg as part of their armoury. One sick old sod would administer punishment by paddling a pupil's arse whilst reciting:

Father heard his children scream,
So he threw them in the stream,
Saying as he drowned the third,
Children should be seen and not heard.
Mother's shrieks he could not bear,
So, he popped her in the Frigidaire.

Mr Topping with two fingers missing from his right hand, was a cruel bastard. He had a golf ball stitched into the wings of his gown which he would whirl around his head like a dervish before "twatting" some poor kid around the back of their head. One Christmas during assembly the golf ball wielding teacher attacked a Sixth Former, who, when reading the lesson, referred to the Three Kings' gifts to the baby Jesus as "gold, Frankenstein and myrrh." He picked the wrong kid that day. He was captain of the First Eleven Cricket Team and knocked out "Bomber" Topping with one punch.

My fellow pupils came from well-heeled families, whilst I was lucky to have two heels on my shoes reinforced with Blakey's segs. Being sons of restaurateurs, bank managers, business owners, company directors, writers and broadcasters, they all made me feel inadequate. These kids had foreign holidays, went on school skiing trips to St Moritz, and their parents were no doubt friends of the Aga Kahn and received racehorses for Christmas. I was on the outside peeking inside and feeling out of my depth. I had much difficulty keeping up with the diverse curriculum, and, intimidated by the ferocity of some of my teachers, I was reluctant to ask for help. I remember showing dad my maths homework when I was stumped, and he cried. As for geography, I couldn't ask my beautiful mum because she thought that the North Pole was cold, and the South Pole was hot. They were not illiterate or ignorant, just poorly educated, but they had great life skills, integrity and love in abundance. My dad had to pay one penny a week to go to school, and he had a slate to write on – no paper. They had a damp rag to clean their slate after lessons, and that is where the saying "wipe the slate clean" originated.

A school full of young boys was a magnet for the deviant teacher. Bert Howard was a well-known academic, head of our history department and regular broadcaster on the BBC. He was a rotund, scruffy individual with an oversized gown with pockets containing sweets for his favourite "sweeties". I hasten to add that I was not one of his brood. Dirty Berty would unfurl his gown around his prey and in return for as many sweets as their little hands could hold each was expected to pleasure his "secret place". Some boys would extract money from him when they engaged in activities in the flat that he shared with his brother who was of a similar persuasion. His fiddling was no secret, but he evaded the long arm of the law until the debauchery got out of hand during one of his "parties". He and his brother were about to be arrested when he was tipped off by an Old Newtonian "high up" in the Leicester Constabulary. Overnight they disappeared to Amsterdam and vanished without trace.

Hector ffenton Gaskell was our head who appeared strict but at the same time downtrodden by the cavalier behaviour of some of his staff. Many of my teachers had returned to the profession after WWII bringing with them both physical and mental battle scars. A couple had been flyers who were interned in POW camps. Hector reluctantly dispensed the cane, though a couple of the masters relished the opportunity not to spare the rod.

I was always "broke" and anxious to have a pocket full of ten-bob notes like my contemporaries, though I wasn't about to importune myself for a few quid from Dirty Berty and his chums. My interest focused on an out-of-bounds bibliothèque across the road from the school, but in line of sight of the headmaster's office. Leon's Lending Library had an ample selection of well-fingered back copies of *Spick & Span*. These saucy stocking-top and suspender "glamour" magazines featured the tantalising charms of Susan Douglas, who was also an actress, TV presenter and host of government safety infomercials shown in cinemas and by the BBC. These publications were not lurid, or pornographic, and could be rented from Mr Leon. In the back room there was a cornucopia of 8mm cinéma verité movies of Voluptuous Liz and Luscious Lucy, and books from the *Naked as Nature Intended* and *Nudes of the World* film producer Harrison Marks. Again, more "tit and bum" than porn. Under the counter was the "real-deal"- reserved for adult eyes only.

I suppose I was Leon's "agent provocateur", peddling soft porn to classmates too timid to enter the hallowed halls of his legendary lending library. It was a bit of a cloak and dagger adventure as Hector's office overlooked his emporium. I thought I had gotten away with my "tit trade" until one morning, with a satchel full of fun. I was confronted by the headmaster's secretary. To a 13 year old boy's eyes she was more glamorous than *Spick & Span's* Susan Douglas and my every sinew trembled as she pouted her Diana Dors' shaped lips. "Just be careful. I've been watching you, and so far Mr Gaskell hasn't seen you YET!" She smirked and winked and vanished. That lunchtime, I was about to make a furtive return to the bazaar of beauty when a nasty sprog grabbed hold of my satchel and threw it across the playground, possibly only a few feet above the decomposed remains of King Richard III. My stock of "Spick" spewed over the burial site. "Scraggs" went up the cry as eager kids gleaned my stock, and I was left with a school bag, empty except for a book of Common Prayer.

Being a weedy, sickly 13 year old lad without the proverbial pot to piss in, socially at school I wasn't part of the in-crowd. Attending an all-boys grammar there were only two ways to go and I was certainly not interested in going "the other way", though, if one had the inclination, there was an abundance of opportunities to "bat for the other side".

From a young age I can only remember playing with girls, as my mates lived the other side of Stocking Farm. Pat, next door, was the same age as me, and Janice, her sister, was five years older. Their mum was divorced, and in spite of attracting interest from several men, to her credit there was no scarlet lamp above her door. Mabel Cook was a good, care-worn, fastidious woman, struggling to look after two girls on little money, yet she was able to maintain a clean and tidy home. Janice, from the age of fourteen, was more than a "bit of a bugger". A cute, cheeky teenager who attracted the attention of the milkman, the butcher, the baker and the candlestick maker – make of the latter what you will. I may have only just turned seven at the beginning of 1953, but I was influenced by two main events in my life. Sweets had just come off ration and Janice was becoming curvy in all the right places. I fantasized that if she were still around when I was fourteen Jan would certainly occupy a prime place on my subs bench – she was a flirty thing. When I reached fourteen, she had flown the nest, but a "summer the first time" event happened that year which I will allude to later.

By 1953 radio had become my favourite toy. With one turn of the tuning knob I was in contact with the world. At an earlier age I had been introduced to Radio Luxembourg and AFN by my dad, and now I was able to search the ether for stations from afar. English language stations were a bit thin on the ground on medium wave, apart from transmissions from Radio Éireann in Dublin, Radio Luxembourg, and the British Forces Network, but short-wave broadcasts were global and sustainable providing it was dark and the weather was kind. Occasionally reception was good enough to capture sounds from the USA and Canada. By 1955 music was not so old-fartish and rock 'n' roll was seeping into our home. In 1956, when I was ten, Elvis came a rocking into my world. We had an old wind-up gramophone with shellac 78s, but Pat and Janice shared a record player with an auto-change that accommodated a stack of vinyl 45s. Elvis' voice was so different from any sound that I had experienced previously. Who was he, what was he, and where did he come from? I found nothing about him in the *Leicester Mercury, the Daily Sketch*, or the *News of the World*. Janice had some pictures she had clipped out of *Reveille*, but there were no stories in *Woman's Realm*.

One thing was for sure, *Heartbreak Hotel* was streets ahead of Bill Hayley's *Rock Around the Clock*.

My folks always managed to take me away for a week each summer and occasionally over bank holidays. One of my dad's brothers ran the Market Tavern in the centre of Norwich so we would doss down there if we couldn't afford "digs" in Great Yarmouth or Gorleston-on-Sea. My Uncle Reg and Auntie Leah lived in Norwich with their diminutive twin daughters, Jean and Gloria, and they would come to Great Yarmouth with us. When the weather was fine, we would be on the beach all day. More often than not it *pissed* it down, so we holed-up in the Holkham Pub next door to the *'musements.* The penny arcades were fabulous with slots which paid out a handful of pennies, a single damp cigarette, an often-stale Club chocolate biscuit or occasionally a naughty playing card. And there were flipper machines and a jukebox, I would spend hours in there with my cousins. If my dad won on the races, then it was a café meal for everyone. If it was a big win then it was a posh restaurant on Regent Road with free melba toast. On one occasion, we sat on tables adjacent to Lonnie Donegan and Des O'Connor. If there was no win, then it was mushy peas and mint sauce from the market. My Uncle Reg would always get drunk and one time he was so "steamed-up" that we had to take him back to the train station in the rain, draped over a borrowed pushchair. They were fun times.

We would go to end-of-the-pier shows, if we could afford it, to see comedians such as Arthur Askey, Max Wall or Tommy Cooper. I was walking along Marine Parade and coming towards me was Billy Fury and the tallest man I had ever seen. The big man was Marty Wilde who over the years has become a good friend.

By the late 50s and for most of the 60s it was all pop music acts. As well as Billy and Marty, I saw Joe Brown, Lonnie Donegan, Susan Maughan, Lulu, Johnny Kidd, Vince Eger, Gerry & The Pacemakers, The Searchers, The Swinging Blue Jeans, The Merseybeats, Manfred Mann, The Fortunes, and the Tornados. Pop music aristocracy, the Beatles, performed at the ABC Great Yarmouth.

(Almost all of these acts, except for the Beatles of course, have entertained our Elvis Presley Fan Club audiences, either in Great Yarmouth/Hemsby, or at our Elvis Conventions. Paul McCartney is rumoured to have visited in mufti during one of our week-long fan club bashes at Pontins Camber Sands in the Autumn of 1981.)

With shed loads of homework during term time, entertainment was limited to occasional visits to the Checketts Road Working Men's Club at weekends. WMC's in the Midlands and the North of England were amazing places. All over Leicester on Friday, Saturday and Sunday evenings these 1,000-seater concert halls were packed with families who were treated to a variety of entertainers, interspersed with a couple of games of bingo. The acts would range from wartime music hall comedians who were stars in the 40s, but surpassed by new television talent, to 60s bands waiting for their lucky break. Comedians, solo singers, female impersonators, magicians and strippers, made a good living going from club to club around the country. Local singers, Jerry Dorsey and Bill Maynard, would tread the boards across the county before becoming mega stars - Jerry being Engelbert Humperdinck, and Bill one of this country's finest character and comedy actors.

Cockles, whelks, oysters and shrimps were purchased from a basket carried by a seafood seller who would follow in the footsteps of the glass "snatchers". They gathered up the empties which were returned to the back of the fifty-foot long bar, dipped into water and reused in an instant. You could bring your own food if you preferred, but not fish and chips because they would "stink the place out". You could, however, scoff on hot boiled potatoes draped in Colemans, and steamed black pudding sold from a shitty little lean-to, built on the side of a terraced house near the club, which today would never ever pass health and safety or food hygiene regulations.

Going to school in the centre of Leicester was an adventure. My home city is vibrant, cultural and historically rich. Its existence can be traced back over two millennia, making it one of the oldest cities in England. An iron age settlement occupied by the Romans in 47AD, it served as a watering hole between Lincoln and Exeter along the old Fosse Way on the banks of the River Soar. The remains of Ratae Roman Baths *(Ratae being the Latin name of the settlement)* are within walking distance of the site of my old school. The baths are overlooked by a Holiday Inn, the first hotel in the UK opened by the Memphis-based chain.

When Sam Phillips sold his Elvis Sun Records contract to RCA in 1955 for $40,000, he gave $5,000 to Elvis, and invested the rest in a local lodging firm which needed a few bucks to expand. That investment was extremely shrewd because that business became the Holiday Inn Corporation.

Leicester is the county town of Leicestershire and has a renowned reputation for quirky food production statistics. The Walkers' crisp factory produces a staggering ten million packets each day. The Walkers Pork Pie Company produces 3 million pies each week, well ahead of Pukka Pies who bake a modest 50 million every year. Cofresh, Sara and Geeta's brands produce ethnic snacks and food items for export around the world, and fromage fans love Blue Stilton and Red Leicester. All can be washed down with a pint of Everards beer (incidentally the name of the imaginary friend of local comedian Larry Grayson). And if you want a tingle fresh mouth Fox's Glacier Mints are a Leicester favourite.

M & S knickers and bras were made in Leicester by Corah which had statues of St Michael and St Margaret outside their factory. There was also a reproduction of New York's Statue of Liberty perched on top of the Liberty Shoe Factory. Adorning the clock tower in the city centre there is a statue of the founder of my school, Gabriel Newton, along with Simon De Montfort, Thomas White and William Wyggeston. And finally, next to Leicester Railway Station, we have a bronze likeness of Thomas Cook, the founder of the now defunct travel agency empire. His first trip was an open topped train ride from Leicester to Loughborough for the local Temperance Society.

In the analogue days, if you went into any BBC radio or television studio, the clock on the wall was made by Gents of Leicester. Their electric clocks could be found in railway stations and public buildings around the world, particularly in India. The trading name still survives but there is no time for clocks, now it is a business of fire alarms and security equipment. The most famous brand of typewriter was made in Leicester, though after 1975 the Imperial Typewriter Company ceased trading. No British pop and rock band could be seen without a Premier drum kit. Amongst the great and good with a kit: The Who, Genesis, Iron Maiden, Jimi Hendrix Experience, Radiohead, Style Council, Hollies, Rage Against the Machine, Massive Attack, Blondie and The Beatles. Not forgetting Bostik glue because "I'm stuck on you", and Mazda Lights that stay brighter longer.

Leicester City Football Club, Leicester Tigers Rugby Football Club and Leicestershire Country Cricket Club are amongst the nation's most successful clubs, and let's not forget the World's most respected fan club - the Official Elvis Presley Fan Club of Great Britain, which I based in Leicester from August 1967 for almost 40 years, before being re-located in Staffordshire.

Not being able to enter the Sixth Form for financial reasons, like many others when reaching 16 and awaiting my GCE results, I had to decide what career path to take. Being a feeble, weedy guy I wasn't destined for a factory or a building site, so it was either office work or something practical. There was no *Holby City* or *Casualty* on the telly but there was *Emergency Ward 10* on BBC TV. This weekly TV series enjoyed a variety of A-list actors including Charles Tingwell, Desmond Carrington, Joanna Lumley, John Alderton, Jane Rossington, Peter Barkworth, Dandy Nicholls, and my favourite squeeze,

Jill Browne, who played the part of Nurse Carole Young (I still have the autographed picture she sent to me). If all the nurses looked as good as Jill Browne then a hospital job seemed exciting. I couldn't be a doctor or nurse but radiography appealed. The interview at Leicester Royal Infirmary went well. The job was mine subject to exam predictions which were to be supplied by the school. My school exam invigilator calculated that I wouldn't pass the necessary Physics GCE, so the hospital offer was withdrawn. I ended up working for Leicester City Council, and guess what? I got 82% in my Physics exam. Bollocks!

Chapter Two – Work Work Busy Busy Bang Bang

After an induction course which included visits to Rotherby Nurseries to see the delights of flora and fauna (plants and farm animals) and City Farms (the poo processing plant), my first day in the Leicester Town Hall as a worker involved being assigned to a department. I had GCEs in Technical Drawing and Mathematics, so I was despatched to Leicester Water in Bowling Green Street. The head office was located behind the beautiful Town Hall Square, with a central feature of an ornate bronze coloured cast iron fountain, with a lion on each quadrant, spewing forth gallons of water. At least once a month, Saturday evening revellers would empty bottles of Fairy Liquid into the base producing enough bubbles to put a foam party to shame.

I never had a Saturday job, so the Water Board was my first experience of any paid work except for when I was a choir boy. My weekly remuneration was two pounds thirteen shillings and five pence. Girls who lived nearby were earning ten pounds doing piecework in hosiery factories. After paying my folks for board and lodging I was left with two little quidlets. Having embraced pop music for years and being fascinated by Elvis Presley, I was able to buy an Elvis and Brenda Lee LP every other month from the record stall on Leicester Market, and an "oakie" from Eric's Ice Cream kiosk. Every week I wouldn't miss the *NME* and *Disc* pop music papers, and *Elvis Monthly* when I spotted it on the magazine shelves. I would never have guessed that in the future I would own that title and buy the fan club from publisher Albert Hand. I listened religiously to Luxembourg each evening and, whilst getting ready for work in the morning, the Dutch language Radio Luxembourg service also broadcasting on 208 metres on medium wave. Great pop music, especially American acts, punctuated by the odd “cloggie” Cliff cover.

I was in an office with men, all of whom were re-living the horrors of WWII. One emaciated poor sod, with sunken cheeks, had been a Japanese prisoner of war who slaved away building the Burma Railway as depicted in the movie *Bridge over the River Kwai.* There were girls too - two or three years older than me.

I had three tasks. Every Monday I would stand in reception to log complaints from housewives who would appear with jam jars full of *Asellus aquaticus,* a transparent freshwater crustacean resembling a woodlouse. It is known by common names including “tap water shrimp”, "waterlouse", "aquatic sowbug" and "water hoglouse”. “*Monday is washing day, is everybody happy?”* You bet your life they weren’t.

Job two was issuing PUSWA notices to the gas board and electricity suppliers. The Public Utilities and Street Works Act notices were mandatory alerts prior to digging up a road or footpath to fix, amend and install additional water services for existing customers and new-builds. Not overly exciting until one day our gangers cut through the hot line between the White House and the Kremlin. Shit hit the fan big time with the army, MI5 and the police storming up the A6 to arrest everyone. As this vital link between the super-powers was top secret nobody in Whitehall had thought to tell us where it was, so our lovely Irish navvy chopped it in half with a shovel and a pick and a rhubarb stick.

The third job was a clandestine operation. Office manager, Frank Turner, had one bad leg, ravaged by polio, and a wooden leg replacing a limb amputated following a motorbike accident. Frank was the fishing correspondent for both the *Leicester Mercury* and its competitor the *Leicester Mail* – he wrote under a pseudonym for the *Mail.* Every Thursday I would visit the editors of both newspapers with his articles and on the way back I would pick up 5lbs of bloodworms and a similar weight of maggots.

By 1957 the Russians were ahead in the Space Race and launched Sputnik, the first satellite to orbit the earth. At the end of the year Sputnik Two carried a live payload, a dog called Laika which perished during the flight. Man's first space flight occurred in April 1961 when Soviet Air Force pilot and cosmonaut, Yuri Gagarin, orbited the earth in Vostok 1. The following month a Freedom 7 Spacecraft put America's Alan Shepard into space.

For me, the launch of Telstar on 10th July 1962 captivated my imagination. Telstar was an orbiting satellite which transferred television and telephonic signals from the USA to Europe during a 22-minute window when the space vehicle was in line-of-sight of the transmitting and receiving stations on earth. The satellite could be tracked for transmission every two and a half hours. Telstar carried live TV news reports to and from the USA but nothing of entertainment value. I came up with a suggestion which would enable Elvis to appear on British television live from the US with the pictures delivered by Telstar. It was a project that dominated my every waking hour when I was not at work. News of President Kennedy's assassination on 22nd November 1963 in Dallas, Texas was relayed to the BBC via Telstar. The satellite carried live information from the USA including things we had never seen before – commercials.

Telstar was an orbiting satellite. The next challenge was to position a communications satellite in space so that it would travel at the same speed as the rotation of the earth. A geostationary satellite would then link Europe to the USA and vice versa 24 hours a day. Scientists around the world were experiencing immense difficulties in understanding the associated maths, but a Brit, Arthur C Clarke, science fiction writer, science correspondent, futurist, inventor, undersea explorer, and television series host came to the rescue. He computed that the optimum position was 22,236 miles above the equator – subsequently known as The Clarke Belt. Arthur wrote the book and screenplay for the 1966 motion picture *2001: A Space Odyssey*. The theme tune for the film, *Also sprach Zarathustra,* composed in 1896 by Richard Strauss, was the opening piece played as Elvis Presley walked onto the Las Vegas Hilton Hotel stage.

Telstar captured the imagination of record producer Joe Meek who composed an instrumental of the same name for Billy Fury's backing band The Tornados. It was so innovative, weird and haunting that the single sold 5 million copies worldwide topping the UK charts. The Tornados became the first British group to take top spot in the American Billboard Hot 100. (It wasn't however the first British instrumental to top the American charts. That accolade was achieved a month earlier by Mr Acker Bilk with his clarinet solo of *Stranger on the Shore*).

The publicity from my "Elvis Via Telstar" concept would soon be opening show business doors, and whilst I was on the outside of this fabulous industry, it gave me a glimpse of the inside together with the opportunity to sample and experience some of the delights and horrors of the world of entertainment. I was able to meet movers and shakers, the rich and the famous together with a cornucopia of celebrities and ten years later, Elvis Presley himself.

I was eventually drafted away from the mundane PUSWA form filling onto the engineering draft board. I was now officially a draftsman, planning when and where water mains and new domestic services would be installed underground. It sounded unreal that I could decide on which side of the road a water main would be buried, but I had the power. OK, ok, I'll admit it – it was easy, and pretty soon it was more mundane than the PUSWA notices. One advantage was sitting next to the mini-skirted Sheena who was truly blessed with legs that went all the way up to her armpits.

I wrote letters about my "Elvis Via Telstar" campaign in *Elvis Monthly, Pop Weekly*, *NME* and *Disc*. I'm sure many of my mates thought that I was a bit "tapped" spending all my spare time and money writing to everyone in the media, but I was on a mission. The idea was even announced on the *Teen & Twenty Disc Club* shows on Radio Luxembourg. As a result, I started to receive daily bundles of mail from Elvis fans anxious to get involved, so we launched a petition for Colonel Parker to consider the opportunity.

RCA product was distributed in the UK by the Decca Record Company, and my suggestion was having such an impact in the business press that in April 1963 I was invited to the director's dining room in Decca House, overlooking the River Thames at 9 Albert Embankment, London SE1. I was there to meet the big boss man of the company, Sir Edward Lewis no less. Unofficially, Sir Edward said that he could not get involved because Decca was a licensee of RCA product, but he suggested that I keep knocking on the door of Radio Luxembourg as it was an international broadcaster across Europe.

Decca's sponsored radio programmes on 208 were hosted by an eccentric Yorkshireman called Jimmy Savile. This new, not quite so young kid on the block quickly established himself as one of the big four DJs on British radio, the others being Alan Freeman, Pete Murray and David Jacobs. Recorded music on the BBC was limited to a couple of hours each day spread across their three networks - the Home Service (mostly talk), the Third Programme (Classical music), and the Light Programme (entertainment). Pop music could only be heard on the Light Programme for one hour each day during the morning show *Housewives Choice* hosted by Desmond Carrington, an actor from BBC TVs *Emergency Ward Ten*. At the weekend, there was *Two Way Family Favourites*, another request show linking service men and women with their families back home via the British Forces Network studios in Hamburg, West Germany. Jean Metcalfe anchored the programme from Broadcasting House in London, and former Squadron Leader Arthur Clifford (Cliff) Michelmore read out the requests in Germany. There were no other radio service operators in the UK, so evening broadcasts from the Grand Duchy of Luxembourg were the only alternative source of a dedicated English language radio station.

Still holidaying each summer in Great Yarmouth, I was pleased to see that Jimmy Savile was the compere of the Helen Shapiro show at the Royal Aquarium. He had met Elvis in January 1961 when he was introduced to him by Colonel Parker on the 20th Century Fox set of *Wild in the Country*. Jimmy was there to present Elvis with a Gold Disc for a million UK sales of *It's Now or Never,* and came back with a picture of himself with Elvis which he sold on air with the proceeds going to the Duke of Edinburgh's Playing Fields Association. Savile bragged "He was a bit impressed with the style of it, and me and the Duke have been pals ever since."

Sharing fish and chips with Helen Shapiro, joking around with Ronnie Corbett, and having basic tap-dancing lessons from Roy Castle, I was living the dream. I was there every afternoon and evening for a whole week, getting to know Jimmy Savile and talking "Elvis via Telstar" at every opportunity, punctuated by seeing him soaping his nuts in the sink, sucking ferociously on Bassett's Sherbet Fountains, eating tinned prawns and clamping a Castella between his yellowing teeth – "as it 'appens."

Weeks later I was knocking at the door of 38 Hertford Street and mixing with the doyens of commercial radio. On my first trip to London to see Jimmy record his programme, I took my mum. In Studio A, with her son, was Agnes Savile who he referred to as the "Duchess". Savile presented his show sitting at a grand piano. A mike on a boom, dangling above the keyboard lid, was positioned by studio engineer Alan Bailey. The top of the piano was covered in fan mail with requests for a dedication and always a postal order for membership of the Teen and Twenty Disc Club. Gals got a bracelet with a TTDC charm, and guys a necklace with a medallion – the same size as the charm. Everyone had a membership card. My number was 45204, and Elvis Presley was member number 11321. My mum and Jimmy's got on very well, and they both went into a back room to make a cuppa, as the "Hi there guys and gals" presenter started. "F***ing brilliant move Doctor Todd bringing your mum. You've gone up in my estimation. Next time come down on your todd – you can help." I replied, "Why is there a job?" "Yes, cleaning the bogs – you 'ave to start at the bottom and as it 'appens there's a lot of arseholes here use that crapper."

Sitting in on recordings of the TTDC, rubbing shoulders with 208 station manager Geoffrey Everett, who topped and tailed the Horace Batchelor football pools adverts, and meeting Pete Murray, Alan Freeman and David Jacobs – who wouldn't want to work for Radio Luxembourg in the early 60s? I thought that I might bore everyone rigid talking about "Elvis via Telstar", but, unless they were being extremely polite, my utterings appeared to be attracting great interest. The fact is everyone wanted to talk about Elvis Presley. Elvis was not only the most prolific vocalist of all time but he was also both an icon and a curio.

Going back to work, proper work, was tedious, and the obligatory night school classes about local government practice were a nightmare. I needed to move on. Even the delights of Sheena, the long-legged girl with the short dress on, Barbara in the typing pool, and Fay on the front desk, were not temptation enough for me to stay, not even for just a little bit longer. I left my chums at the water works and off I went to that old mill by the stream - British Steam.

I was working now within the cogs of industry. British Steam Specialties (BSS) was the UK's leading supplier of pipeline equipment and, by luck more than judgement, I appeared to be fast tracked from the drawing board into the factory, on to marketing, next into promotion and then sales. It was a fun place with great people and my career path was developing rapidly, but I hated the work. I was a charlatan. I went on block release to Leicester College to get an engineering diploma, and management trusted me with research and development. But, to my shame, I didn't understand a bloody thing that I was doing. I was sent to Belfast at the height of the Troubles. I attended conferences and exhibitions in Paris and Brussels. I dined with one of the directors of Saab in Stockholm, and I scurried around the shipyards of Trieste and Genoa to locate and replace faulty equipment with a hairy-arsed fitter who spent all our expenses getting shags in brothels on both sides of the Italian coast.

Being on the road so much I was able to set my own agenda, satisfying the demands of my employer, whilst at the same time dovetailing my Elvis meetings up and down the country. BSS did get a pound of flesh in return for my salary. My company travel expenses enabled me to get to Elvis appointments at no cost. My overnight stays for business cost the firm nothing as I was always dossing down with my Elvis friends, both in the UK and overseas. I walked a tightrope, occasionally being spotted dancing in the audience of *Top of the Pops*. One time, when visiting our Glasgow office, I was seen on Scottish Television, sitting next to Marty Wilde as a guest on a chat show.

When I was overnighting in the "smoke" I would stay at the Aaland Hotel in Coram Street, Bloomsbury. Jimmy Savile had the biggest room there for seventeen bob a night (17/-). The room I used was twelve and a tanner (12/6d) including breakfast. There was another B& B, the Adrian around the corner in Hunter Street, which was owned by the same woman. If I was in town for BSS I could have stayed in much more palatial accommodation, but the Aaland was a great base.

If Savile wasn't there, I could use his room. It reeked of cigar smoke and there were columns of Coca Cola cans in crates covering an entire wall. It had no bathroom but it did benefit from a cock-high sink. Curiosity got the better of me and, rooting through papers, books and personal effects, I came across what could only be described as a framed wedding picture. It appeared to show an incredibly young Jimmy Savile in a tidy suit next to a pretty girl in a wedding dress.

As well as permanent residents, both hotels doubled up as theatrical digs and there were a few celebrities that I came across. Goldie & The Gingerbreads, The Hollies, and a boxing promoter Henry Henroid. He was representing an American DJ working for the English service of Radio Monte Carlo.

Tom Jones had earlier been to meet Joe Meek at his recording studio above a handbag shop on the Holloway Road. On his first visit Meek wouldn't see him. "He's come all the way from Wales" said his assistant Patrick Pink. The curt response was, "Well, he'll know the way back then!" Joe was eventually persuaded to record half a dozen songs that he peddled to various record companies without success. Hearing that Jimmy Savile was staying at the Aaland, Tom Jones arrived on the doorstep. He knew that the TTDC was a Decca show so he thought the DJ might be able to open the door for him. I didn't know the Welsh vocalist from Adam. No one did at that time and I sat with him in the lounge talking about "Elvis via Telstar" until Jimmy arrived. I never missed a chance to enlighten folk on my vision. Jimmy Savile offered to help Tom, taking a demo to Colin Bostock-Smith. *It's Not Unusual* topped the charts a year later. In his autobiography Tom Jones has said that although the name of Jimmy Savile is not to be brought up in polite conversation he also adds, "It would be churlish of me not to acknowledge the help that Jimmy did for me to get me a recording contract with Decca." I must endorse Tom's sentiment. The help that Jimmy Savile gave to me, to the Elvis Presley Fan Club and to Elvis cannot be ignored. At my invitation Jimmy was a surprise guest at the London Elvis Presley Appreciation event on 10th January 1965, and again at our Elvis Week at Pontins to receive a cheque for £35,000 raised by the fan club for the Stoke Mandeville Hospital Appeal. That said, his lurid behaviour which came to light after his death sadly tarnished the legacy of the British Pop Music industry.

Jimmy was based in both Leeds and Manchester. Whilst still managing Mecca Ballrooms, he travelled to London every Thursday to record his Radio Luxembourg show in the Hertford Street studios, produced by Alan Bailey. In his time at 208 Alan recorded sessions with Marty Wilde, Billy Fury, Cliff Richard and the Beatles – he was one of the most respected studio managers in British broadcasting.

Savile often had American guests and on occasion when he knew he would be late, and with all his people based up north, he would ask me to travel from Leicester to London to meet them at Radio Luxembourg prior to his arrival. I would get them some "scran" at the caff in Shepherds Market. "Get a second-class ticket, sit in the first-class diner and have breakfast. Eat slowly and you travel first class for free."

Sonny and Cher arrived from Los Angeles and were booked into the Hyde Park Hilton, a two-minute cock-stride to Hertford Street. They were not allowed into the four-star dining room for breakfast because they were dressed like a pair of prats. I took them to a nearby greasy spoon and ordered a "full English" - pork sausage, bacon, eggs, black pudding, tomatoes and toast. As their food arrived, smoke and flames billowed out of the kitchen and we had to vacate PDQ. Just as well as I hadn't known that they were Jewish. We went back to the Hilton to get their clobber, as an accompanying TV producer suggested that they perform their new single outside of the hotel entrance, capitalising on the publicity of their eviction. I had to hold a battery-operated record player as Savile arrived, took off his shirt and cavorted around as Sonny and Cher lip-synced to their hit *I Got You Babe* for CBS TV news.

Ike and Tina Turner were my next charges to feed. They had no religious dietary issues and Ike gobbled down the lot, speaking at the same time and discharging bits of toast with his loud excitable dialogue. He told me how Elvis would sneak in to watch their shows from the wings in clubs in Beale Street, Memphis. Tina said nothing. Ike baffled the server by asking if they had any grits, and to be honest he had no idea what Telstar was. Ike hadn't heard that the tune of the same name, recorded by the Tornados on Decca, had topped the Billboard Hot 100 Stateside.

The BBC launched *Top of the Pops* and it was initially broadcast from an old church in Manchester. Jimmy Savile presented the first show which featured Dusty Springfield with *I Only Want to Be with You*, the Rolling Stones with *I Wanna Be Your Man,* the Dave Clark Five's *Glad All Over*, the Hollies *Stay,* the Swinging Blue Jeans *Hippy Hippy Shake* and the Beatles *I Want to Hold Your Hand* - that week's number one. There was also a brief link to Alan Freeman in London to preview the following week's programme. Throughout its history the programme always, with very few exceptions, finished with that week's chart topper. Three weeks later I was with Savile as he was the "brief link" from a church. We tied a rope around his ankles and he was suspended upside down with the rope draped over the rafters. Along with a female studio assistant I held the other end as he did his piece to camera announcing the stars appearing on the next edition. The studio assistant discreetly whispered in my ear, "We've made a mistake Todd, this rope should be 'round his f***ing neck!"

Jimmy Savile had the reputation of being a tightwad, someone who would skin a turd for a ha'penny and steal a penny knife to do it. He wasn't a person who would ask what your choice of meal might be, you had to eat the same as him. We went to dine in a scruffy Indian Restaurant yet the food was unexpectedly fantastic but his manner of ordering was somewhat obtuse. "We'll have two curried chicken, not babies' motions - the dry stuff, one rice to share and if that comes with free chapattis, we'll have two each." During the "snapping" he instructed me to find a club in Leicester. "We'll make it an all Elvis nightclub and you can run it. All the pineapples you can handle. I'll come and open it. Come to Manchester, I'll show you how it operates. You can kip at my place."

I arrived at Manchester Piccadilly, and there he was waiting at the wheel of a Roller. I had never been in a Rolls Royce before so another dream experience. We drove to Denton and pulled up at a dilapidated overgrown mansion. It was a shit-hole. Inside there was a huge lounge with a couple of double beds, two bedrooms, a bathroom and a separate bog. It was all painted black a la Rolling Stones. It was damp, dank and dismal, with only one electric light. Within an hour a few guys arrived. David the Judge (a real Rinder), "Ugli" Ray Teret (a DJ now doing time), Dave The Rave (a DJ cum lacky), a Detective Inspector, and a couple more high-ranking members of Manchester Constabulary. A lot of guffawing and innuendoes ensued, and then in came the girls, accompanied by another guy with bags of chips. I was daft enough to enquire where I might be sleeping, and was told by Teret, "In the bath".

It wasn't long before the fumes of fornication filled the air. The girls were in their late teens, certainly legal, but not in their twenties. I felt a child amongst men but, being only just 18 myself, I thought it was nothing more than the spoils of showbusiness fame, and I wasn't about to judge, even though there was a judge in the house. At this point there was no hint or rumour of paedophilia.

That evening, with a change of car, we went to see his nightclub. It was a dingy dive, The Three Coins in Fountain Street. On the way we drove slowly past the queue of fans waiting to see the Stones at the Opera House. With the top down on his white E-Type, I had to hold the steering wheel whilst he flailed his arms around letting rip with his trademark "ahhh – a – ahhh – a – ahhh" throated yodel in the direction of the queuing "pineapple chunks".

We met Danny Betesh, boss of one of the country's largest entertainment agencies - Kennedy Street Enterprises. At the time Danny had finished working for Mecca Ballrooms and had signed up Herman's Hermits, Freddie & The Dreamers and Wayne Fontana. I spoke about "Elvis via Telstar" and he seemed curious, but not in funding an Elvis Night Club in Leicester. I looked around the club, used the unisex bog where girls were popping pills, but I was more staggered by the environmental brutality of the gaff. Then, it was back to the "black pad".

Plod had reconvened and the Denton den of debauchery continued with a new flock of birds expected to arrive at any moment. I was knackered – I needed to sleep. "You share that bed Doctor Todd - with the fat bird – not a bad f*** as it 'appens." I grabbed a bundle of previously used blankets and like the classic line from the News of the World reporter,

"At this point I left the building." I followed Teret's suggestion and kipped in the bath. Thank goodness it wasn't going to be used as a pissoir. The crapper had its own cubicle.

I needed a bath, but the bloody thing didn't work, so it was a whore's wash in the sink. Breakfast was at a taxi rank in the centre of Manchester, then in the afternoon we went to Belle Vue Zoo as Jimmy was going to fight wrestler Gentleman Jim Lewis later that day. I then had the honour of accompanying *Coronation Street* actress Pat Phoenix (Elsie Tanner) to her seat ringside. In the evening it was back to the Elizabethan Ballroom in the zoo for the biggest disco ever, as 2,000 pop fans danced to the top tunes of the time spun by Savile. The weekly event was billed as the *Top Ten Club.*

Then it was back to reality. Once again Jimmy drove me to Piccadilly Station in Manchester for my return journey to Leicester, not in the Roller, not in the Jaguar E-Type, but this time in his BMW Bubble Car.

On my second stay at the "black pad" I had the use of a bedroom but was told to stay behind closed doors when a Monseigneur of Catholic persuasion appeared to give "communion" to the fallen. Being driven around Manchester in his Rolls Royce in the thick of night, to the sound of Dionne Warwick singing *Walk On By* from 208 was somewhat poignant. Jimmy was aware that Elvis fans were loyal to those who supported the King, and knowing that they could vote him the number one DJ in the music paper polls, I guess associating with me was advantageous.

In 1965 I met up with Savile's nephew Roger Foster. He had come to London to accompany his uncle who was compering the NME Poll Winners Concert in Wembley Pool Arena. Roger had dyed his hair blond which Jimmy had taken exception to. Tugging at his own hair he said to young Rog, "these are my working-clothes" and slapped his face. "I don't want f***ing earache off your dad for what you've done to your barnet". We drove to the venue in silence and as the rear gates opened we were backstage with The Beatles, The Stones, The Animals, Donovan, Twinkle, Dusty, Tom Jones and dozens of others. As Savile announced the acts with Keith Fordyce, I spent much of the afternoon talking to the adorable Cathy McGowan who was co-host with Keith on the best music TV show *Ready Steady Go!* She introduced me to Elkan Allen, the producer of Associated Rediffusion's RSG, and we met up for lunch to discuss Elvis Via Telstar. I had been in contact with ABC Television in New York and the seeds of the idea appeared to be taking root. Parker had said to Savile on the set of *Roustabout,* when presented with our petition, that he would think about it although at that time, he joked, he had no representation of Elvis on the moon.

(We took our first members' group to see Elvis in Vegas in the summer of 1972, when Colonel Parker and Elvis simultaneously announced that he was to do a satellite show from Hawaii in January 1973. Game, set, and match).

Chapter Three – Tune In And Turn On

In 1913 Michael Joseph O'Rahilly was a founding member of the Irish Volunteers, who were negotiating with the British for Irish independence. He learnt that there was going to be an uprising on Easter Monday, 24th April 1916 and, despite his efforts to prevent the skirmish, he joined his friends in the Volunteers. They were garrisoned at the General Post Office in central Dublin during Easter Week. On Friday 28th April the fighting between the volunteers and the British Army intensified. A British machine-gun at the intersection of Great Britain and Moore streets shot him and several of the others. "The O'Rahilly", as he was known, slumped into a doorway on Moore Street, wounded and bleeding badly but, on hearing the English marking his position, made a dash across the road to find shelter in Sackville Lane (now O'Rahilly Parade). He was wounded diagonally from shoulder to hip by sustained fire from the machine-gunner. Even after surrender Michael was left bleeding for 19 hours until he died. Michael O'Rahilly's grandson was named Ronan, and his parents purchased from British Railways a deep water port and dock in Greenore village on Carlingford Lough, County Louth.

Ronan O'Rahilly ran the Scene, a club in London's Soho district and managed a handful of pop music artists, including Georgie Fame and Alexis Korner. Ronan recorded a Georgie Fame track on his own independent label. Unable to get airtime for his acts on either the BBC or Radio Luxembourg, and encouraged by Scandinavian and Dutch pirates, in February 1964 O'Rahilly obtained the 702-ton former Danish passenger ferry, mv Fredericia. It was secretly converted into a radio ship in the family's Irish port. Greenore was isolated enough not to attract any attention from the authorities. Locals who questioned the transmitter tower were told it was an inverted periscope which would be lowered onto the seabed to detect the presence of oysters, jellyfish and octopuses.

Radio Caroline was funded largely by financier John Sheffield (great uncle of Samantha Cameron, wife of our former prime minister), Carl Ross (creator of the Ross fishery frozen food business and grandfather of David Ross, the co-founder of Carphone Warehouse), together with publisher Jocelyn Stevens (owner of the high-society magazine *Queen*).

On 28th March 1964, with their words having been pre-recorded since they were too nervous to broadcast live, Chris Moore and the then unknown actor Simon Dee announced, "This is Radio Caroline on 199, your all-day music station." Then the Rolling Stones record *Not Fade Away* was played and dedicated to Ronan O'Rahilly. Caroline was on the air! The monopolies of the BBC and Luxembourg were compromised, and UK radio was changed forever. When Radio Caroline's audience figures were calculated, it was evident that 12,000,000 listeners had deserted the BBC who were apoplectic. As a concession to Radio Luxembourg Caroline decided that they would initially only broadcast from 6.00am – 6.00pm leaving the evening audience to 208. I heard the station on its first day by accident, twiddling the knob on an early Pye transistor radio that my dad bought me for Christmas. Rediffusion, who operated one of the first radio and television cable systems in Leicester, carried

Caroline's programmes during the day on the channel that was dedicated to Radio Luxembourg each evening. Within two weeks the Post Office made the company remove the station.

In 1964 when the Beatles, Stones, Dave Clark, Cliff, and Dusty were dominating the charts, Elvis released three singles and only one, *Kissin' Cousins* made the top ten, in at number 10. The original Caroline DJs - Carl Conway, Simon Dee, Chris Moore, Doug Kerr, Gerry Duncan, and especially Tom Lodge, all included Elvis on their playlists mostly as Revived 45 play. The original jocks were former "resting" actors but as the months passed and the station amalgamated with Radio Atlanta there were changes. Tom Lodge took the Caroline ship to the Isle of Man with fellow presenter Jerry Leighton and this became Caroline North. The Mi Amigo ship, formerly Radio Atlanta, became Caroline South with Ken Evans becoming the land-based programme director for both stations. I met Tom Lodge when he visited the London studios of Radio Luxembourg after he had just returned to work on the South ship and sold him on the "Elvis Via Telstar" project. Tony Prince, who later became our honorary Elvis Presley Fan Club president, did the business for us on Radio Caroline North. These were amazing times. I had fantasized about working on Radio Caroline and I went out to the station with Tom Lodge a few times. On one occasion I was on the Mi Amigo to read the news. I was crap and lasted two days – once again I was a child amongst men.

If you've seen the Pathé newsreel from 1965, the piggy looking Dutch skipper of the tendering vessel Offshore One was a great character who would tune into the station on his journey from Harwich into the North Sea. On my very first visit to Radio Caroline I fondly remember hearing Herb Alpert's version of *Casino Royale* blasting across the waves of the North Sea over the boat's Tannoy. I can't summon up the words to describe my excitement that day. The Mi Amigo (Spanish: My Friend) was originally a three-masted cargo schooner that later gained international recognition as the most famous offshore radio station. She was built as the schooner Margarethe for German owners. A sale in 1927 saw her renamed Olga and she was lengthened in 1936. During the Second World War, she was requisitioned by the Kriegsmarine and served as an auxiliary ship for the German Navy between 1941 and 1943. In 1953, the ship was lengthened to 133 feet 9 inches (40.77 m). In 1959, she was sold for conversion to a floating radio station and was renamed Bon Jour. Subsequently, she was renamed Magda Maria in 1961 and Mi Amigo in 1962. She served intermittently as a radio ship until 1980, when she sank in a gale.

The food served on Caroline South was fantastic, and whilst on the Mi Amigo for a few days with Tom Lodge, Robbie Dale, Emperor Rosko, Rick Dane and DLT, when the ship's clock reached 7.30pm, they all gathered in the mess, not to plan their programmes but to watch *Coronation Street.* Here were the nation's greatest DJs, rock 'n' pop giants of the time obsessed with *Corrie*. Fabulous stuff.

Caroline's dominance of commercial radio was short lived. Just before Christmas 1964 the MV Galaxy appeared out of the mist. It was formerly a WWII American minesweeper. Like the other pirates it was a rust-bucket, but much sturdier and with a more powerful transmitter. It boasted the best station idents ever and an unbeatable programme formula. Wonderful Radio London was directed by Texan radio people who knew how a US Top 40 station clawed in an audience and made the listener feel part of the picture. It was a revolutionary radio experience for a UK audience, and we embraced both the professionalism and the characters who made up the broadcast team. Tony Blackburn and Keith Skues left Caroline, joining Tony Withers (now Windsor) from Radio Atlanta, together with other professionals from forces radio and the colonies. Different from Caroline, the Big L had news bulletins with Paul Kaye re-writing feeds from the BBC, ITN and the American Forces Network. It was not long before ships and old wartime forts dotted around the British Isles were pumping out pop music to an eager audience who celebrated the opportunity of now having a choice. Elvis fans were clamouring for each one to play more Elvis tracks and flooded the new stations with "Proud of Presley" request cards.

The British Government were anxious to close the dozen or so stations operating "offshore". They said that these broadcasters were interfering with other stations on the continent, that they were stealing music by not paying any royalties, and that their transmissions were causing danger to the coastguard emergency radio services. All of these claims were untrue, as too were their assertions that there was insufficient capacity to accommodate additional broadcasters. In the UK we now have 700 FM and 200 AM broadcasters operating from a total of 2,000 transmitter towers. The irony at the time was that the British government's trade associations were supporting the pirates by buying ads. Our police forces would ask the ships to broadcast SOS emergency messages to their huge audiences. A USAF pilot was rescued by the broadcast ships' tender crew when his plane crashed into the North Sea.

The pirates were hugely influential in sustaining interest in what we were doing as fans and maintained Elvis' position within the changing world of pop music. On my final trip back to land from Caroline I was the only passenger on the tender Offshore Two until we reached the MV Galaxy when newsreader Paul Kaye and DJ John Peel climbed aboard. The journey to Harwich and customs clearance took about 90 minutes. After we left the Radio London ship the skipper noticed that he had not unloaded a crate of 20 small bottles of Carlsburg. *"Gooi die krat in de zee - we zullen in de problemen zitten als ze dat aan boord zien als we in Engeland zijn"*. Paul Kaye did throw the crate of bottles into the sea as the captain had asked, but only after he had necked the contents of all of them. Paul died of liver failure in 1980 aged 46.

When the Marine Offences Act became law, it made it illegal for British advertisers to use the offshore stations. Pirate broadcasting ceased apart from the two Caroline stations which transferred their offices to Holland and continued to operate until their funding sources dried up.

The most successful DJs from the ships and forts either joined BBC Radio 1 (the network's new pop service) or went to the Grand Duchy to staff a re-vamped Radio Luxembourg.

In 1967, whilst still working for BSS, I bought the Official Elvis Presley Fan Club from Elvis Monthly publisher Albert Hand. I had freelanced for Albert's magazines for some time and he was very aware of my involvement in the UK Elvis Scene.

I acquired the world's most famous fan club at a time when Elvis' chart successes had diminished. Elvis' album sales, however, were buoyant, mostly because of the budget RCA Camden series which repackaged old tracks together with a handful of previously hidden movie soundtrack songs. Elvis Presley's films were no longer blockbusters, but each one still made a profit because of the continuing devotion of Elvis Fan Club members.

I rented office space in the Leicestershire village of Thrussington, and local Fan Club Branch Leader, Anne Knight, with her friend Barbara Pendle, dealt with the mail and subscription list. After Anne married, Barbara worked as a full-time staff member for many years at our Empire Road office in Leicester. Memberships were directed to our well-known PO Box 4 Leicester address.

All our DJ chums were now working for the BBC or 208 and they remembered the support that they received from Elvis' UK fans at the start of their broadcasting careers and were happy to support us. All I had to do was to tread water for a few months before amazing things in the Elvis World started to happen. I hosted my first Elvis radio show on BBC Radio

Leicester – the first local radio station to come on stream following the demise of the pirates. I might not have been broadcasting to millions of people all over the UK and the continent, but I was speaking to “the great incontinent” across the great East Midlands. Also in my favour was my daft name - Todd Slaughter – a name that was not easy to forget.

Chapter Four – How Can I Be Sure – In My World That's Constantly Changing?

On 13th August 1967 I helped Albert Hand organise what was to be his last Elvis Convention at the Nottingham Palais. Ballroom manager, Michael Knight, came from the Jimmy Savile stable of Mecca managers. The Mecca group was run by Eric Morley who was also responsible for the Miss World Contest. The annual show attracted 22 million viewers in the UK and was seen in countries around the world. When the domestic organisers in South Africa were told by the Government that only white women could enter the competition due to existing apartheid laws, Morley took on the politicians and won.

At our Nottingham event we had Radio Caroline programme director, Tom Lodge, who was leaving the station at midnight in advance of the Marine Offences Bill becoming law on 14th August, and DJ Robbie Dale who, along with Johnny Walker, was defying the law and going back out to sea. Tom told me I could go with them if I wanted, as they would be short staffed. I declined because on 16th August I took control of the World's most respected fan organisation - The Official Elvis Presley Fan Club of Great Britain. Nottingham club DJ Stevie Merrick joined the rebel broadcasting lawbreakers.

Superfan and avid collector Ian Bailye had been to Memphis some years before with his wife Pat in an attempt to meet Elvis. Gary Pepper, a great friend of Elvis, ran the Tankers Elvis Presley Fan Club. Gary suffered from cerebral palsy and, although our main man was in Hollywood, Gary contacted Vernon

Presley and he gave Ian some of Elvis' clothing. From the outset Ian joined me running the fan club and for many years operated his own Vintage Elvis Club. Together we travelled around the country with his mobile DJ and movie equipment helping local branches with their entertainment programmes. Bob Bacon, his brother Andy and his family also helped with Conventions and our holiday functions in Great Yarmouth.

On 21st July 1968 the first Elvis Presley Fan Club convention was held at the De Montfort Hall in Leicester. We had a bevy of DJs including Tommy Vance, Johnny Moran (Scene & Heard), Tony Prince and Peter Aldersley. Emperor Rosko broadcast the first Radio 1 Roadshow from the event. (Mike Pasternak had to get special permission from the Beth Din to broadcast as our event coincided with Yom Kippur). Rosko is the son of late MGM film producer Joe Pasternak who directed two of Elvis' MGM movies. Chart topper, Anita Harris, was a surprise guest, and there was a special screening of *King Creole*. Live entertainment was from Dave Kaye & The Dykons, a Heanor band managed by Elvis Monthly editor, Albert Hand, who also spoke about his meeting with Elvis, and from the Playboy Club in London the Buddy Loren Band accompanied by three Bunny Girl Dancers. As a side note British Elvis fan Winifred Innes and her husband, whilst on a trip to Hollywood, managed to get tickets to see the recording of the *1968 Special* at the NBC studios in Burbank. Outside the venue they bumped into Elvis and he and Priscilla signed their Leicester Convention tickets which were sold recently at an auction at Christies for £1,188. The publicity that the Fan Club enjoyed following our successful events swelled our membership and our Empire Road office was buzzing with activities and visitors from around the world.

I had started seriously to date a beautiful Scottish girl, Vikki Allardyce, so I wasn't about to run away to sea. I often wonder what would have happened had I joined the Caroline crew. When we married, we honeymooned in Luxembourg with Tony Prince and Paul Burnett. An unconventional start to our life together visiting the Blow-Up nightclub with the 208 team and incurring the wrath of newsreader Paul Kaye who had joined the station after leaving Wonderful Radio London. We also spent some time in Brussels with Marie du Bois de Vroylande who edited *Elvis Mensuel* (the French language version of Elvis Monthly distributed in Belgium, France and Canada). Marie was also the cookery editor of *Femmes d'Aujourd'hui*, a French language women's weekly published in Mechelen, Belgium. Founded in 1933, it is one of the oldest magazines in the country and the premier Belgian women's magazine. In the roof of her apartment she and her mother hid British airman and Jewish families out of sight of the Gestapo during WWII.

We started our married life in a rented flat on the Upperton Road, and like most couples scrimped and saved for a deposit to buy our own house. We ended up with a semi in Oadby, South Leicester. Opposite was Invicta Plastics, a factory that manufactured Mastermind, an all plastic peg board game that sold worldwide in millions. Vikki worked for Invicta for a while and I continued to travel to Leicester each day to *do the do* at British Steam.

What has made this Fan Club so unique is that it has always enjoyed celebrity and media support and continues to do so. When Elvis was working in Hollywood very few Brits got to meet him and reporters were kept at arm's length. Apart from a handful of British actors, only Tom Jones, Peter Noone, Savile and Albert Hand enjoyed a connection with Elvis. Everyone in the media grew curious to know more about Elvis, and as such latched onto our Fan Club.

The NBC *Elvis 68 Special* is judged to be the first uncut television event, twelve years prior to the launch of MTV, which focused on this style of presentation. Colonel Parker, Elvis' manager, agreed that the British Fan Club should be able to screen the programme to a capacity audience of 2,000 devotees before it was seen at large outside the USA. This screening at the De Montfort Hall in Leicester on Sunday 22nd September attracted an array of A-list celebrities including a young Tim Rice, and some chart-topping British acts of the time. On hearing of the audience reaction, the head of the newly launched BBC2 colour service, David Attenborough, requested that the NBC print we were screening be taken to his BBC office to audition. Subsequently, he secured the UK broadcasting rights to the programme for his new channel. A ticket for our convention screening was signed in Las Vegas in 1970 by Elvis, Colonel Parker and Vernon Presley (Elvis' father) and sold for £624 at a Bonhams auction in 2008.

On 20th July 1969 Neil Armstrong became the first man on the moon and uttered those immortal words,

"One small step for man, one giant leap for mankind". Eleven days later, on 31st July, a nervous Elvis Presley took one small step onto the stage of the Las Vegas International Hotel and one giant leap to reignite his live entertainment persona. That historic performance at the International was played before a star-studded audience. In the last paragraph of its review, *Variety* declared *"Presley took all things in fine stride throughout the invitational VIP preview, with most star acts on the Strip in attendance and a total of about 2,000 comped. No verbal hurrah or musical fanfare accompanied his slouching, grinning amble from the wings, dressed in open-neck black blouse and bell trousers. He was immediately affable and, although nervous, very much in command of the entire scene as he went on to prove himself as one of the more potent Vegas lures.*"

Elvis closed at the International on 28th August 1969. Two weeks later *Variety* reported the numbers. During the engagement's 29 shows, Elvis set Las Vegas attendance and gross records. With the minimum charge set at $15 per customer, the 101,509 attendees paid a total of $1,522,635 to see Elvis. Average attendance in the 2,000-seat capacity show room was 1,750. Weekends were standing room only. Following Elvis at the International were his recent movie co-star, Nancy Sinatra, along with the Osmond Brothers

Yes indeed, a couple of months before we screened the *68 Special*, Elvis had returned to live entertainment in late July of 1969 at the newly constructed International Hotel in Las Vegas. It was an amazing year for Elvis fans even those of us outside of the USA.

Elvis had recorded a couple of dozen terrific songs at American Sound in Memphis including *In the Ghetto, Don't Cry Daddy, Suspicious Minds* and *Kentucky Rain*. It was noticeable too that he was including in his repertoire compositions from British writing teams: Arnold/Martin/Morrow, The Gibb Brothers, Harrison, Lennon/McCartney, Fletcher/Flett, Reed/Stephens, Howard/Blaikley, Westlake/Most, Wickham/Napier, McColl, and McCaulay/Greenaway - the material gleaned by Carlin Music boss, Freddy Bienstock, who I had previously met in his Camden offices. Freddy was a business associate of Colonel Parker and he met with Elvis during his Army Service in Germany and showed him the sights of Paris during his furlough visits to the French capital. (Film producer Hal Wallis was in Germany in 1960 filming location segments for his soon to be released, after demob epic *GI Blues*.) Gosh, it was exciting times for everyone concerned.

In the autumn of 69 I contacted the Elvis fan clubs in Holland, Belgium, France, Germany and Scandinavia suggesting that we hold a summer convention in 1970 in Luxembourg. This tiny country was in the centre of Western Europe and, apart from iron and steel, its main industry was broadcasting. Tony Prince and the other DJs, who were resident in what was becoming known as the "sound-state" of Europe, were anxious to be involved. MGM was due to make a rockumentary of Elvis' Las Vegas concerts and Colonel Parker thought it would be good for both the fan club and the movie if he could convince MGM to include us in *Elvis: That's The Way It Is*.

I looked for a tour operator in Leicester to see who might help me carry a group of Elvis fans to 208 territory. As an overview of what and why this was happening, I wrote the following piece when asked to produce copy for a special screening of *Elvis: That's The Way It Is*.

In the mid to late 60s The Beatles, The Rolling Stones, Tom Jones, Engelbert Humperdinck, Herman's Hermits, and the Dave Clark Five were all out-selling and out-performing Elvis Presley in the charts, on the concert circuits, and in Las Vegas. The British Invasion had certainly rattled Elvis. The world's greatest superstar was locked into movie contracts by a manager who, for the first time in his professional career, had miscalculated his non-existent five-year plan for Elvis, and at the same time hadn't appreciated a massive change in the social strata of the time.

The Colonel thought that Elvis' pinnacle of achievement was always to have in place a Hollywood contract. The shunning of television and live appearances for the majority of the 1960's had opened the floodgates for a massive onslaught of British talent, none of which was in the slightest bit interested in movie contracts. Anxious to appease an unhappy Elvis, who was refusing to sign more movie deals, in October of 1967 Colonel Parker opened negotiations with NBC's Tom Sarnoff for a Christmas 1968 Special that would give Elvis his first television outing in eight years. The Colonel had always looked for million-dollar movie deals, and with NBC the money was matched for a one-hour television special. Recorded in Burbank on 27th and 28th June 1968, and broadcast to a massive US TV audience on 3rd December of the same year, the show was an astounding success. Elvis was able to prove that he had lost none of his on-stage sparkle whist being locked away for almost a decade on the movie lots of California.

On the very day that Neil Armstrong walked on the moon, Elvis Presley was locked into rehearsals at 6363 Sunset Boulevard - the West Coast home of RCA Records. "We were there for six nights in total and learnt almost 150 songs;" James Burton recalls. They were there rehearsing for Elvis' return to live entertainment which was to take place ten days later at 10.15 pm, on the 31st July, on the stage of the International Hotel, Las Vegas. Going back to sing on stage in Las Vegas for the first time since 1956 was certainly one giant step for Elvis, who only minutes before was in a state of near collapse with violent feelings of panic and nausea. He need not have worried - his celebrity audience was on its feet for almost the entire performance.

After the show, the Colonel concludes his famous table-cloth contract with hotel president Alex Shoofey guaranteeing Elvis $1,000,000 for two four week seasons each year for five years. Quite a deal for the hotel, as Elvis and the Colonel are left to pick up the expenses. From 31st July - 28th August Elvis performs a total of 57 shows, before an estimated audience total of 150,000. Although only licensed for 2,200 seated guests, the hotel was known for "crammin' 'em in". It was a wonderful deal for the hotel. For less than twelve dollars-a-piece the hotel was able to present Elvis. Everyone was happy, especially hotel magnate Kirk Kerkorian. Elvis returned to Vegas for a further 57 shows on 26th January 1970, and by 1st March the Colonel was prepared to let Elvis appear outside of the Las Vegas environment, in possibly one of the biggest indoor venues in the world - the fantastic Houston Astrodome. A staggering 36,000 packed the "dome" for the first show that first evening, a figure which was replicated for each of the six shows staged over the three days of the Houston gig, with the Saturday late show achieving a record of 43,000. The "dome" was so big that it "hosted" its own weather system within the complex and would occasionally rain without prior notice. Thankfully it didn't rain when Elvis appeared, and as always, he walked away over a million dollars richer! (It's a pity our Dome didn't enjoy similar attendance figures, but it couldn't, could it? Greenwich didn't have Elvis as the main attraction.) By now, RCA was receiving dozens of calls from its licensees and affiliates around the globe demanding the inevitable "World Tour". For almost 15 years RCA staff in every country had been trumpeting Elvis' success to their domestic media, and for the same period, that media had been asking "when is he coming here?" In the words of British singer Johnny Wakelin in his "Tennessee Hero" song, "Elvis Presley, you've been away too long. We've seen the Rolling Stones, And then came Elton John You've been star now for 20 years or more But no one knows what you've been waiting for The population says what we all know, Yeah, we want to see an Elvis Presley Show" (That's out of context really, because Wakelin didn't record the song until 1975, but the sentiments were the same, we all wanted to see an Elvis Presley show.)

For the first time the Colonel's back was against the wall. Tom Diskin was sent to New York to fend off RCA executives, and he also stopped off in Memphis to calm down Elvis who by this time was itching to perform outside of the US. "The Colonel says that there are no suitable venues." Elvis sends some of his cronies to Britain to check out available locations, but they come back and reported to Elvis that what the Colonel says is fact. "There is nowhere big enough Elvis". "Ah, Shit, so where did the Beatles play?" replies Elvis. Had the "Mafia" been got at, we ask? "Kerkorian Snowed The Colonel" The Colonel had to placate RCA, so he dreamed up the idea of a pay-per-view deal, where Elvis would appear in cinemas around the world, and perform a live closed-circuit theatrical concert. (The Colonel told me just six months before he died that he got the idea from my 1963 "Elvis via Telstar" project, and, of course, he eventually presented “Aloha From Hawaii" - by satellite in 1973.) The million-dollar deal fell through, but MGM Studios owner, Kirk Kerkorian, came to the rescue with a half million-dollar guarantee linked with the proposed "Elvis: That's The Way It Is" documentary movie project which, of course, had to be filmed at his Las Vegas International Hotel. Kerkorian not only owned the venue, the on-stage rights to the artist at that time, but also the movie company. He had snowed the Colonel!

The filming was to take place between 10th August and 15th August - the first part of a third season at the International Hotel, 58 performances this time and an extra show planned for the Labour Day holiday period.

Producer, Dennis Sanders, had earlier travelled to Europe to film this fan club's convention in the Grande Duchy of Luxembourg. The location of the venue was selected because of our club's affinity with the broadcasting company Radio Luxembourg. Its DJs, including Tony Prince, were firm favourites with Elvis fans, and being in the centre of Western Europe it meant that all major European Fan Clubs could support the event. For us it was a fantastic success, but Sanders chose to concentrate on the bizarre aspects of the gathering, which both devalued our people, and elsewhere in the film it showed Elvis enjoying the support of fans who were selected for their bewilderment. That said, at the time we were delighted, and thankfully Elvis must have wet himself when he saw our footage selected to be included in the 1970 biopic.

Meanwhile, in January 1970, just off the Essex Coast, anchored a multi-coloured ship with a huge radio tower. Radio North Sea International (RNI; German: *Radio Nordsee International*; Dutch: *Radio Noordzee Internationaal*) was a pan European offshore radio station run by the Swiss firm Mebo Telecommunications, jointly owned by Swiss engineer Edwin Bollier and his business partner, Erwin Meister. RNI broadcast for less than five years in the early 1970s and, courting both disaster (having been bombed by a group working for the well-established Dutch pirate Radio Veronica) and success (especially for us as it promoted the fan club), made a modest financial profit. DJs Mark Wesley and Chris Carey both rallied to our cause.

Page & Moy of Leicester were synonymous with motor-racing tours for enthusiasts. It all started back in 1959, when Tony Moy went to Le Mans with friends in a 1½-litre Riley, the year Salvadori and Shelby won for Aston Martin. Moy was so impressed with this unique race and the joys of continental travel that he decided something should be done about both. At the time he and his friend, Leon Page, were working at different jobs but they decided to make another visit to Le Mans in 1961, but organised as a simple tour, using the Dover-Dunkirk ferry and a small motorcoach, at a cost of 9½-gns. a head to those fellow enthusiasts who accompanied them. They had no office, not even a telephone, and their brochure was just a duplicated sheet. By 1969 Page & Moy Limited had offices on Belgrave Gate and a staff of 30 employees. I met with the directors explaining that I wanted to take a few hundred British fans to Luxembourg the following year, and a similar number to Las Vegas to see Elvis Presley in 1972. They freely admitted that they knew nothing about music and even less about Presley. They were doubtful that we would fill 4 buses, but they found someone in the office who was a music fan to put together a tour visiting Belgium, Holland, Germany and finishing up in Luxembourg. We didn't fill four buses, we filled twelve! The guy appointed to run the tour left to work with the Kent Messenger Newspaper group managing their reader travel offers. Our operation was passed on to a new recruit, fresh from an American Express office on Woodbridge/Bentwaters US Airforce Bases in Suffolk. He was a very amusing guy who claimed to be a reformed hippy and it was assumed that he had no interest in Elvis Presley. His name was David Wade.

Rodney Burbeck had previously been a journalist with the *Daily Sketch* and moved to CBS Records in the mid-sixties as head of press and publicity. In the spring of 1970, he moved into the RCA building on Curzon Street which also accommodated the London offices and studios of NBC Television. Amongst his first duties was the promotion, in tandem with MGM, of the movie and supportive album release for *Elvis: That's The Way It Is*. Another RCA body was in Las Vegas and had received another kind of tandem – this time a bicycle made for two – presented to Peter Aldersley by Elvis. The tandem was a prop used by Elvis when peddling between sound stages at MGM. Actors were encouraged to cycle around the studio complex to avoid any vehicular noise, which might bleed into audio recording.

Filming was almost completed when RCA London received a call from Denis Sanders in Hollywood. Producer Sanders said that immediately after "wrapping" Elvis, he and his crew were instructed to fly to Luxembourg to film a British Elvis Fan Club convention. Dennis Sanders asked Rodney Burbeck, "Where the f*** is Luxembourg? Is it close to London?"

To find out that MGM were flying over to record our European convention activities for inclusion in an Elvis motion picture was unbelievable! We were the envy of all the fans Stateside.

Upon arrival in London, the MGM crew with Sanders transferred their kit into a chartered plane and were joined by RCA's Aldersley (a former Radio Luxembourg DJ), and RCA press man Mr Burbeck together with some hand-picked music journalists that he had selected and who had a passion for Elvis.

We did not expect there to be any problems getting into the country of Luxembourg. Having piled a million dollars' worth of film equipment onto two trolleys, the entourage was halted by two over-enthusiastic Findel Airport customs officers. "Bonjour bienvenue au Luxembourg. Qu'est-ce que vous avez ici? Avez-vous un carnet pour tout cet équipement?" A carnet (pronounced kar-nay) is an international customs and temporary export-import document. It is used to clear customs in 87 countries and territories without paying duties and import taxes on merchandise providing that the items will be re-exported within 12 months. Oops!

I met Rodney who passed through immigration with only his suitcase and we set about resolving the dilemma. Both his and my schoolboy French was piss-poor. We taxied into town to the Palais Grand-Ducal located on Rue du Marché-aux-Herbes. We explained to an equerry that an MGM film crew from Hollywood was being "quarantined" at the airport together with their equipment because they had no carnet. We didn't have to wait long before the equerry informed us that His Royal Highness, the Grand Duke of Luxembourg Jean Benoît Guillaume Robert Antoine Louis Marie Adolphe Marc d'Aviano, had requested that the customs officers take an early lunch and leave a side gate unlocked.

Fan Club members from all over Europe attended the event held in the New Theatre which was built on the occasion of the millennium of the city of Luxembourg, according to the plans of the Parisian architect Alain Bourbonnais. Prior to our convention it hosted the Eurovision Song Contest. It boasts that it embodies the spirit of European collaboration as the building materials and fittings came from Luxembourg, Belgium, France, Germany, Austria, Switzerland and the Netherlands. Not a nail or screw came from the UK as we were not a member of the European Union until 1973, but then again, neither was Switzerland. Perhaps the country had a lot of Swiss Maids working in hotels, "one time a long time ago".

The entertainment included an Elvis tribute from each country including Dave Kay & The Dykons from Heanor representing the UK. We had the European premier of the movie *Change of Habit*, but the Belgian projectionist drank too much Bofferding beer and was too p***ed to change the reels. It was, however, an amazing experience to meet so many fans from other countries and during our stay we were entertained by Tony Prince and the gang from the radio station. MGM filmed five hours of content at the event and followed fans around the city, including some hairy scenes of Tony Prince and Peter Aldersley riding through the narrow, cobbled streets. I presented the bike to the winner of our charity raffle, Bill Ross from Northampton. Ian Bailye, who helped run the fan club and operated our local UK branch network of events, purchased the bike from Bill, and it was last seen in the Fingerprints of Elvis exhibition, as part of the Beatles Experience at the wonderful Albert Dock in Liverpool.

Elvis: That's The Way It Is was premiered by the Fan Club in London in February 1971. The following day I went to Paris to attend an exhibition and conference for BSS and that evening I went to the French premier as guest of the "Treat Me Nice" fan club president Jean-Marc Antoine Gargiulo.

Vikki and I took our first trip on Tor Line from Immingham to Gothenburg and then drove to

Stockholm to see a recent acquaintance, Sten Berglind, and his partner Christina Ollén. Sten was a journalist for Expression and a huge record collector and Elvis fan. It was our first visit to Scandinavia and we took a trip to his birth town of Västerås. Several years later we would return to this beautiful town with Sten. We went to meet his best friend who had an 8-year-old son, Peri-Erik Jonnson who played piano like Jerry Lee Lewis and looked like a miniature Elton John. I got him an audition with Hughie Green on *Thank Your Lucky Stars.* This programme was originally on Radio Luxembourg and was now a major ITV show. Peri-Erik passed the audition but due to Equity Union regulations he couldn't appear on British Television.

On 7th December 1971 we had our first son who we named Gregory St John Slaughter.

Plans were now afoot to market our Fan Club's first trip to the States to see Elvis. In the early 70s few people travelled from Europe to the USA. Up to that time only people who won a competition prize off the back of a Kellogg's Corn Flake packet made it across the Atlantic.

Colonel Parker advised Emilio Muscelli, the maitre d' of the Las Vegas Hilton, who arranged the seating in their showroom, that we would be bringing 180 members to see Elvis. Within a month we had sold all the seats on our chartered World Airways flight! Chicago based travel consultant, Peter Dallow, who booked all the coaching and hotel accommodations for Page & Moy, did an exceptional job. Our itinerary included Nashville, Tupelo, Memphis, Las Vegas and Los Angeles, with an optional crossing from San Diego into Tijuana, the Mexican border town.

In advance of our trip I contacted all the local media and TV stations in every town, and the response was amazing. When we arrived in Nashville, we received free tickets to a TV show hosted by Porter Wagoner. He had a girl guest singer who was an instant hit with our passengers. Everyone returning from the tele-recording was overwhelmed with the singer with the big titties. She was, of course, Dolly Parton, though nobody on this side of the pond had heard of her or Porter Wagoner. His syndicated television program, *The Porter Wagoner Show*, aired from 1960 to 1981. There were 686 30 minute episodes taped, the first 104 (1960–66) in black and white and the remainder (1966–81) in colour. At its peak, his show was broadcast in over 100 markets, with an average viewership of over three million.

The show usually featured an opening performance by Wagoner with performances from Norma Jean, or later Parton, and comedic interludes by Speck Rhodes. During Parton's tenure, she and Wagoner usually sang a duet. Each episode also featured a guest who would usually perform one or two songs. A spiritual or gospel performance was almost always featured toward the end of the show, generally performed by either Wagoner or Parton or the show's guest star, or occasionally the entire cast. After Parton left the show, Porter began taping his programme at Opryland USA in various locations around the park.

The shows had a friendly, informal feel, with Wagoner trading jokes with band members (frequently during songs) and exchanging banter with Parton and announcer Don Howser. In 1974, Parton's song *I Will Always Love You*, written about her professional break from Wagoner, went to number one on music charts around the world. It was a song that Elvis wanted to record but she was not prepared to give him half of her song-writing royalties.

Wherever we went it was a culture shock for us. The south bore no resemblance to the America we had seen in movies filmed in and around Los Angeles. The south was virgin territory for us Brits, and wherever we went we were a *curio en masse*. “Where’y’all from?” “England.” “Wow, wherever did you people learn such good English?” This was posed so often that we gave our reply before the local townsfolk completed the question.

We had special permission to drive our buses down a native Chickasaw and Choctaw Indian migration route now known as the Natchez Trace. The Natchez Trace Parkway is a national parkway in the “southeastern portion of this here United States” that commemorates the historic Natchez Trace and preserves sections of that original trail. Its central feature is a two-lane road that extends 444 miles from Natchez, Mississippi, to Nashville, Tennessee. Access to the parkway is limited, with more than fifty access points in the states of Mississippi, Alabama, and Tennessee. The southern end of the route is in Natchez at its intersection with Liberty Road, and the northern end is north-east of Fairview, Tennessee, in the suburban community of Pasquo, at an intersection with Tennessee State Route 100. In addition to Natchez and Nashville, larger cities along the route include Jackson and Tupelo, Mississippi, and Florence, Alabama. Commercial transportation is not allowed on the Parkway ordinarily but we, the Official Elvis Presley

Fan Club of Great Britain, enjoyed a special dispensation.

If Nashville was a culture shock, then Tupelo was an explosion. Here, everyone turned out to see our cavalcade of coaches and wanted a happy snap with a Limey, or a Cloggie, or a Froggy because we had a sprinkling of Dutch, Belgian and French fans in our group. Our black bus drivers were hysterically funny guys and pre-warned us that when we crossed the state line into Mississippi they would be treated differently. Gosh that was true. The police referred to them as "boy" and one old biddy asked me if we had "negras" in our country.

Elvis' birthplace, the shotgun shack surrounded by a white picket fence, was not much bigger than a garden shed. A little restoration had taken place around the modest homestead but it had not yet geared up for tourists. A mayoral welcome greeted our bus convoy, preceded by the chief of police with his blues and twos flashing and his "narh-narh" sirens blaring. Motorcycle police outriders put on a show as they weaved in and out between coaches. A speech from the Mayor, a prayer, another speech, an acapella song from a local police officer, and a speech of reply, all in bright sunlight heating up the onlookers to a cool one hundred and ten degrees Fahrenheit.

The Mississippi-Alabama State Fair and Dairy Show played host to Elvis Presley on the 26th September 1956 at the Tupelo Fairground. Elvis did two shows in downtown Tupelo, diagonally across from the Tupelo Hardware Store where Gladys bought a guitar for him as compensation for an unaffordable bike. The day started with a small reception in the presence of the mayor, followed by a parade through the centre of the city. A donation of $10,000 to the government followed later on that day.

Our 1972 group visited all the important Elvis-related sites and were treated to Perspex pint glasses filled to the brim with ice cubes and what appeared to be Coke. Disappointingly for us it was iced tea. The police motorcycle outriders gave some of the girls pillion rides around Elvis Presley Park and Tony Prince took centre stage standing on his head on one of the saddles. It wouldn't be the last time he pulled that acrobatic stunt.

On the way out of town we stopped at the Tupelo Hardware store, before heading north to Tennessee and Graceland. We checked into the Peabody hotel in the centre of the city. Being the Fan Club president, my wife Vikki, our son Gregory and I were given the presidential suite on the twelfth floor. It was an amazing place, but it needed more than a bit of TLC, TCP and DDT.

As downtown Memphis decayed in the early 1970s, the hotel suffered financially, and the Sheraton-Peabody closed in December 1973. We were possibly one of the last groups to occupy the hotel before it was given a makeover. We still loved it, and the Peabody Ducks in the centre of the public lobby were a fascinating feature. An Alabama investment group purchased the hotel in 1974 and reopened it briefly under its original name, but they declared bankruptcy on 1st April 1975, and it closed again. Isadore Edwin Hanover bought the hotel from the county on 31st July 1975, for $400,000 and sold it to his son-in-law, Jack A. Belz, for the same amount. Belz spent the next several years and $25 million renovating the landmark structure. The grand reopening in 1981 is widely considered a major catalyst for the Memphis downtown area's ongoing revitalization.

On the first evening we explored Beale Street. Two hundred white folk in what was still a mostly black area were certainly a feature, but it was bloody fantastic. We all got a bit drunk, with Tony Prince singing *What'd I Say* standing on his head in the Rum Boogie Café. Oh yes, Radio Luxembourg's top DJ had brought a little bit of English soul to the land of rock 'n' roll and the blues. All our passengers were out of their minds with excitement, and our black bus drivers were our minders. Even five decades later, thinking about what we did back then brings tears to my eyes, and there are guys in those Beale Street Bars today who are now old men yet still remember our 1972 British Invasion. We were walking in Memphis, walking with our feet ten feet off of Beale, walking in Memphis and yes, we really felt the way that we'd feel.

Elvis' uncle, Vester Presley, was keeping guard on the gates of Graceland the following day when we arrived outside Elvis' home. For us it really was "where the heart is" and we were allowed to walk up the drive and stand on the steps leading to his front door. We never envisaged that our entire group would be allowed to tread the hallowed turf in Elvis' garden. Colonel had alerted Vester of our impending visit. Although we had seen pictures of the house over the years, it looked much smaller than we had expected. Years later, talking to D.J. Fontana and he recalled that during a visit to London he received an unexpected call from George Harrison. The former Beatle invited him to stay at his home for a couple of days and D.J. thought that he might live in a house like Graceland. "Man, George lives in a f***in' castle." So sad that D.J. and George are no longer with us.

During our three day stay in Memphis we had a party at the Peabody, toured Sun Studios, drove past Elvis' former homes, and visited Humes High School. Non Elvis related sightseeing included the Lorraine Motel, where Martin Luther King Jnr. was assassinated, and we all went on a Mississippi River boat ride where we were all bitten to buggery by the gnats and mosquitoes. As an aside, but nothing to be proud of, one of our passengers was arrested for exposing himself in Walgreens Drug Store. Our Peabody party included a local DJ who had no idea how to either wire the kit or use it, so Tony Prince stepped in, did the business and stood on his head singing "What'd I Say."

Although it was frowned upon, we involved our Continental Trailways bus drivers in all of our festivities, and when we left "fat city" we shed a tear leaving behind our new friends who we saw again and again every time we returned to Memphis.

Chapter Five – Viva Las Vegas

Viva Las Vegas, the 1964 American musical film directed by George Sidney and starring Elvis Presley and Ann-Margret, was titled for a while in the UK *Love in Las Vegas.* This film is regarded by fans and film critics as one of Elvis Presley's best, and it is noted for the on-screen chemistry between Elvis and Ann-Margret. It also featured a strong set of ten musical song and dance scenes choreographed by David Winters and features his dancers. *Viva Las Vegas* was a hit at film theatres and was number 14 on the Variety box office list of top grossing films of 1964. The title song has also been embraced by the Vegas Tourist Office as their trademark anthem. When it was released the image of the city was improved immensely, from being a den of debauchery to somewhere that could be family friendly. Such rebranding possibilities excited Howard Hughes, eccentric hero of the American aviation industry and noted entrepreneurial financier with connections to long established networks in the country. In 1966 he relocated to Las Vegas, initially staying in the Desert Inn. Hughes refused to vacate his room and instead decided to purchase the entire hotel. Howard Hughes extended his financial empire to include Las Vegas real estate, hotels and media outlets, spending an estimated $300 million and using his considerable powers to take over many of the well-known hotels, especially the venues connected with organized crime. He quickly became one of the most powerful men in Las Vegas. He was more than a bit of a nutter, not washing too often and never cutting his hair or fingernails. He and Elvis were both instrumental in changing the image of Las Vegas from its Wild West roots into a more refined cosmopolitan city.

In the meantime, Elvis had done much to improve the city's image and he returned to live entertainment on the newly constructed International Hotel stage in 1969, having been buoyed up by the success of Tom Jones who broke the mould at the Flamingo Hotel in 1968.

Elvis went with Priscilla to see Tom at the Flamingo while Michael Grade was in town to see if his Morecambe & Wise act might be suitable for a Vegas audience. Grade was the nephew of Lew Grade, the founder of ATV back in 1955. Lord Michael Grade has followed in his uncle's footsteps and can certainly be described as television royalty having been the boss of London Weekend, Channel 4 and controller of the BBC. Speaking to him recently he told me that Elvis was thrilled to see his friend Tom making his mark in Las Vegas. Jones' success gave Elvis the confidence to embrace the Colonel's bidding and agree to be one of the opening acts at Kirk Kerkorian's new International Hotel and casino.

By the time our group arrived to see Elvis in 1972, the hotel was still the "new digs on the block" and had been rebranded as the Las Vegas Hilton. The Hilton was not on Las Vegas Strip but number 3000 on Paradise Road. It was so huge that it looked like it would only be a 15-minute walk from Las Vegas Boulevard South but in 40 degree heat it was a hard 45 minutes.

Our flight touched down at McCarran International Airport but a delay meant that Colonel Parker, who had come to the airport to meet us, had already returned to his suite at the hotel for a meeting. Knowing where our group was billeted Vikki, my eighteen-month-old son Greg and I hadn't been in our room for more than five minutes before Colonel was on the phone. I rounded up Tony Prince and Ian Bailye and we headed for the Hilton.

I was not expecting the level of hospitality that we three, and later in the week our entire group, received from Colonel Parker and his second in command, Tom Diskin. Over the years we had all seen the Christmas ads that Elvis and the Colonel placed in the music press and some of our tabloids, thanking fans for their continued support. Now we were in his office in the Las Vegas Hilton being entertained by Parker's antics. No matter what you have heard about the Colonel, make no mistake - he was a naturally funny guy, full of one liners and tales about Elvis and their activities over the years. He showed genuine appreciation that we had travelled to the USA. He wanted to meet all of the group, and we never expected that he would host a party for everyone in his private function rooms. For our last night in Las Vegas on 4th September 1972 he arranged "tipping free" prime booth seating for our entire party in the showroom. "Follow That Dream", the Elvis collectors label, recently released that concert when Elvis addressed our Fan Club from the stage. The promotional blurb reads: *To honour all the fans worldwide who travelled to see Elvis Live in 1972, especially the 200 British Elvis fans for whom Elvis gave this special show on September 4, 1972. Re-live the experience when many Elvis fans from around the world saw Elvis for the first time in Las Vegas, September 1972. The 16-page booklet includes 'eye-witness' accounts from fans who actually met Elvis backstage. It features stories from fans who were there in the front-row seats including 200 members of the British Elvis Presley Fan Club.* The album was conceived by Robert Frieser and produced by Ernst Mikael Jorgensen and Roger Semon.

On the morning of 4th September, there was a press conference at the Las Vegas Hilton hotel to announce the upcoming worldwide telecast of an Elvis concert in Honolulu on the island of Oahu, Hawaii. The announcement was made by the president of RCA Records, Mr. Rocco Laginestra. Elvis was also present and told the press he hoped he wouldn't let his fans down. Mr. Laginestra announced that the upcoming programme would reach the largest audience in the history of television. The concert would be broadcast to Southeast Asia via satellite. In Europe the concert would be seen in 28 countries the day after the concert. The U.S.A. (mainland) would not see the programme before April 1973. This was the concert for which I had been campaigning the last 10 years since the Telstar satellite had been launched.

If the Colonel was not playing roulette, he was always available to talk to any Elvis fan. To those members of our group who were from Holland he spoke to them in Brabantian, a dialect of Dutch. To those fans who wanted an autograph he would find a picture of Elvis and sign it. What we didn't realise, until sometime after, was that there were fans who asked him if they could meet Elvis. Colonel would "umm and ahh", then ask them to return just before showtime and take them backstage. He would instruct them not to tell as he couldn't take everyone, but he always did his best. On that first trip Tony Prince and I worked out that over thirty people from our group got to meet the great man. As the comedian, Jackie Kahane, started his warm up routine, Tony Prince, me and my wife, Ian and his wife, David Wade and his fiancée Janet, together with half a dozen others were taken by Parker to a "green room" to spend a few minutes with the King. We presented Elvis with an award from the *New Musical Express* supplied to me by the paper's news gatherer, the Alley Cat himself Derek Johnson. Tony did a discreet interview for Radio Luxembourg, with the Colonel turning a blind eye.

The Colonel was born in Breda and travelled several times in his younger days to Harwich and Liverpool. Having business associates in Europe, and particularly the UK, he knew what was going on over our side of the pond. He knew about the BBC, Radio Luxembourg and pirate radio. One of his relations had a tendering business that serviced the Dutch offshore station Radio Veronica and occasionally Radio Caroline. Breda is in the south of Holland close to the Belgian border. It was the home of Oranjeboom (the Netherland's oldest and largest brewery), and the location of the factory that makes the Mentos brand of mint sweeties. During WWII the Nazis occupied the area and treated the residents appallingly, rounding up many and shipping them to the death camps. The city was liberated, not by the British, but by the 1st Polish Armoured Division of General Maczek, on 28th October 1944.

Even in Las Vegas local TV news filmed our group arriving at the Hilton to see Elvis, and included some rare film footage of him on stage in their report.

Not wishing to miss a trick during his reception for our members, the Colonel sold, at a discount, souvenirs which were on sale in the showroom, including the treasured giant hound dogs. I received an 8 foot tall version which was officially presented to me and Tony by Hilton boss Henri Lewin. (Just so you know, the Colonel gave all the money from the souvenir sale to me for a farewell party in Los Angeles at the end of our tour.)

After escaping from the tyranny within Nazi Germany via Shanghai, Henri arrived in the United States in 1940. He and his brother became highly successful in America operating hotels and catering. He made a name for himself working his way from waiter to president of the famous Fairmount Hotel in San Francisco. Lewin left the Fairmount for the Hilton chain. Barron Hilton, son of Conrad Hilton and Lewin's boss, called the gaming executive a "brilliant leader. He was a talented hotel executive who left his mark in San Francisco and Hilton's western region before running our Las Vegas operations," Hilton said. "He took to the gaming business and was instrumental in building the convention market in Las Vegas."

There are two questions always asked of me (well three, but the third will be left until later). The obvious one is what was Elvis like when you met him? I met Elvis three times in 1972, 1973 and 1977. I could say that I spent hours with Elvis and few would doubt me but on each occasion it was a matter of minutes, though let me tell you that every second was precious. Also, at the time my mind was on slow-mo although I had a lot to do. Did it help that previously I had met a good number of celebrities? No, not at all. Those past encounters were generally one-to-ones, here are three of them.

Experience one: I was talking with record industry giant David Hughes, when I was reminded of one of my most embarrassing gaffs. David was a journalist initially working for the *Kent Messenger* (it's a small world after all), *Disc & Music Echo*, then in charge of press and publicity for Polydor. He now owns "Collectors Vinyl". The Disc newspaper editor was the lovely Penny Valentine who at the time was trying to organise a Disc Reader Poll Winners event, with only a handful of staff. As I had given her Elvis stories in the past, she invited me along to help. I was happy to do it as I was freelancing for BBC Radio Leicester. I took with me a Uher reel to reel tape recorder and was asked by the station to capture any star interviews. Kenny Everett, Lulu, The Bee Gees and The Walker Brothers were all willing to give a few words. I got there early and so did a black dude with big hair. A really nice guy and I became his manservant plying him with drinks and snacks. As the other celebs arrived they gravitated in our direction to speak to him. I had no idea who he was – he was Jimi Hendrix. Young Hendrix was particularly fond of Elvis. At school Hendrix created a colour drawing of Elvis two months after attending the concert at Sick's Stadium (Seattle) on 1st September 1957, Jimi had taken notes during the concert itself, in which he wrote down the entire line-up of songs he heard Elvis sing that night. Several biographies have told the story of Jimi attending an

Elvis Presley concert at Sick's Stadium. This story originated from Jimi's brother, Leon Hendrix, who said that Jimi couldn't afford a ticket and so watched the concert from a nearby field with a view of the stadium. Both documents can still be seen at the Rock and Roll Hall of Fame in Cleveland, Ohio. His reverence to Elvis Presley continued even into adulthood. In late 1968 he attended a late night screening of *King Creole* during his time in Paris. He credited this particular viewing with giving him the additional strength and inspiration he needed to further his career after his first uneventful appearance in London.

Experience two: I was backstage at the De Montfort Hall in Leicester with David Lingham, boss of the City Council Entertainments Department. I was there to discuss a forthcoming Elvis "do". I could hear the superstar singing her heart out. Lingham had gone elsewhere as the stunningly elegant performer, drenched in sweat, scurried back to her dressing room. "Come 'ere you, you're gonna have to help me get this off" as she dragged me into the privacy of her quarters. Her tight-fitting frock was stuck to her torso. "Be careful, don't f***in' rip it". Someone who I had seen on *Top of the Pops* was glistening naked before me. "Thank you, sir", said Mary Isobel Catherine Bernadette – the one and only Dusty Springfield.

Experience three: Ken Woolley was the best man at my wedding to Vikki. He was a fanatical Cliff fan so I offered to get him a backstage pass for Cliff's next concert in our area. Permission was granted and Ken gave me a good camera with which to take pictures of him and his hero. Cliff was accommodating to the extreme and we spent a good hour talking with him, obviously about Elvis and Cliff's attempt to see the King when he visited his Bad Nauheim home in Germany in 1959. Elvis was in Paris at the time. I took lots of pictures, but when developed the film was blank.

Backstage with Elvis I was as nervous as hell, popping like a two-stroke. The Colonel shouted, "Todd, introduce everyone to Elvis, we don't have much time." When Elvis entered the room, he came through the door without a 20th Century Fox fanfare or searchlights. There was no aura around his head and for some seconds we didn't see him – it wasn't 'til the Colonel bellowed that I was "on duty". I went down the line of our platoon, repeating, "Elvis this is", "Elvis this is," "Elvis this is" then there was a kiss and a scarf for the girls, autographs for the guys, official photographs and happy-snaps. Tony and I made the NME presentation which was reproduced as a full page in the *New Musical Express* after being wired to the publisher in London by Bruce Banke, press officer for the hotel. A quick interview for Radio Luxembourg, then it was "Hi and Bye" time. Oh my god it was exhilarating and fabulous! Elvis, who in the past would have only been used to meeting a couple of people at a time, had been faced with an entourage. He came across as being a very modest and polite gentleman. On the way back to our seats Mr 2IC Tom Diskin said to me, "You've pleased the Colonel. Most people dither and mess up. You controlled it Todd."

Just as we sat down, Tom came back to get Tony Prince. "Colonel wants you to talk to the audience Mr Prince."

The Royal Ruler punched his way through the join in the tabs, acknowledging our group and claiming that we were the mountain coming to see our Mohammad. The audience applauded as our mob shrieked with delight. Tony introduced himself as a British DJ working for Radio Luxembourg but resisted the temptation to stand on his head and sing *What'd I Say*. He walked off stage and within minutes the curtains opened, the band played and Elvis materialised into the spotlight like manna from heaven.

I was the catalyst for everyone to agree to come and see Elvis in Vegas, and I was justifiably proud with what we had achieved. I spent as much time looking at our group, who were transfixed on Elvis, as I did watching Elvis. He acknowledged where we were all sitting and glided through a repertoire punctuated with exhilarating vocal crescendos and dramatic gestures. He communicated with facial expressions which made you feel as if he was singing just for you which of course he was, and in return we shared our emotions with him for 90 minutes.

As we exited the showroom a "gaggle" of GIs (if that is the right collective noun) surrounded Tony, saying how much they preferred 208 to AFN when they had been stationed in West Germany. Most of 'em ended up around our hotel pool talking about their postings on our side of the pond. A few had furloughed in Luxembourg too. Great times!

During our stay in the "bright light city" those amongst us, who could afford to, saw two Elvis shows every night and many tipped a hundred bucks to the table captains to get tables that fronted the stage. In the daylight hours some of our more adventurous passengers went into the desert with our Royal Ruler to ride horses hired from a Dude Ranch. Before becoming a disc jockey Tony was a real jockey, an apprentice along with Willie Carson, so he was able to show our eager "ranch hands" his riding skills including standing on his head on top of a horse and saddle.

The following day we boarded coaches and drove westward through the Mojave Desert towards Los Angeles, stopping off on the way for some prospecting. Calico is a ghost town and former mining town in San Bernardino County, California. It was founded in 1881 as a silver mining town and today has been converted into a county park named Calico Ghost Town. Located off Interstate 15, it lies 3 miles from Barstow and 3 miles from Yermo. Giant letters spelling *CALICO* can be seen on the Calico Peaks behind the ghost town from the freeway. Walter Knott purchased the town in the 1950s, restoring all but five original buildings to look as they did in the 1880s. Calico received a California Historical Landmark award and in 2005 was proclaimed by then-Governor Arnold Schwarzenegger to be California's Silver Rush Ghost Town.

We stopped off at a couple more watering holes before dropping down through the San Bernardino Valley and heading to our base in Los Angeles, the Hollywood Roosevelt Hotel.

In 1956 when Elvis Presley arrived in Hollywood, he and his entourage stayed at the Hollywood Roosevelt Hotel. One day he got into the elevator. "What floor?" asked the operator. "Tenth please." The operator looked at him with disdain. "You can't go up to the tenth floor., Elvis Presley is staying there. No one is allowed there."

Four days to visit Universal Studios (where Elvis filmed *Change of Habit*), Disneyland, Knott's Berry Farm, and an optional day trip across the border into Mexico to Tijuana. Hollywood Boulevard, Sunset Boulevard, the Pier and the beach at Santa Monica, we did it all. To top off our stay "The Destination USA Farewell Party", paid for by Colonel Tom Parker, had a special surprise guest, bandmate John Wilkinson who shared messages from Elvis and the Colonel. Guess who stood on his head and sang *What'd I Say?*

The realisation that we had taken 180 like-minded souls to our "promised land" was the ultimate satisfaction. What we had achieved was much more than that, it was a cultural exchange, a meeting of the minds, an experience for us Elvis fans, and for Elvis himself. It was so good that in our heart of hearts we knew that we could never equal these feelings, but we tried in August 1973.

More pictures were supplied to the NME when we returned to the UK, and, in October 1972, Tony Prince hosted an Elvis Special with me, Ian and David from Page & Moy Limited, all of us recalling the magical times in the USA. We used that opportunity to promote our 1973 tour.

Chapter Six - We Sailed On The Sloop John D in 1973 And We Flew Back To Memphis

RCA, the record label, had benefited hugely from international press coverage of our caravan of fans visiting America to see Elvis. It was at a publicity meeting at their London offices that I met Boppin' Bob Jones. He was *the* cutting engineer genius whose remarkable mastering abilities earned him praise from record companies in Britain and elsewhere in Europe. Bob worked on countless UK Elvis and Rock 'n' Roll releases over 3 decades. He was feted for injecting new life into the music of Elvis from the 50s. Bob gained employment with Decca Records in 1960, became cutting engineer at Pye Studios in the 1970s, and worked for CTS Studios in the 1980s. In 1991, he was one of the founding members of Sound Mastering. Bob also launched the reissue label Detour Records. On all record companies' vinyl product which he cut, Bob secretly engraved his trademark "Boppin" logo onto the surface, out of sight to the uninitiated but visible to the collector. He invited me on a tour of the Wembley recording facilities and, upon opening the door of one sound stage, there performing were 50 musicians from The City of Prague Philharmonic.

The orchestra was recording the theme and incidental music for the series *The World at War*, conducted by composer Carl Davis, and which Bob was soon to be mastering for Thames Television. Davis said that he went for an eastern European, Slavic flavour, and there is definitely a hint of Dvorak as well as more contemporary composers such as Wojciech Kilar. Narrated by Sir Laurence Olivier, and made in association with the Imperial War Museum Trust for transmission on the ITV network between 1973 and 1974, *The World at War* was a 26 episode documentary series chronicling the events of World War II. In its day it was the most expensive documentary series ever made, costing £900,000, which in today's money is the equivalent of £11,000,000. For me, the experience of those haunting refrains being put down in perpetuity was an emotional adventure that has lived with me to this day.

Aloha from Hawaii Via Satellite was the Elvis Presley concert that, for ten years, I had been trying to convince Colonel Parker to initiate. It was broadcast live via satellite on 14th January 1973. The concert took place at the Honolulu International Center (HIC) in Honolulu (now known as the Neal S. Blaisdell Center) and aired live in over 40 countries across Asia. Europe received the telecast the next day, also in primetime. Despite the satellite innovation, NBC did not broadcast an edited version of the concert in the United States until 4th April 1973 because the concert took place the same day as Super Bowl VII. The decision paid off handsomely for the network, attracting 51 percent of the television viewing audience to become NBC's highest rated programme of the year. *Aloha* was the most expensive entertainment special of its time, costing $2.5 million, $1.5 million was the cost of the satellite transponder for an hour. Today a 60-minute transponder lease would cost no more than $5,000 for HD transmission, or free on Whatsapp! My, how technology has changed over the years. When the album *Elvis: Aloha From Hawaii* was subsequently released it became the first quadraphonic album to reach number one.

Elvis taped a 12th January rehearsal concert as a fail-safe in case anything went wrong with the satellite during the actual broadcast. This concert was eventually released as the *Alternate Aloha.* For both shows, he was dressed in a white "American Eagle" jumpsuit designed by Bill Belew. The broadcast was directed by Marty Pasetta, who was then in charge of directing the Oscar ceremonies.

Colonel Parker insisted that the audience tickets for the 14th January concert and its 12th January pre-broadcast rehearsal should be free. Each audience member was asked to pay whatever he or she could afford. The performance and concert merchandise sales (given free from the Colonel's stock) raised $75,000 for the Kui Lee Cancer Fund in Hawaii.

Due to a contractual difficulty between NBC and the BBC, *Aloha* wasn't screened in the UK at the time of broadcast, and then not until four years after Elvis' death. Non-English speaking territories, such as mainland Europe, paid a moderate foreign language fee of between $10,000 and $30,000 per country but the UK was asked for $400,000 which was way outside the BBC's budget for a live feed.

On Friday 23rd March 1973, Tony Prince and I went to the Rainbow on Seven Sisters Road to see Thin Lizzy and the Electric Light Orchestra. Mel Bush was the promoter and he wanted to speak to us about the possibility of doing an Elvis show in England, having been extremely successful with concerts for Led Zeppelin, David Bowie, Elton John and The Osmonds. We agreed that we would sound out Colonel Parker when we went back to Vegas in August. Through the grapevine we heard that there was a private bash going on aboard a party boat on the Thames called the “Sloop John D” (no idea why it wasn’t named the John B, possibly it was a Beach Boys’ trading name). Tony bumped into Eric Clapton waiting at a river landing stage. He had known Eric since March 65 when he was in the Yardbirds and Tony had promoted their first hit *For Your Love* on Radio Caroline. We decided to gate-crash behind “slow-hand” who had an invitation, but he had no idea what the party was about and jumped aboard the launch taking VIPs out to the vessel. It was a private party alright, a birthday “do” for Elton John with all of London’s pop glitterati in attendance. From caviar to the finest Premier Cru it was all there for the taking. Ringo Starr was as p***ed as a fart after joining Tony in a drinking contest. I didn’t have to participate as Elton gave me a bottle of vodka and I sat in the corner watching the madness with Lynsey de Paul. I had met her before at another Disc bash, but I can’t remember where because I was well hammered. I had a feeling that she might have been dating Bernie Taupin; I didn’t know if he was on the boat but, if he was, I wouldn’t have known him if I fell over him. Tony had booked accommodation for us overnight, then he buggered off with Ringo and I had no idea where I was supposed to be billeted.

Following the death of Albert Hand, I was asked by his business partner, Peter Keegan, to leave BSS and run the company Heanor Record Centre Limited. This Derbyshire based business in the former mining town was established to sell Elvis records to readers of *Elvis Monthly*. In 1962 if you wanted to sell singles and LPs you had to have a retail outlet. A small shop was acquired on the Derby Road which also became the editorial offices for *Elvis Monthly*, *Fury Monthly*, *Mods Monthly* and *Pop Weekly*, the latter jointly owned by Australian impresario Robert Stigwood, who eventually went on to manage the Bee Gees and make the movies *Grease* and *Saturday Night Fever.*

For a while Stigwood had a relationship with Joe Meek, promising that he would find him acts for his recording studio. Until the Sexual Offences Act of 1967 decriminalised homosexual activity, Messrs Meek & Stigwood were discreet but in the business became known as the "Pink Mafia". It was said that their casting couch activities were an unwritten clause in their early recording contracts. Bored with Meek's erratic behaviour and horrified by his arrest for importuning in a public toilet, Robert Stigwood dumped his playmate and formed a business association with NEMS, owned by Beatles manager Brian Epstein.

Vicki Wickham, who was an assistant producer of the 1960s British television show *Ready Steady Go!*, was fashion consultant for Mods Monthly. Vicki was best known for being Dusty Springfield's manager and co-wrote (with Simon Napier-Bell) the English lyrics to Springfield's only British number 1 hit, *You Don't Have to Say You Love Me,* adapted from the Italian song *Io che non vivo senza te.* This song was a showstopper in the movie *Elvis: That's The Way It Is.* With Penny Valentine, the editor of *Disc*, Vicki co-wrote *Dancing with Demons*, a biography of Dusty Springfield.

One would have thought that the mighty Heanor Record Centre, with such an illustrious past pedigree of movers and shakers within the 60s music industry, would be cash rich. Far from it, it was trading insolvently. I had to bring to the party the Official Elvis Presley Fan Club which I had bought from Albert Hand six years earlier for £2,000. At the time of purchase the Fan Club had no assets, no mailing lists, no stock, no nothing. I had made the Fan Club viable and now I had to use its assets to bankroll a failing *Elvis Monthly*. I was only successful in doing so as I had an address book full of music industry friends and associates, and a daft name that once heard no one forgot.

To make matters worse *Elvis Monthly* was in debt to the printing company owned by Peter Keegan. Printhouse Limited was managed by a wonderful guy, Tony Atkinson, who had been editing *Elvis Monthly* for several years as Albert was terminally ill. Smoking three packs a day it was, of course, lung cancer.

Tony was a go-between with many of the aforementioned businesses, and for some unknown reason was printer to Doctor Stephen Ward. The good doctor was alleged to be a procurer of high-class call girls, notably Christine Keeler and Mandy Rice-Davies for the Westminster Establishment, including John Profumo MP.

On our way back from Leicester, after picking up a bunch of Elvis pictures from my home, we were driving up the A46 in the direction of Nottingham. We stopped at the Halfway House pub and hotel for a pint. I was served by an extremely attractive young woman who looked over my shoulder and said, “The man you came in with, is his name Tony?" "Yes, it is" I replied. "Ask him to come to the bar, please." "The drinks are on me".

"Drink your pint Tony love, then f*** off and don't tell anyone I'm here, or I'm dead and so might you be - and your friend." We shot out of the bar like shit-off-a-stick. "Who the f*** was that?" A red-face Tony Atkinson responded "That was Mandy Rice-Davies, and don't tell a soul."

The *Elvis Annual* was a big selling Christmas gift, generally bought by aunties for their nieces as a "stocking filler." The ten-year-old recipient probably wasn't interested in Elvis, but Auntie Ruth got to read and drool over it first before she wrapped it. The pictures I had collected from home had been sent to me by Colonel Parker and were due to be included in the Elvis Annual 1974.

World International were the Manchester publishers of the majority of Christmas celebrity titles, including our Elvis annual, and the following day we went to their offices just next to Granada TV. Tony was a reckless driver, possibly because he always had big cars, but he was "not far enough to be out of the ground to be healthy" (northern expression for being small) to be able to see over the steering wheel. As he spun the car opposite the entrance of the TV studio the entire cast of *Coronation Street* had to scatter. The meeting went well, they liked the pictures and the print run was 100,000.

Tony Atkinson was a soldier during WWII and was captured by the Germans in Normandy during the D Day invasion. He was interned in a variety of POW camps ending up in Czechoslovakia. He escaped many times but, because he was a mere foot-soldier, he was of no importance to the resistance who were only interested in the repatriation of airmen. Tony walked a couple of thousand miles to Paris hiding in hedgerows overnight, crossing borders and minefields, living on root vegetables and stealing eggs. Chickens were available, but he could never kill one although he did eat a few worms. Being a printer, he did a bit of forgery for the resistance and was paid in proper food, accommodation and wine with promises of joining the Comet Line escape route across the central Pyrenees into the Basque country. It never happened as he wasn't a pilot.

During an Elvis Fan Club trip to Paris my dad, John Slaughter, joined up with Tony and he walked my father around the back streets to some of the bordellos he used to visit when he was on the run.

Vikki and I along with Greg had moved from the south of Leicester to Loughborough which was in the north of the county and close to junction 23 of the M1. The Heanor exit was just three junctions up making the daily commute only 40 minutes.

In June 1973 on my first day in Heanor, it was a strange feeling sitting in the seat that was once occupied by Albert Hand, but there were no Elvis pictures on the walls, only LP and magazine stocks that were visible on the shelves. All the Elvis items that Albert had collected over the years had vanished. All the movie stills had "evaporated" and the place needed a bloody good clean.

We had problems with the heating so with my BSS hat on I went into the cellar to find the boiler. Standing in the corner was an apparition. If you remember the

1980s Southern Television series *Worzel Gummidge* starring Jon Pertwee, then the Heanor Record Centre ghost was the spit of Jon Pertwee.

Jack and Lizzie Newbrooks were the only staff left, along with Albert's father who worked for a couple of hours each day in the postal room. Lizzie said, "You've seen Jakey. I can tell by the look on your face." I had not been smoking any weed, but I did see a ghost. Jakey had to go into hiding in the 1850s as he had impregnated the mayor's daughter. Cornered and knocked unconscious he was thrown into the flooded cellar and left there to drown. The cellar still had water problems, but a small pump sucked up the occasional flood and despatched it through a pipe and spurted it into the road.

What had once been a thriving publishing company had been hung out to dry. The proceeds from royalties of sales across all the magazine titles and associated advertising revenues had been diverted to form another unrelated warm air business, and printing company. *Elvis Monthly* was reduced to a hand-to-mouth operation, and sales were dwindling with every issue. Amalgamating with my Official Elvis Presley Fan Club of Great Britain doubled the turnover in a stroke and guaranteed its survival. For the company to grow I had to find another subscription magazine.

It was soon time to return to Memphis and Las Vegas with trip number two. London Weekend Television tried to make a deal with Parker for their crew to accompany our group with presenter David Frost and for him to interview both Colonel Parker and Elvis. The Old Colonel was having none of it so on this occasion there would be no documentary.

Our itinerary was roughly the same as the previous year with a few alterations. We would overnight in Tupelo at the Ramada Hotel and, as the Memphis Peabody was closed for renovation, we would be based on Union Avenue in another Ramada. In California we would stay on the seafront in Huntington Beach.

Although we had no TV company on board, again we enjoyed coverage from all the local broadcasters who trailed behind us. However, we did have some media people travelling with us. Journalist Peter Moeller and photographer Deborah Thomas from the *Daily Mirror*, Sten Berglind from *Expressen* (Swedish Daily Express), and two anonymous reporters from *De Telegraaph* (Dutch Daily Telegraph), anxious to get a scoop on Andreas Cornelius van Kuijk (Colonel Parker). We had known about Colonel Parker's ancestry since 1961 when Hans Langbroek wrote a fan booklet about Parker's Dutch family. In June 1961, his elder brother Ad van Kuijk spent 17 days in the Colonel's apartment in LA. The trip was financed by the Dutch magazine *Rosita* but, although we all knew Parker came from Holland, the news never reached the USA. The Colonel introduced Ad to Elvis.

Our time in Tupelo was amazing, meeting everyone from the Mississippi state governor to Miss Mississippi. The beer was due to flow at our party except for the fact that it was a Sunday and on the sabbath Mississippi is a dry state. We got 'round that problem with the help of hotelier Jimmy Papas who allowed us to drink our liquor store purchases spiked with locally distilled Moonshine sourced by our bus drivers.

When we reached Memphis, the news coming out of Las Vegas was not good. For some inexplicable reason, the management of the Hilton's Showroom International had cancelled all reservations from the UK. We had a party of 250 who each had bookings for, on average, four tickets apiece, so one thousand of our Elvis tickets had been reassigned. Their concierge refused our calls but I did manage to get in touch after several attempts with Colonel's second in command Tom Diskin. It appeared to him that the hotel was full, and unusually everyone staying needed tickets for the Elvis show, and as our group was billeted elsewhere our tickets were being reassigned to their guests.

Informing our passengers that we were travelling to Vegas to ensure that everyone got tickets to the Elvis shows, Tony Prince and I flew there two days before our people were due to arrive. Peter Moeller, who had an extremely upper-class English accent, called the hotel's press officer while we were in the air in the guise of a BBC newscaster and spoke to the Hilton's publicity director Bruce Banke. Guessing that he was to give an interview about the success of Elvis in their hotel, Bruce agreed to take the call. Moeller did just that for a couple of minutes before interrogating Banke about the fans from the British Fan Club having their pre-booked ticket allocation "confiscated". We believe that his photographer also joined in the ruse and called, posing as a reporter from the *Daily Mirror* the world's biggest selling tabloid weekday newspaper.

When Tony and I arrived at the Hilton we went straight to the ticket office and met up with a very "pissed off" Emilio Muscelli. As a revered Las Vegas maitre d', Emilio seated thousands of locals and visitors for the Rat Pack's performances at the Sands in the early 1960s so knew how to manage a two and a half thousand-seater casino cabaret showroom. Tony Prince employed his broadcaster's eloquence and Muscelli threw his handwritten seating plans at us and told us to select 250 names, to hand write those names on cards, and pass them individually to our people when they arrived in Vegas.

It was a nightmare, Tom Diskin told me to calm down and with Tony Prince we did as we were asked. At least everyone would get one ticket.

When giving out the precious cards we instructed everyone to learn the name written thereon and keep the card out of sight. So, on the night of the show, there were 250 Brits all dressed in C&A and M&S clothing edging their way into the showroom nervously uttering their assumed names. It worked, but I was close to having a coronary.

Colonel Parker had agreed for me, my wife, Sten Berglind and a few others to see Elvis and present him with another NME award moments before he went on stage. A picture of the event, taken in colour, surprisingly appeared some years after Elvis' passing on a Somali Republic postage stamp. After the presentation, my wife Vikki, in true Glaswegian style, decided that Elvis should know about the grief inflicted on his British fans by the hotel and the stress caused to her husband. Elvis was stunned and his men moved in to remove her and we all left the building. I conducted an onstage interview with Red West during one of our Elvis Week events near Great Yarmouth in the late 1980s and he remembered his kerfuffle with my then wife.

Tony and Christine Prince, 208 programme controller Ken Evans, *Daily Mirror* staffers Peter Moeller and Deborah Thomas, plus a few fans, met Elvis before the midnight show and recorded another interview for Radio Luxembourg. For the rest of our stay in Vegas our people were able to get to see as many shows as they wanted, Elvis had spoken to the management.

I am not ashamed that we contrived a deception to obtain tickets for our group, and years later, during a dinner in Vegas, the Colonel said that he admired my tenacity.

I felt so upset after that debacle that I took comfort from a bottle of vodka and a gallon of Coca Cola – things go better with Coke. We had tickets for more shows but we bumped into four Brits, not in our group, who had come to Vegas. There were no tickets available to see Elvis so I gave them ours.

The rest of the tour was a breeze and not long after our return I flew out to the Grand Duchy for another marathon Elvis session. Little did I know that over the next few years I would be visiting the radio station's London offices more frequently than I had during the 1960s and that I would be travelling to Luxembourg on a regular basis.

Back in the Heanor office I worked on a variety of projects to ensure that the wheels were not going to fall off and talked to my phantom friend, Jakey. No, I wasn't going mad. I did see him a few times and I did speak to him and he nodded back in recognition. I must confess that I was freaked out when driving home to Loughborough one rainy evening with the bogeyman sitting next to me in the passenger seat.

Once the majority of the offshore radio stations ceased broadcasting, the BBC hurriedly cobbled together 20 or so local stations. These didn't impact on Radio Luxembourg's audiences but then something happened.

Today, LBC (originally the London Broadcasting Company) is a nationwide London based phone-in and news talk show radio station. It was the UK's first licensed commercial radio station and began to broadcast to Londoners on Monday 8th October 1973, a week ahead of Capital Radio. The launch of LBC also saw the beginning of Independent Radio News, providing a service to all the independent local radio stations soon to be launched nationwide. Whilst the London Broadcasting Company was all talk, Capital was all music. The chairman of the board of directors of this new station, Richard Attenborough, was the first voice to be heard on Capital and, having a roster of "named" broadcasters, it was to become a serious player. With independent commercial broadcasters opening in Glasgow, Birmingham, Nottingham, Manchester, Liverpool, Edinburgh, Sheffield, Plymouth and Newcastle upon Tyne over the following months, 208's bosses had to look at ways to protect their position.

Ten years earlier Alan Keen had been working for the Daily Mirror Group, selling advertising space in its newspapers and magazines. It had been his job for the previous sixteen years, twelve of them with the Mirror. Prior to that he had been involved with parliamentary reporting. One day Alan arrived at his office to be told that a man called Philip Birch, who worked for the advertising agency, J. Walter Thompson, had been trying to contact him. Alan called Philip and they agreed to meet, but not at the agency. They had a secret rendezvous at the Hilton Hotel on London's Park Lane. Birch told him he was about to leave JWT to launch an offshore radio station. Radio Caroline and a couple of smaller operations already existed but Birch told him this was going to be bigger and better than any of them. He offered Alan a job as a sales executive. Alan took a while to think about it, discussed it with his wife and, despite her reservations, decided that it might be fun. In August 1964 Alan formed Radlon Sales Ltd., the airtime selling department for the new station which was to be called Radio London. Philip Birch was managing director and the secretary was Margaret Greville. With its formula broadcasting playlist and a personalised set of the latest PAMS jingles from Texas, BIG L was an anglicised version of BIG D in Dallas, the biggest and hottest Top 40 station in the USA. (Big D was also the first major broadcaster to form a promotional partnership with Colonel Parker to market Elvis' shows across Texas from 1956 onwards.) It wasn't long before Wonderful Radio London eclipsed all the other pirates.

Following Radio London's closure Alan joined the English language service of Radio Luxembourg in August 1970, initially as general manager then Managing Director, based at 38 Hertford Street. He took with him Dennis Maitland, Richard Swainson and Godfrey Morrow from BIG L.

Aware of what we were doing with Elvis, Alan and Tony invited me to London to discuss opening Club 208 in tandem with the magazine Fabulous 208. It was to be a listener's club, with its own weekly request show hosted by former *Record Mirror* journalist Rodney Collins, publicity director for the station. As well as a members' magazine, there would be listener trips to Luxembourg City to meet the DJs and visit the RTL transmitters and studio complex located in the majestic Villa Louvigny, located off the aptly named Allée Marconi.

Taking 208 fans to Luxembourg was an adventure. In the days of watery radio, girls would risk life and limb to "pedalo" from Frinton-on-Sea to the anchorage sites to catch a glimpse of their favourite boss-jocks. Occasionally some would be invited aboard, but others had to be rescued by the Coast Guard when their lilo proved an inadequate form of transport across the North Sea.

The noun *anorak* comes from the Greenlandic word *annoraaq* which is an insulated outerwear coat worn for most of the year north of the Arctic Circle. Hooded "parkas" became the favourite garb of mods in the 60s which also became known as "anoraks". In the 80s the term "anorak" described a geek, nerd or an obsessive. Pirate radio DJs referred to the fans who came out to the ships, especially after the Marine Offences Act came into force, as "Anoraks", principally because they all wore them for protection from the sea spray. A boatload of "anoraks" was a welcome distraction from the isolation of their Knock John Deep anchorage. These clandestine networks delivered food, booze, newspapers and letters from home. I used them to take Elvis and other RCA records out to the broadcasters, a secret that I shared with Elvis record producer, Joan Deary, when she came over to speak at one of our Elvis Fan Festivals at Pontins Hemsby during the 80s.

The fans we took to Luxembourg were certainly not anoraks. These were mini-skirted girls who made the journey to spend a few days in the presence of their idols. Tony, Peter, Mike, Mark, Spangles, Kid, Bob, Dave, Paul and Stuart were all pin-ups in the eyes of our listeners. Yes, there were a handful of male enthusiasts who were anxious to see the studios, the equipment and the broadcast towers, but in the main it was party time with the DJs in the pubs, clubs and the bar at the Holiday Inn, with everyone wanting to stay in room number 208.

For three years Club 208 was a huge success taking us up to 1977.

In 1973 and out of the blue I was called by Michael Levy, who I did not know from a bar of soap. After I took over the Elvis Presley Fan Club in 1967, and whenever we got our hands on additional funds, Ian Bailye would buy 16mm Elvis films. He found an unexpected source in Africa that had loads. These prints had been sold off by the South African Broadcasting Corporation to a dealer and we bought every title that became available. We showed these movies at Elvis functions around the UK and Europe because there was no such thing as portable video projection at that time. I allowed Caroline TV to borrow a few of our Elvis films. Ronan O'Rahilly had leased a couple of Super Constellation aircraft which had been converted by the US military for broadcasting propaganda during the Vietnam War. Ronan planned to fly these over the North Sea in a figure of eight to give the UK an additional terrestrial TV channel, broadcasting music video material and pop movies. When the backers of this airborne pirate project withdrew their investment, the Caroline team concentrated once again on their radio business and Ronan returned our Elvis movies.

Along with our collection of Elvis films we received a couple of dozen small reels that had been sent in error. These were 16mm pop songs that fitted into a cassette housing in an amusement arcade visual jukebox. Two of these reels were songs performed by Shane Fenton, *Moody Guy* and *Cindy's Birthday*. Michael Levy wanted a meeting.

With singer/songwriter Peter Shelley, Levy had started Magnet Records and had initial chart successes with Shelley's *Love Me Love My Dog* and *Gee Baby*. He also created the persona of a glam rock idol called Alvin Stardust and recorded *My Coo Ca Choo*. Peter was not wishing to appear on *Top of the Pops* out of character. Shane Fenton came to mind, so he was quickly fitted out in black leather, a high pompadour quiff hair style, black eyeliner, and hey presto, here was the new Alvin Stardust. His accurate lip-syncing to Shelley's vocals, enhanced with sexy, moody gyrations, helped the track storm to the top of the charts. Michael Levy wanted good quality film of Bernard Jewry's early hits when he went under the name of Shane Fenton, and someone to organise a riot at one of Stardust's early promotional appearances to build up an untouchable portfolio of publicity opportunities.

One of Magnet records other acts, guitarist Chris Rea, said of Levy, "He is extremely tough, one of the hardest bastards I have ever met, but I would leave my children with him rather than anyone else." Reading that quotation recently I am no longer surprised that, at my initial meeting, Levy was on the phone arranging for someone to "have their fortune told."

I provided the films and arranged for a riot to occur in front of a bevy of paparazzi photographers during a guest appearance at the Nottingham Palais. To me Michael Levy was a gentleman, a man of his word and I was well rewarded. We also published an Alvin fanzine. Alvin would ring Vicky Molloy in our office just to hear her say, "Hello, me duck, are you ok?"

Alvin Stardust was a good friend and great company. He appeared for us many times, including at our Hemsby Elvis Week just three weeks before he died in October 2014.

Chapter Seven – The Curzon Street Meet

A three day week was one of several measures introduced by the government to conserve electricity, the generation of which was severely restricted owing to the effects of the 1973–74 oil crisis. Later, industrial action by coal miners further compounded events. From 1st January 1974 commercial users of electricity were limited to three specified consecutive days' consumption each week and prohibited from working longer hours on those days. Services deemed essential were exempt: hospitals, supermarkets and newspaper printing presses. To conserve electricity both the BBC and ITV television services were required to cease broadcasting at 10.30pm every night during the crisis. Consequently, Radio Luxembourg enjoyed its biggest regular night-time audience in twenty years. It was also a year of IRA terrorist bombings across the UK, killing in total almost 100 innocent people.

Colonel Parker phoned to ask if I could take a call from a good friend of his, a lady called Olive. She had seen American television coverage of our fans' trips to see Elvis, so I took the call. Olive Osmond wanted to discuss the possibility of bringing UK fans of The Osmonds to their hometown of Orem, Utah. Within days complimentary airline tickets arrived and we were on a flight to Salt Lake City, the spiritual homeland of Joseph Smith, founder of the Mormon Church. We were met at the airport by Jay Osmond, and driven to their ranch and office complex which doubled up as a television and recording studio. An Osmonds fan club trip was arranged to Utah and I was given *The Book of Mormon* and an accompanying volume *This We Believe.*

I remember that Jimmy Carter's brother was there filming and he was so drunk that he missed the urinal in the gents and pissed all over my feet. Although his family business was farming peanuts, Billy was more interested in brewing beer and distilling liquor and drinking it. When Jimmy Carter was elected President of the United States, he was nicknamed President Peanut. Billy died of liver failure in 1988 aged 51.

Upon returning to the UK, I met Maureen Street, the boss of the Osmonds UK Fan Club who had previously worked with Rosko and Dave Clark, and then operated out of the Polydor Press Office alongside David Hughes, the record company's PR guru. The trip was arranged through our travel partner and 200 Osmond fan club members travelled to Salt Lake. They met the boys at their home, enjoyed a BBQ served to them by the group (what a thrill that must have been) and they travelled onward to see a concert.

That year I couldn't afford to go to Memphis and Las Vegas, so Mark Wesley and his wife Pierrette travelled with our group, representing the Radio Luxembourg team who were always at hand to support our efforts.

As it was a lean time for Elvis' chart success, I worked night and day planning functions, local events and an Elvis Fan Club convention in Luxembourg with Marty Wilde. There were, of course, several Club 208 visits to the Villa Louvigny.

A dreadful thing happened to one of our passengers during the journey to Luxembourg for the Elvis bash. When we left Victoria Coach station there was a skinny old biddy who was dancing in the aisle of the bus all the way to the ferry. When we reached Belgium, we stopped at a service station at Bastogne in the Ardennes where, during WWII, the famous Battle of the Bulge occurred. *Disco Granny* wanted to take a leak but had no coins for the plate-lady at the entrance to the ladies' bog. She disappeared into the lorry park, hid behind a 16-wheeler and whilst she was peeing the truck reversed over her.

Freddy Bienstock, the boss of Carlin Music, wanted to meet up again. During his career Bienstock worked with such songwriters, performers and music business executives as Leiber & Stoller, Cliff Richard, Bobby Darin, Ray Davies, U2, John Sebastian, Tim Hardin, Eric Burdon, James Brown, Peter Allen, William Bolcom, Ernesto Lucuona, Norman Dello Joio, Carol Bayer Sager, Kander & Ebb, Koppelman & Rubin, Marvin Hamlisch, Stephen Sondheim and, of course Elvis Presley. Bienstock worked closely with Elvis and Colonel Parker who always relied on the publisher to choose the songs Elvis recorded, both in the studio and for movie soundtracks. With representatives in New York, in the legendary Brill Building, and in Denmark Street (London's Tin Pan Alley), Freddy had his finger on the pulse of the song writing and popular music industry. He introduced Elvis in the late 60s and throughout the 70s to a vast catalogue of suitable songs from British composers. He visited Elvis when he was in Bad Nauheim, West Germany with the US Army, and accompanied him to Paris introducing him to the sights and the ladies working in the seedy nightclubs.

After emigrating to the US before the start of World War II, Bienstock began his career in the stock room of publisher Chappell and Company, later becoming its chairman. Bienstock, who served on the National Music Publishers Association's board of directors for nearly 20 years, founded Carlin Music in 1966 by acquiring the Belinda Music Company and built it into a catalogue of over 100,000 songs.

Today, the Carlin catalogue boasts an extensive collection of classical, country, classic pop and standards, as well as being the world's leading Broadway musical publisher.

When the MGM movie *Elvis: On Tour* was being shown in cinemas there was no new material to justify RCA releasing a soundtrack album as they did with *Elvis: That's The Way It Is*. Freddy told me that a follow-up film was in the early stages of planning and his brief from Elvis was to find new material written by British songsmiths. The Colonel was fearful that the record company giant would lose interest in Elvis' new music especially as they had acquired all of Elvis' back catalogue of recorded material pre-1973 in a $6 million dollar buyout. Our meeting started in the London offices of RCA in Curzon Street, just around the corner from Radio Luxembourg, on the same road as the former studios and offices of pirate broadcasters Wonderful Radio London, Britain Radio, and Swinging Radio England. A right turn off Curzon Street takes you towards 6 Chesterfield Gardens, still identified as Caroline House. We then relocated to a booth in Wheeler's Fish Restaurant in Hertford Street for more discreet discussions. (I recall entertaining *Paradise Hawaiian Style* co-star Suzanna Leigh in Wheelers one lunchtime during a break from meetings with Rodney Collins at Radio Luxembourg opposite.

Halfway through lemon sole her denture plate snapped in half.)

Freddy asked if the British Fan Club membership would support another documentary film that might include an overseas visit. Remembering the Mel Bush offer at the ELO Rainbow concert, I said I would investigate. Freddy was very excited and we were all sworn to secrecy. Bienstock was born to a Jewish family in Switzerland on 24 April 1923, and relocated to Vienna with his family when he was three years old. After the Anschluss, he emigrated to the United States in 1938, just before the outbreak of World War II, with his brother Johnny Bienstock, who later founded Big Top Records. The family ended up settling in New York City after his parents came to the US in 1940. Freddy, after being in the States and the UK for almost 50 years, still retained a charming smiling Swiss dialect when he said, "Don't tell the Colonel!"

For those fans unable to travel to Luxembourg we held a convention at the Nottingham Palais with the Swinging Blue Jeans topping our bill. Major Bailye drove the turntables – still only vinyl in those days. We had a surprise guest, Brighton country singer Johnny Wakelin came along with his band to premiere his forthcoming single *Tennessee Hero*.

"Elvis Presley, you've been away too long. We've seen the Rolling Stones and then came Elton John" Great lyrics.

When it was released the following year on Pye Records sadly it didn't chart. Wakelin did have UK chart success though with *Black Superman* and *In*

Zaire, both songs in tribute to his other hero Muhammad Ali. I had the honour of meeting Muhammad Ali at a dinner in London in later years when he was attending a charity event in support of the Parkinson's Society. By that time, he was wheelchair bound and completely debilitated by the disease, but he still managed to make people laugh even having lost his ability to speak. Many Elvis fans met Muhammad in Memphis when he visited Graceland in 1984.

Chapter Eight - A Crash Landing Of Emotions

1975 was a strange year. It was the last time consultants and junior doctors took industrial action when they decided to withdraw non-emergency services. The consultants worked-to-rule and suspended all "goodwill activities" between January and April of 1975, protesting against proposed new contracts which they said would force them to abandon private practice. The action was called off when the then social services minister, Barbara Castle, agreed to consultants switching to part-time NHS contracts whilst still preserving their private practice commitments. Later that year, doctors again took on Ms Castle over plans to phase out private work from NHS hospitals, and, in the autumn, junior doctors walked out. During the strike William Hartnell the first actor to play the role of *Doctor Who* died. He was born on January 8th, 1908, and I remember meeting and talking to this fine actor as I sat next to him on the Piccadilly Line underground service from St Pancras Station to Hyde Park Corner, my exit for 38 Hertford Street.

We were invited by Fan Club secretary, Maureen Street, to see The Osmonds at Earls Court in May 1975. Donny flew by wire just over the heads of the audience, sprinkling red rose petals on everyone at the start of the show. When she was told that we were bringing a party of Elvis fans to Memphis in the summer, Olive Osmond arranged tickets for our passengers to see the boys. Their appearance at the Mid-South Coliseum, the day after Rod Stewart & The

Faces, coincided with our stopover in Elvis' hometown before we headed to Las Vegas. Rod and some of his guys were also in the audience.

Wearing costumes designed by Elvis' stage clothes designer, Bill Belew, it should have been a fitting warm-up to seeing Elvis at the Hilton, but it didn't work out that way. As our plane touched down in Nevada I was informed by the captain that Elvis had cancelled the rest of his season at the Las Vegas Hilton and had been flown back to Memphis.

As our passengers were transferring to coaches for a guided sightseeing tour prior to hotel check in, I jumped into a taxi and headed for the Hilton. Only two years earlier I had done the same thing when our members' ticket allocations had been cancelled. I had the daunting job of boarding every bus as it arrived at our hotel and sharing the bad news that Elvis had left the building and was now at the Memphis Baptist Memorial Hospital. Two hundred fans had lived on beans on toast for a year to be able to afford to travel to America to see Elvis, and now I had smashed everyone's hopes and dreams with one sentence.

Amongst our group was Dutch cartoonist Ger Rijff, who was nominated to fly back to Memphis on our behalf and take flowers to the hospital. A collection was taken and we raised enough money to buy a florist. Who would have thought that two years later, and every August thereafter, we would be buying flowers once again only to end up on Elvis' grave?

Ger Rijff was a comic artist who gained notoriety with his hippy comic strip *De Vogels* (also known as *Daan en Dodo*, 1970-1971), drawn for audiences of rock fans. He was notorious for contributing to various sex parodies of popular comic franchises, such as *Tintin, Lucky Luke, The Smurfs* and *Suske en Wiske*. Yet it would be condescending to categorise him simply as an obscure cartoonist of lewd spoofs. Rijff was equally respected as an expert and author of various articles and books about Elvis Presley.

When he arrived in Memphis Ger managed to reach the 16th floor of the hospital but wasn't allowed to enter the room. Although he never met him personally, Rijff did see Elvis perform three times, albeit in the twilight of his career, namely 1976 and his final two concerts before his death in 1977. From 1976 onwards "Jerry" published a huge amount of (photo) books about Presley and 1950s rock 'n' roll, including *Elvis Presley: Echoes of the Past* (1976), *Long Lonely Highway* (1984), *Faces and Stages: An Elvis Presley Time-Frame* (1986), *Florida Close-Up* (1987), *Elvis Close-Up* (1988), *Memphis Lonesome* (1988), *Elvis: The Cool King* (1989), *Elvis: Fire in the Sun* (1991), *The Voice of Rock 'n' Roll* (1993), *Growing Up With The Memphis Flash* (1994), *Inside Jailhouse Rock* (1994), *60 Million TV Viewers Can't Be Wrong* (1994), *Songs of Innocence Rattle & Roll* (1995), *Shock, Rattle & Roll* (with Michael Ochs, 1997), *Steamrolling over Texas* (1997), *Studio B Blues* (1998), *Inside King Creole (*1999), *The Hottest Thing That's Cool* (2001), *Inside Loving You* (2003), *The Rock 'n' Roll Years: My Wish Came True* (2003) and *Inside G.I. Blues* (2006).

Ger Rijff was a prolific bootlegger, and his Fort Baxter label was a precursor to the Sony licensed "Follow That Dream" Elvis Fan Clubs' collectors label. In the height of summer when the temperature was 100 degrees, he would arrive at RCA's offices in

New York, Nashville and Los Angeles in a long thick coat which was customised with huge internal pockets. Having befriended RCA executives, he would be accompanied to the vaults, and with the connivance of label management left with pockets bulging with master tapes packed with outtakes, alternate takes and the odd previously unreleased gem such as *Black Star*, the original title song for the movie which was eventually renamed *Flaming Star*. He was the first to capture the, "I'll take a piss in every fountain" version of *Heart of Rome*.

We filled our time in Las Vegas by going to see other shows, and visiting the Hoover Dam, the Grand Canyon and the odd Ghost Town, but it wasn't good. Our hotel bar took a load of money and a couple of our passengers who had guitars entertained us with repeated versions of *Rhinestone Cowboy,* a big hit at the time for Glen Campbell, and the Eagles classic *One of These Nights*.

Colonel Parker was still at the Hilton, and having been harangued by fans phoned me and said, "Friend Todd come see me in Los Angeles at MGM please." To be fair, those Brits who approached the Colonel in the reception area leading to the showroom were each given a bunch of photographs, posters and brochures but it was small consolation for not seeing Elvis on stage.

The journey through the Mojave Desert included the usual stops at Calico and Barstow, and eventually we were at Huntington Beach with the possibilities of "*slicin' sand*" and meeting Mickey Mouse. Over the following subdued days our tour escorts did everything to rally spirits but it was not easy.

I followed the Colonel's instructions, headed to Burbank and went through the movie studio gates into the sound stages and outdoor sets of the giant MGM empire, not part of a tourist trail. I was taken to Parker's office. I found the man despondent and somewhat peeved at being judged as the bad guy for not allowing Elvis to tour overseas. Beating his walking stick on top of a well-worn mahogany desk which must have been a discarded prop from *Gone With The Wind*, he commanded me to "Go get an offer for Elvis to play England and take it to Mr Vernon."

Jim O'Brien, Tom Diskin and a couple of MGM executives were present when in walked Freddy Bienstock. "Hello Todd, how nice to see you. Are you here for the meeting?" questioned the head of Carlin Music. "How do you know Todd Slaughter?" retorted Parker. "In England everyone knows Todd Slaughter!" answered Freddy. That fluffed up my feathers!

So, there *was* a meeting, to discuss a follow-up movie to "Elvis on Tour". Was this the film which might include an overseas concert that Freddy had alluded to in the private cloisters of Wheelers Fish Emporium? There was a lot of preliminaries up for discussion but I had a feeling that the MGM execs weren't convinced. If a London concert had been on the table at that time I believe the idea would have grown legs, lots of legs!

At the end of the meeting Colonel suggested that the Fan Club plan a trip for the December season in 1976 when the Hilton would not have to keep so many seats back for hotel residents.

The following day I was advised by Freddy to go and talk with Mel Bush when I returned to England and to see what he could come up with for the spring of 1977. When you think this through, I was just a guy who runs a fan club, yet I was expected to be the go-between for Colonel Parker, MGM, Carlin Music and the Mel Bush organisation. It really didn't add up but I did my best.

Chapter Nine – Wings Over America

I met up with Bournemouth based impresario Mel Bush just after Christmas 1975, and he proposed an Elvis concert at Windsor Safari Park. "Why on earth would Colonel Parker want to play Elvis in a zoo?" I asked. Mel responded, "Well he is a fairground man, and he likes elephants, doesn't he?" He went on to explain that the accommodation for Elvis would be secure in the middle of the lake. He would arrive from the US at Heathrow, be transferred by helicopter and arrive in the same way as seen in the TV show *Aloha From Hawaii.* "Colonel will like that."

Billy Smart Sr. bought the St. Leonard's Estate in the mid-1960s. After his death, the Royal Windsor Safari Park was founded in 1969 by his sons, the Smart brothers: Billy Smart, Jr., David Smart and Ronald Smart. Built on St Leonards Hill in Windsor in Berkshire, England, the 144 acre estate of rolling parkland included a 110 room country house owned by the American Horace Elgin Dodge Jr (son of Horace Elgin Dodge of Dodge Motor Cars) and occupied by the Kennedy family during World War II, when JFK's father was US ambassador to the UK.

A key attraction at Windsor Safari Park was Seaworld, a dolphinarium complex housing dolphins, a killer whale, penguins and sea lions each performing acrobatic displays for members of the public.

Windsor Safari Park was proactive in dolphin research and conservation, employing many wildlife experts and academics. Research efforts included the development of a fishing net warning system for dolphins and the Dolphin Research Project aimed to raise funds for other research on sonar communication and behaviour.

The Safari Park owed its success in part to the natural roaming habitats that had been created for lions, tigers, cheetahs and baboons. A Serengeti zone was also added (featuring camels, llamas, giraffes, zebras and buffalo), an elephant enclosure, a hippo lake, and a monkey jungle.

The Safari Park attracted up to 2.5 million visitors per annum, from when it opened. It grew significantly throughout the 1970s and 1980s.

Young "Lord" William Smart Junior used to come to our Elvis events in South London, and it was only when I noticed that he was dropped off by the family chauffeur in a Bentley I thought there was something odd going on. He tuned out to be the grandson of Billy Smart.

A flight was going to New York, full of Daily Mirror staff and fans off to catch a concert at Madison Square Gardens on 24th May. It was Paul McCartney's "Wings Over America" tour so I scrounged a ride and upon arrival I transferred to a Memphis flight. I checked into the Ramada on Union and met the director of Sales for the Ramada Group. He "compt" me a poolside room on the roof of the hotel and, as my following day was free, I decided to chill big time. As we used that hotel for our fan club groups, I was wined and dined by the Sales Director. We had an amazing surf and turf banquet on the terrace and imbibed beaucoup de bouteilles de vin rouge. It was a beautiful gnat-free evening, but the *Blue Hawaii* track *Let's Go On a Moonlight Swim* was not re-enacted. The moral of this story is "don't swim when you are inebriated".

My meeting with Vernon Presley, arranged by the Colonel, was on the morning of the 25th. I got a cab to Dolan Avenue, knocked on the door and his *nurse* Sandi Miller took me into the lounge for a meeting. Armed with a plan of Windsor and a bushel of documents, I was about to do chapter and verse on the proposed Mel Bush project when Vernon said. "If only I had remembered, you could have come here last night. Elvis was here and we were watching the fight between Ali and that English boxer Richard Dunn. Do you know him?" "No, I don't" I replied, "but my dad used to spar with his trainer in Leicester." I was so deflated but I did the sales pitch adding, "Can you get Elvis over here?" "No son I can't he'll be asleep now all day, because he is leaving tomorrow with the guys for the start of a tour somewhere in Indiana."

I had done what Colonel Parker had asked. Paul McCartney paid for my flight but I guess he never knew it, and Ramada gave me a free room. I called Parker and told him that I had given the documents to Vernon and headed back to New York and the hotel where the Wings people were staying. I didn't have a room so I slept in the closet where everyone had parked their baggage. I was woken up by a pretty young thing, one of the passengers who was from Denmark. I remember that her name was Inger, and on the flight back to Heathrow I was told by one of the tour escorts that she was so friendly she was now called, behind her back of course, "Inger Outer".

Within two weeks of my return to the UK I took my first ever phone call from Tom Diskin, who told me diplomatically that no one in the office had been able to talk to Elvis about my discussions with his father.

At the time I wondered whether Vernon had even spoken to his son, but days later I heard from journalist Bill Burk at the Memphis Commercial Appeal saying there was "Trouble at Mill." Elvis had isolated himself in his upstairs quarters at Graceland seeing no one apart from Billy Smith. Smith's wife Jo was looking after Lisa. Even George Klein had disappeared into the oblivion. Schilling, Esposito, Fike and Hodge were nowhere to be seen, and Messrs West, West, and Hebler, who had heard that they were about to be "retired from service", had negotiated a book deal with one of Rupert Murdoch's publishing houses.

The summer of 1976 heatwave led to the second hottest average temperature in the UK since records began. At the same time, the country suffered a severe drought. It was one of the driest, sunniest and warmest summers of the 20th century. Much further north in Scandinavia there was such an intense heatwave that it melted both the ice cap and the permafrost. Over on the Swedish side of Lapland, well within the Arctic Circle, a WWII British plane became visible, with three crew members perfectly preserved and obviously killed on impact when the reconnaissance aircraft crashed. According to the pilot's log there should have been four airmen on board. The two main newspapers, *Expressen* and *Aftonbladet*, were chasing the story of the navigator and as features editor Sten Berglind was unable to contact anyone in the London bureau of *Expressen*, I was put on the case. The missing airman had a most unusual name, which I am not able to reveal, but he was identified as coming from the Wirral, a peninsula in Cheshire just below Liverpool. I tracked him down and attempted to interview him.

Aftonbladet had been on the phone five minutes before me and were going to fly someone over from Stockholm to get the story. I phoned *Expressen* and the chief editor said, "Offer him £1,000." I got back to Mr Navigator and I said, "speak to me now and there's five hundred quid in it for you. When the other journo arrives tell him you have been interviewed by the *Daily Express* in London." I got the scoop but I needed a picture. I rang a photographer I knew on the *Liverpool Echo*. "I can't help, we're all out on f***ing strike again." I offered him the other £500 and he took a picture of Mr Navigator, got into the newspaper offices and wired the photo to Sweden. The story was fascinating. Crashing in Sweden, which was a neutral country, he would have had to be "interned" for the duration of the war by the Swedish authorities. Saying that he had crashed in Norway, which was occupied by the Nazis, meant that he could be classed as an escapee when crossing into Sweden and, under the terms of the Geneva Convention, he had to be repatriated back to Great Britain. *Expressen* couldn't pay me for my front page exclusive because I wasn't a member of the NUJ so they gave me a quantity of Tor Line travel vouchers.

Over the following weeks I realised that nothing would come of my efforts to get an Elvis concert in the UK and Freddy Bienstock said that a follow-up to *On Tour* was now dead in the water. Privately he confided that, because of rumours of a tell-all book which was about to be serialised in a British newspaper, Elvis' spark had disappeared. In today's climate of understanding and compassion one would openly say, without condemnation, that Elvis was possibly experiencing mental health issues. Any appearance outside his USA "comfort blanket" was now unrealistic. Three years earlier, aboard the Sloop John D when Elton John had given me a bottle of vodka, he was thrilled at the prospect of meeting Elvis the next time he toured the United States. His wish came true in late June '76, backstage at the Capital Arena in Maryland, but he was shocked by Elvis' appearance. The guys looking after Elvis were not administering their duty of care, and, "he already seemed like a corpse." Freddy told me that Colonel was desperately looking for something to rekindle the fire in Elvis' soul.

The British television talent show *Opportunity Knocks*, hosted by Hughie Green on Radio Luxembourg, was bought by ITV. Associated Rediffusion, the network which championed my "Elvis Via Telstar" project, launched the show in 1956. Some of the contestants became big stars after appearing on Hughie's programme including Freddie Starr, Su Pollard, Paul Daniels, Darren Day, Middle of the Road, Mary Hopkin, Bonnie Langford, Les Dawson, Peters and Lee, Lena Zavaroni, Frank Carson, Max Boyce, Pam Ayres and Paper Lace. (Freddy, Su and Darren have all appeared on stage at our Fan Club events.) When Hughie Green retired, ATV launched *New Faces* hosted by the network's midland region newsreader Derek Hobson. Unlike "Op Knocks" the programme had a panel of judges including composer and record producer Mickie Most (brother of David Most who wrote *How The Web was Woven* for Elvis), Tony Hatch (husband of singer Jackie Trent who had a brief fling with Elvis when he was serving in Germany), Lionel Blair (no relation to our former

Prime Minister, Tony Blair), and Clifford Davis (journalist, magician, and an unlikely president of the Daily Mirror Pop Club – he was a friend of newspaper proprietor Robert Maxwell who became known as "The Bouncing Czech" following his embezzlement of his workers' pension fund.)

Along with a couple of *Daily Mirror* prize-winners, Clifford Davis and his mistress travelled with us on our December 1976 trip to Las Vegas to see what turned out to be Elvis' final season at the Hilton. Also booked onto the holiday was Dee Bradford, a Bunny Girl from the London Playboy Club and a previous model in *Playboy Magazine*. As I sat next to her on the bus transfers, she was recognised by a couple of the male passengers but, never being a subscriber, I didn't know her from a bar of soap. (I was doubling up as Tour Escort on that trip as one of our regular couriers failed to show up at the airport).

Having been seconded as one of the Elvis Presley Fan Club Travel Service team and "on-duty" every day, I was too busy to meet Colonel Parker. I did arrange for Clifford Davis to meet the old man and hand over the Radio Luxembourg "Battle of the Giants" all time winner's trophy. Elvis proudly held this up on the stage and acknowledged our group and me personally during his show. Although some of the UK tabloid reports about Elvis' stage performances had been dreadful and US after show reviews were mixed, we thought that Elvis looked great and performed well. To me he did not appear overweight or sluggish in his performance. The three shows I saw were very entertaining, and I did not experience any ranting which apparently did occur a couple of times during that two-week season.

Clifford had been instructed by Robert Maxwell to ask if Elvis would headline a 1978 charity concert in London to celebrate the 75th anniversary of the *Daily Mirror*, in the presence of HRH Prince Phillip, with proceeds going to the Duke of Edinburgh's Award scheme. According to Clifford the Colonel loved his silly magic tricks and said that he would consider the offer. *The Mirror* offered to pay £500,000 in expenses to have the kudos of Elvis Presley topping the bill. Elvis would only be required to perform for 30 minutes.

Our magic man was satisfied with his discussions with Parker, so Clifford, his girlfriend, and I went to see Dean Martin. I was so looking forward to hearing "Whiskey Dean" croon his way through his back catalogue of classics. Boy, was I disappointed! He told unfunny-to-me political jokes which angered sections of the audience, sang half a dozen songs but didn't finish any of them, argued with hecklers and drank a bottle of fizz, whilst at the same time floundering around the stage like a stranded seal. I was devastated - he was shite! How the mighty had fallen.

Chapter Ten - Merry Christmas, Glad Tidings of Great Joy From The Colonel

When the Colonel calls you immediately ask, "What's in it for him?" When the Colonel calls and wishes you "Merry Christmas" you know that there must be a plan. "I would like your people in England to see Elvis in concert. You'll be getting a call from Tom Hulett – he'll explain."

I found out that Tom Hulett ten years earlier had founded the Pan-American concert promotion company, Concerts West. He was instrumental in establishing a national musical events business, beginning with tours for Jimi Hendrix. In the 1970s, Concerts West, headed by Hulett, promoted more than 500 events a year and worked with artists such as Elvis, Cher, Eric Clapton and the Rolling Stones. It could be an interesting call as I had met all his acts previously. A few weeks passed, and no call.

I had corralled the telephone, calculated the time in Vegas and just as I decided to ring the Colonel the phone rang and it was Tom Hulett. "Get a flight to Seattle to see me, then one to Los Angeles to meet with Colonel Parker. I've got 200 $15 tickets for Cincinnati and 200 $15 tickets for Indianapolis. Bring cash and I won't have to charge you state tax. Shows are 25th and 26th June, is that OK for you?"

Within a month I had "hitched" a free ride on an empty Wardair 747. I really was the only passenger aboard a Canadian charter airline along with 20 cabin crew flying direct to Vancouver. That in itself was an odd sensation. In my carry-on I had secreted $6,000, and now I felt like a money launderer. I had no invoice, no paperwork, and not even an address for Concerts West in Seattle. My connection to Seattle was on time and when I arrived at the appointed Holiday Inn, even though it was March, it was warm enough for a swim. It had a good coffee shop with an all-day breakfast meal on the menu with real hash browns. I spoilt myself with a triple shot Screwdriver on the side (Smirnoff and orange juice). A couple of Bloody Marys (Smirnoff and tomato juice) in the bar and I was ready for bed. Tom Hulett met me for breakfast so it was time for more eggs, more bacon and more hash browns but no grits and no alcohol. Money was exchanged for tickets and a lift to the airport. Did he have an office? Who knows, and who cares? I had the stash!

The distance from Los Angeles International Airport to Santa Monica is only 10 miles, and the Holiday Inn there was my favourite. The distance from my hotel to 6363 Sunset Boulevard (RCA West Coast HQ) was also ten miles. A walk down to the Pier, a foot-long hot dog, a paddle in the Pacific, a bike ride to Huntington Beach, another foot-long, then back to the hotel to rehearse my drinking. I really was living the dream.

The iconic RCA building located at 6363 Sunset Boulevard was the West Coast Corporate Offices for the world's most famous record label. It had three main recording studios, which were used by legendary music stars as well as Elvis Presley. The Rolling Stones, The Grateful Dead, Henry Mancini, The Monkees, Harry Nilsson, Crosby Stills Nash and Young, Jefferson Airplane, Herman's Hermits and others were seen there from the time since it opened its doors on 21st April 1964 through the 1970s. The company was anxious to move staff out of New York.

(On 17th January 1994, an earthquake rocked Los Angeles, killing 54 people and causing billions of dollars in damages. The Northridge quake (named after the San Fernando Valley community near the epicentre) was one of the most damaging in U.S. history. It was 4.31am when the 6.7 magnitude quake struck the San Fernando Valley, a densely populated area of Los Angeles located 20 miles northeast of the city's downtown. With an epicentre 12 miles beneath the earth's surface, the earthquake caused the collapse of several apartment buildings. At the Northridge Meadows complex, 16 people died, all of whom lived on the first floor, when the weak stucco structure fell on them as they slept.

Given the strength and location of the earthquake, it was fortunate that the death toll was not far higher. Two key factors were critical in reducing the casualties. First, the quake struck in the middle of the night while nearly everyone was at home in their beds. A mall parking lot in the Valley collapsed, but no one was killed because it was entirely empty. Several highways also suffered critical failures, but only one police officer died, when his vehicle plunged off an overpass. The other key factor was that the city's building and safety codes were strengthened following the 1971 Sylmar quake that collapsed the San Fernando Veterans Hospital. Every building constructed after the new regulations were implemented stayed intact. Still, the quake caused a huge amount of property damage over a wide area, especially in the beach community of Santa Monica, even though it was relatively far from the epicentre. As much of Santa Monica stands on soil that is less solid than bedrock, it suffered severe ground movement during the earthquake. The partial collapse of the Santa Monica freeway snarled traffic in Los Angeles for months. All told, it was estimated that the earthquake was responsible for $20 billion in damages. After the quake RCA relocated the remaining staffers to Nashville.)

I had absolutely no idea why Elvis' manager had requested my presence after picking up the tour tickets. As I entered his hallowed halls, I was introduced to the Knights of the Hollywood Entertainment Industry. They were each perched at King Colonel's Round Table. Waving his trusty walking stick at me he pointed his Excalibur to where I should perch.

I was amongst the great and the good. The president of CBS Television; the vice president of the CBS Network; Rocco Laginestra - Big Boss Man of RCA Records; George Parkhill - Parker's RCA aide; and Dwight Hemion from Smith Hemion the independent production company. Dwight Hemion worked with Elvis when he was an NBC production assistant on the *Milton Berle Show* back in 1956. There were also a couple of lawyers, one representing the broadcaster and the other the Colonel.

Colonel Parker was desperately looking for a filibuster to prevent RCA putting Elvis' future recording career onto the back burner. He also wanted a project that would relight the fire in Elvis' belly giving him something special to work on, his own one-hour TV show on CBS. He had not been on the CBS

Network since the Ed Sullivan days. The discussions with MGM for a follow-up movie to *On Tour* had faltered and were now forgotten.

With his partner Gary Smith, Dwight Hemion was a mover and a shaker in music television, he had also produced the *Muppet Show* for Lew Grade's UK ATV Network. Dwight Arlington Hemion Junior began working in live television in New York City in the 1950s, particularly for the original *The Tonight Show* starring Steve Allen. In the 1960s Hemion began concentrating on musical variety shows, working with producer Gary Smith on a series of popular Kraft Music Hall specials for NBC TV. Smith-Hemion Productions arguably defined the fast-paced look and glamorous style of the American comedy variety genre and influenced scores of later generations working in television.

Hemion had a knack for balancing both visual and musical elements that made him a master of directing concert performance specials. He worked with such major stars as Frank Sinatra, Bing Crosby, Barbra Streisand, Sammy Davis, Jr., Paul McCartney, Bette Midler, Shirley MacLaine, Julie Andrews, Burt Bacharach and Luciano Pavarotti. Now it was time for him to be reunited with the King!

One of the CBS team suggested that they should meet Elvis prior to the filming. The Colonel responded in typical patois, "I don't think that will be necessary, do you Todd?" (Later, the Smith-Hemion crew were to joke that during their research and prior to filming, Colonel charged them for tickets to see an Elvis concert adding, "No one sees my boy for free.")

Just as the contract was going to be finalised, Colonel refused to sign. Everyone looked on aghast. “This man here is to witness, and he will need written into the contract, something for him.” Wow, was I going to get a few quid for signing the 50 page contract? “Todd Slaughter will need 200 polystyrene *Elvis in Concert* hats, rewrite the contract or I won’t sign, and Mr Slaughter won’t sign either.”

In celebration we took all the executives out to lunch. “Joe, find the best burger restaurant and book a table for 20.” Ashen-faced Joe Esposito returned stating that he couldn’t find anywhere as there was a bread strike. “We can get burgers, but there isn’t anywhere that has bread.”

It must have been something to do with the Egyptian bakers, perhaps the LA bread makers had downed spatulas in sympathy with their Arabian brothers. The Egyptian "bread riots" of 1977 affected most major cities in Egypt. Known as “The Bread Intifada”, the riots were a spontaneous uprising carried out by hundreds of thousands of lower class people, protesting World Bank and International Monetary Fund-mandated termination of state subsidies on bread. As many as 70 people were killed and over 550 injured in the protests, which only ceased with the deployment of the army and the reinstitution of the subsidies. Meanwhile Joan Deary phoned her favourite patisserie, and on the way to the burger shop we picked up a few buns from *Chez Pain.* The Colonel invited me to the Beverly Wilshire Hotel later that evening for chicken soup.

1977 was a year for celebrations. It was Queen Elizabeth’s Silver Jubilee, home computers were available in shops, Jimmy Carter was elected 39th President of the United States, George Lucas' *Star Wars* and Robert Stigwood's *Saturday Night Fever* were released in cinemas around the world, and the Sex Pistols released their classic *Never Mind the Bollocks* album. It was also a year of catastrophes when almost 600 people died in the world's biggest aircraft disaster when two 747 KLM and Pan Am jumbo jets collided at Tenerife airport. For Elvis fans the worst was yet to come.

Back in the UK another tour to the USA in June had to be planned, and we also booked the Nottingham Palais for an Elvis Convention over the weekend of 20th August.

Clifford Davis from the Mirror group called to say that Robert Maxwell wanted me to write an Elvis book as part of their *Pop Club* series. Superfan, Anne E Nixon who had written for *Elvis Monthly* and other fanzines undertook the majority of the research and wrote most of the text. Out of the £500 advance I bought Anne a new electric typewriter.

Club 208 had run its course, but we still maintained a close relationship with Tony and the guys in Luxembourg. Tony Prince was, after all, our honorary president and he always went that extra mile to help the club and me personally. I treasure his friendship.

Chapter Eleven – On the Airport Tarmac

Having to visit both Cincinnati and Indianapolis, two cities never on our travel radar, required a creative itinerary. Flight from London to Chicago for two nights, coach to Cincinnati for one night, then a coach to Indianapolis for two nights finishing up at Niagara Falls in upstate New York for a couple more nights. The return flight departed from New York. During Elvis' career we were the only international group of 250 fans to travel to the USA to see him on tour. We were all so excited even though we were outside our comfort blanket of the Las Vegas Hilton. By this stage though the hotel management had grown hostile to overseas groups not prone to gambling.

In Chicago there is lots to see and we did all the prohibition and gangster sites epitomised in movies starring Jimmy Cagney. Gangsters amassed such unbelievable amounts of money from prostitution, alcohol production and bootlegging that they could afford to buy off most of the police officers and politicians in the districts of the city in which they conducted their illegal activities. Corruption in the government system allowed organised crime to flourish and any officials that stood in the way of their criminal activities could either be "bought out" or "bumped off." Smuggling booze across the lakes from Canada occurred on an industrial scale, with Canadian breweries and distilleries doubling in size overnight to cater for the demand. Across the city "Speakeasies" flourished, secret drinking establishments rife with pep-pills and prostitution, where one would knock on the door and as a hatch opened you would whisper *that Boris sent you.*

As we were bussing along Shoreline, we saw signs announcing that "Elvis is in the Building – Tonite at 8.00pm". Perhaps capitalizing on *Jaws* mania, by 1976 the former Lake Tower now featured a plaster fish head at the entrance of its new Coho Lounge, complete with teeth and eyes that lit up at night. (A "coho" is a rather small Pacific salmon *oncorhynchus kisutch* that has light-coloured flesh, is native to both coasts of the North Pacific and is stocked in the Great Lakes – also known as coho salmon, or silver salmon). Our four-bus procession headed back to the waterfront that evening, startling the manager of his empty club as we filled every seat. The guest Elvis Tribute Act had never performed to a full house or, for that matter, met anyone from England before. He was now becoming a "superstar" in his own lunch-time. Totally understaffed the six hookers went behind the bar to help the beleaguered manager and started pulling pints of Budweiser. As well as pulling pints Effy, one of the hostesses, pulled one of our escorts, an unassuming middle-aged gent, onto the dance floor. Her waltz time eroticism certainly stimulated poor old John Bogie, much to the rapturous delight of our passengers. She cavorted with him to such an extent that she had to take him outside for what is called in polite circles a little "light relief".

It was a four-hour drive to our Cincinnati hotel. A film crew from Smith-Hemion for CBS Television was already set up and waiting to greet our group but we were an hour late because we hadn't factored in the one hour time difference between the two cities. Chicago is on Central Daylight Time whereas Cincinnati is on Eastern Daylight Time. Seated on a signature director's chair Colonel Parker was chomping on his cigar when we arrived. I greeted him with a box of Havana Montecristo I had smuggled in from the UK. Interviewing our passengers was an extremely vivacious producer on a sabbatical from Copenhagen. Annett Wolf was, and still is, a highly acclaimed award-winning Danish director, writer, producer and interviewer for TV documentaries, feature films and stage plays. Between 1962 and 1977, she worked for Danmarks Radio, the Danish Broadcasting Corporation, directing numerous in-depth profiles with artists such as Jacques Brel, Jerry Lewis, Dave Allen, Peter Ustinov and Peter Sellers. Now she was the ground director of *Elvis in Concert.* I was travelling with Ian Bailye and he was responsible for carrying two very precious British industry awards. One was a gold record representing half a million copies of *Elvis in Demand,* a UK LP with tracks selected by fan club members, and the other was a platinum award from Arcade for two and a half million sales of *Elvis' 40 Greatest*. It was our intention to see if we could present them to Elvis, but the lady nicknamed the "Wolf Woman" by Colonel Parker said that there wasn't time for this in their schedule. The Colonel was well on his way to Indianapolis. He always arrived at every venue the day before Elvis was due to appear.

We had never seen Elvis perform in an arena before so it was an exciting opportunity to experience a stadium show. The venue was the Riverfront Coliseum and the audience size was 13,000 including 200 of our folk. Towards the end of his performance Elvis acknowledged the presence of his father Vernon, his latest flame Ginger, and our group to rapturous applause. Back in the hotel bar everyone was buzzing, knowing that the following day there was another show for us to appreciate.

At 5.00am there was a hammering on my door. The sultry, and obviously bra-less, Wolf woman had her business head on and ordered me to pack quickly as she was driving me to a surprise birthday party for the Colonel. It was his 68th having been born in Holland on 26th June 1909. "What about Ian Bailye?" Annett replied, "My car is full of camera kit – we have to go!" Off we trundled along the US 421 south.

Our arrival point was the Indianapolis Airport Hilton. We were early so there was time for breakfast. What happened next could have easily been an extract from an episode of ATVs psychological drama *The Prisoner*, a series written by and starring Patrick McGoohan. A photographer with a wooden leg, a former FBI operative, and a bewildered RCA representative, were told not to use the telephone and to remain together in a room without windows. Seriously, as the saying goes, *you couldn't make it up*.

Colonel soaked up the congratulations and glad-handing as he celebrated his 68th with Elvis' hired help, friends and a sprinkling of industry types, mostly from RCA's record pressing plant on La Salle Street. It was the world's largest vinyl factory.

Difficult to imagine that sixty years earlier, according to his widow Loanne Parker, the eight year old Andreas Cornelis van Kuijk did everything he could to avoid sexual molestation from a perverse family member. He was frequently violently gang raped and received no help or comfort from his parents. When he returned to Holland after his first excursion to the Unites States, he experienced the same abuse. He told his mum that he would never be returning to Europe when he crossed the Atlantic for the second time. She was unmoved by his declaration of independence. He sent her money every month up until the time that she died. She never acknowledged receipt or contacted her son again, even when he offered to fly her to Nashville. When his brother Ad told him of their mother's death Andreas was "broken".

A convoy of vehicles assembled outside the hotel as we were all invited to go to the airport. Just as in Luxembourg seven years earlier, when an MGM crew arrived to film our Fan Club members, a side gate leading into Indianapolis International was opened and a CBS film crew drove directly onto the airport tarmac. With military precision we all assembled to await the landing of the Lisa Marie. On 17th April 1975 Elvis purchased his Convair 880 Jet, recently taken out of service by Delta Airlines, for the substantial sum of $250,000. After refurbishing, the total cost exceeded $600,000. He immediately rechristened it the Lisa Marie. Elwood David was the Captain and pilot of the Lisa Marie. Accompanying him in the cockpit was another pilot, Ron Strauss, and a flight engineer, Jim Manny. Milo High was the pilot of Elvis' 'Hound Dog II' JetStar plane. Also, in 1975, Elvis decided to present the Colonel with his own airplane, a Grumman Gulfstream G-1, which he bought sight unseen. Elvis had it delivered to the Colonel in Vegas on 26th July, but the Colonel didn't really take it the way that Elvis had hoped. "You've got to be kidding", was his first response. He turned it down on the grounds that he didn't need a plane and couldn't afford one.

After touchdown, apart from an appearance by the flight crew, Elvis remained in the aircraft. Colonel Parker positioned himself in his director's chair at the foot of the airplane stairs. The Smith-Hemion team assembled their cameras and, as dusk descended, they had to borrow lighting from the local CBS news affiliate. They were located within line of sight of the forthcoming event but out of camera shot.

As we were waiting, the ground producer Annett Wolf, whispered, "When you get close to Elvis have a good look at him. We have all been kept at arm's length – we have not even been allowed to have a picture taken with him. But our makeup lady says that his skin is not good. He is obviously ill, and she added that she thinks that he has about six months to live." That comment sent shivers down my spine and I became extremely nervous at the prospect at meeting him again. Colonel Parker said, "Joe, make sure Todd can travel with Elvis to the arena."

Elvis gingerly descended down the Delta Airways roll-a-way stairs and was greeted at the bottom by Colonel and his father Vernon. As the cameras continued to roll, into the picture came RCA president Rocco Laginestra ready to present Elvis with a framed copy of *Moody Blue.* I had previously received from Rocco the actual two billionth record pressed at his Indiana RCA plant, which had, of course, to be *Moody Blue.*

Now it was my turn, and here I must confess that I was influenced by Smith-Hemion, not to tell the truth, the whole truth, and nothing but the truth, so help me *Todd* of the nature of the filming that day. It had been the Colonel's wish that I had a video copy of my meeting with Elvis but in no way should I say that it came directly from the production company working for CBS. So, a story was contrived that I gave $100 to the news crew to shoot a few frames for me. What I can say is that it was my suggestion that "our" crew borrowed the news-crew lighting when it became dark.

When Elvis got to the bottom of the steps it was not as seamless as it appears on film. There was a lot of farting about. No one was miked up, because "grips" didn't have any personal clip-ons. The ambient noises from the Lisa Marie, in what was a working airport, meant that a boom mike would not have been suitable so what was shot ended up mute.

With no sound to the film the question always asked is what did I say to Elvis that made him laugh? I did say, "You are going to have to come England to see your fans," Elvis joked, "I will if they let me in. One day, I will." Off camera Joe Esposito said, "Can you two get a bit closer", and I said, "You've stood on my foot." Elvis erupted in laughter and added, "Whenever you come to the States you give me awards. The Colonel and I thought you should have this (he presents me with a trophy for being UK Fan Club president for ten years), Both the Colonel and I appreciate what you do for my English fans. Don't look so nervous, there's only 60 million people watching this – I wish I do could more, but enjoy the show

Todd." It was as simple as that and a couple of minutes later Elvis went back into his plane. On other film that I've seen, I'm walking away turning to wave at Elvis, and what happened next is a bit of a blur. Joe didn't put me in Elvis' car, and I travelled to the Market Square Arena with RCA's Jerry Skidmore.

Did Elvis look as near to death as Miss Max Factor judged? It doesn't seem so when you view the footage. He had a cut on his lip and was careful when he de-planed, his eyes looked tired but other than that I didn't see anything that appeared too alarming. I wondered if he might have problems with his sight as he seemed to have to be "pointed in the right direction." That is also apparent when watching *Elvis in Concert,* and it was well reported that he had been suffering from glaucoma. With 20,000 flash cubes firing off in his face every night, that had to have exacerbated his vision.

I got to my seat as Jackie Kahane finished his comedy routine. I say "comedy" loosely, as to me, his act was about as funny as "thrush". American comedians are good at slapstick. Abbott & Costello, Laurel & Hardy, and The Marx Brothers were fantastic. Stand ups appear to have to throw in a few "f***s" to get any reaction.

As Elvis was 90 minutes late, the Stamps and The Sweets had to extend the pre-show warm ups, and add an interval into the format. When Elvis finally walked on the stage the 18,000 strong audience greeted him with rapturous applause. In previous weeks Elvis had only been on stage for 55 minutes whilst filming took place but, with no CBS cameras on 26th June, he performed for 85 minutes. We had just witnessed Elvis' last concert, and it was bloody brilliant. Elvis wasn't sluggish as he appeared to be in the *Elvis in Concert* CBS Special pieces filmed during the earlier part of that tour. Everyone on our trip was well pleased with both arena shows.

Our tour ended at Niagara Falls, then for all of us it was back to reality. For me, I had a convention to arrange.

AUGUST 16th, 1977

What awful weather. Thunder and lightning, very very frightening. It was a dull, dreary, dismal day for what should have been our summer. ITVs News at Ten was always compulsive viewing. They had a network of world-class news gatherers being affiliated with United Press International and the best newscasters. Being an hour later than the Beeb's offering, ITN was always able to capture the late-night stories. Those ten bongs of Big Ben were our nightly wake up call to pay attention. The news of the day majored on the riots in Birmingham against the National Front, and, just as Sandy Gall concluded the newscast for the evening with football results, he handed over to his co-presenter who announced the death of Elvis Presley. Reggie Bosanquet delivered the information as it was coming through his earpiece. He stalled to say that he was just getting a message that Elvis might still be being treated at the Memphis Baptist Hospital. He signed off saying, "Let's all hope that Elvis hasn't died."

ITN took the unusual step after the commercial break to come back on air, delaying the following programme to allow Reginald Bosanquet to confirm that Elvis had passed away. Mark Wesley, who was 208's *Daily Mirror* sponsored newsreader that evening, announced the death of Elvis to the Radio Tele Luxembourg music fans all over Europe. A distressed Tony Prince threw away the playlist, dropped all the commercials and played only Elvis music all through the night. That evening it was calculated that the English Service of Radio Luxembourg had a pan-European audience of 200 million – the world's greatest listenership to any single English language programme.

My home phone went into meltdown. By midnight a Post Office engineer had arrived with a gizmo, requested and paid for by the *Daily Mail,* to bolster my telephone connectivity, whilst at the same time offering to fly me and a journalist to Memphis. I went on air immediately with Tony Prince and Jimmy Savile. ATV sent a car to get me to their Birmingham newsroom where I was interviewed by TV companies around the world. Acclaimed political correspondent, Reg Harcourt, stayed with me all through the night, acting as anchor, and introducing me to a variety of worldwide TV broadcasters. After lunch Thames Television sent a car to take me to a special cobbled-together tribute programme hosted by Nick Ross. It featured a discussion between me, Jonathan King, Joe Brown, and on the phone from Las Vegas, Tom Jones.

One of the nicest pieces of factual UK news coverage came about when London Fan Club Branch Leader, Caroline Zetland, herself an orthodox Jew, put on a Christian church service in North London which attracted 1,000 local fans.

By the end of the month I had done 40 radio interviews, half from BBC Broadcasting House in London, and 13 TV pieces. I remember being recognised in Woolworths in Loughborough which I wasn't prepared for - feeling vulnerable, embarrassed and threatened. Heaven knows what it must be like being a celebrity, politician or pop star.

The weekend came and our convention at the Nottingham Palais attracted a full house; it *was* a sombre affair. Seven TV film crews arrived but were banned by the Mecca Group from entering the venue. A prudence of vicars was seen amongst our audience and, like the money changers in the temple, they too were evicted. In no way were we going to turn an Official Fan Club tribute for our Elvis into an evangelical crusade. St John Ambulance kindly nursed those caught up in the emotion of the time, and an inebriated guest was asked to depart. Sadly, for him, he attempted to come back into the venue by jettisoning himself at full force through the wire-reinforced security glass doors, getting his head entwined like a submarine trapped in an anti-torpedo net. The paramedics freed his shredded bonce and carted him off to Nottingham City Hospital.

Two weeks after his death, there were nine singles by Elvis in the Top 50 and seven of the Top 30 albums. In America, the vast resources of the RCA corporation could not cope with the demand, while the British subsidiary hastily withdrew redundancy notices issued to 94 staff at its pressing plant in Washington, County Durham. No one in the record industry can recall anything like it. Even the deaths of Jim Reeves and Buddy Holly, which both stimulated enormous sales, were small events compared with the hectic activity of those few weeks.

You couldn't open a music industry trade paper or teenage magazine without being confronted with adverts for Elvis T-shirts, charms, bracelets or books, costing anything from 30p for a button badge up to £75 for a pendant. The Colonel appointed a US firm, Factors Etc Inc, as official merchandising company.

The media noted that somehow it seemed a thoroughly appropriate end to a career which was remarkable, not only for its dedicated commercialism (that would be true of most pop careers), but also for the curious religiosity which surrounded Elvis Presley's name. The world was, and still is, a better place with Elvis being part of our lives.

The Colonel rings. "Fly to L.A. Friend Todd. Harry Geissler will pay your ticket." Harry "The Bear" was the owner of Factors, and he phoned. "Colonel wants you on the team, so you'll get a ticket couriered to you tomorrow. See you next week."

They were all booked into the Beverly Wilshire. I checked their room rates and booked the Holiday Inn, Santa Monica. I was met at the airport and taken to my digs overlooking the Pacific Ocean in a stretch limo. It didn't look the same knowing Elvis was no longer on this planet. I took a stroll and had a pint in what I believed was Tom Jones' pub, the Red Lion. He wasn't pulling pints of Watneys, so I guess not.

The following morning the limo arrived. We reached the junction of Santa Monica Boulevard and Wilshire and the driver shouts "Get under the car". He did and I did. A passenger in the car next to us had just been shot in the head. We were there for half an hour before the police let us continue. When we arrived Harry Geissler said, "Welcome to LA. This doesn't happen in Delaware."

I spent three days with his design team discussing Elvis product ideas and agreeing designs which no doubt had already been agreed. Factors handled all the big licensed names, likenesses and images, including a new brand, *Star Wars*. In the movie world you didn't get bigger.

The Bear sent two limos to take me to the airport, one for my suitcase and one for me. Harry had given me an envelope which I opened in the car. It contained a piece of hotel-headed paper with "Thank You" written on it. Oh yes, and two one thousand dollar bills, a "thank-you" from Factors Etc Inc. I felt like a gangster.

Travelling back on the same flight was David Frost. We both got on together, but he turned left into first class and I turned right and went to the back end. I would never have guessed that in two years I would finally be working with him.

I had a good amount of work to get on with for Factors Etc Inc, including selecting the pictures from our archive for a new licensee, Laurence Prince that I had identified. More than 40 years later that Elvis Presley Enterprises Inc license is still in place with Danilo, the calendar people.

At the risk of being criticised as a name dropper, I received a call from Lord Brian Rix. Brian Norman Roger Rix, Baron Rix, Kt, CBE, DL (27th January 1924 – 20th August 2016) was a British actor-manager, who produced a record-breaking sequence of long running farces on the London stage including *Dry Rot*, *Simple Spymen* and *One for the Pot*. His one-night TV shows made him the joint highest earner on the BBC. He often worked with his wife, Elspet Gray, and sister, Sheila Mercier, who became the matriarch in *Emmerdale Farm*. After his first child was born with Down's Syndrome, Rix became a campaigner for disability causes. He entered the House of Lords as a crossbencher in 1992 and was president of Mencap from 1998 until his death. He wanted me to come to London to look at a script for a new musical about the life of Elvis, written by Jack Good.

Chapter Twelve – Oh Boy!

Jack Good was a British producer for television, musical theatre and records, as well as being a musician and painter of icons. As a television producer, he was responsible for the early BBC and ITV popular music shows *Six-Five Special*, *Oh Boy!*, *Boy Meets Girls* and *Wham!!* Good managed some of the UK's first rock and roll stars including Tommy Steele, Marty Wilde, Billy Fury, Jess Conrad and Cliff Richard. He joined the BBC on the magazine-format show *Six-Five Special*. He wanted full-on music and movement. Good had sets built but, shortly before the show started, he had a change of mind, dragging them out of view and filling the space with bopping bodies. This was live television so once the programme started, Good had to maintain a vibe as spontaneous as possible. The running order was sketched out on Friday morning, then the only complete run-through happened immediately before transmission. The show launched the hand jive and Jack Good even wrote an instruction book, *Hand Jive at Six-Five*. None of the *Six-Five Special* shows were recorded as video tape wasn't invented and kinescopic capture was expensive (positioning a 16mm movie camera in front of a cathode-ray tube), but a low-budget film based on the show survives.

Although Jack had given the BBC a show that was attracting 12 million viewers, he was paid only £18 a week. He left for independent television and launched *Oh Boy!* in June 1958 for the ITV franchise holder Associated British Corporation, owners of Associated British Cinemas (ABC). After trial broadcasts in the

Midlands it went national, in direct competition with *Six-Five Special*, on Saturday evenings. *Six-Five Special* stuck to its mix of rock, jazz, skiffle and crooners, but Good was in his rock 'n' roll element with *Oh Boy!* The programmes were broadcast from the Hackney Empire, London, and made a star of Cliff Richard, as well as showcasing Billy Fury in several editions. *Oh Boy!* was non-stop rock and roll. Each show was 26 minutes, and no song lasted more than a minute.

In 1964, he made a one-off programme *Around the Beatles*, but regular rock 'n' roll television had disappeared from British screens apart from *Ready Steady Go*, which made heavy use of Good's technique of building excitement and interest by allowing the audience to mill round the singers.

Jack Good championed the rise of rhythm and blues and went to the United States in 1962, where he spent $15,000 of his own money to produce a pilot show for the American market. After trying for a year to persuade television executives to take the show, he gave up and returned to the UK. A year later, a disc jockey gave the tape of the pilot show to an American television executive, who then sent for Jack. This led to the production of the first *Shindig!* show, broadcast by the American Broadcasting Company (ABC) on 16th September 1964. *Shindig!* had a half-hour spot until January 1965, when it was extended to one hour, before switching to twice-weekly half-hour episodes in the autumn. Occasional broadcasts came from London. Jack fell out with ABC executives and walked away from the project. He had a bit part playing the role of Hathaway opposite Elvis in *Clambake*.

So here I was sitting amongst the doyens and luvvies of the London theatreland. At the meeting there were some of the West End's finest, including choreographer Carole Todd, musical director Keith Strachan, producer Ray Cooney, Laurie Marsh, Brian Rix and Jack Good. Oh yes, and my good friend Freddy Bienstock. I was a sort of consultant. I was to provide Elvis photographs for the brochure, press release and programme, sit in on rehearsals, and, most interestingly, watch the girl dancers limber up every morning. There were to be three Elvii: Tim Whitnall (young Elvis), Shakin' Stevens (rock and movie Elvis) and James Proby (the Vegas Elvis).

Tim was a budding actor who got his big break co-starring in Elvis The Musical. Shakin' Stevens had been a well-known and respected act on the rock 'n' roll circuit prior to being launched into the pop charts following his success in this amazing show. And PJ Proby (James Marcus Smith) born in Houston, Texas in 1938, under the tutelage of Jack Good was one act who profited from being embraced by UK pirate radio, having 10 singles in the charts from 1964 to 1967 including *Hold Me*, *Somewhere* and *Maria*.

Being launched within months of Elvis' death this skillfully crafted musical had to be a success, and playing at the recently converted Astoria theatre, it won the coveted Evening Standard Best Musical Award. Loads of celebrities came to watch rehearsals including a few cast members from *Emmerdale*, Warren Mitchell (Alf Garnett), Bruce Welch (Shadows), plus Arthur Lowe and Bill Tarmey from *Coronation Street*. I learnt a lot about musicals from Lionel Bart who was in the stalls overseeing the construction of *Elvis The Musical*. Lionel Bart was a British writer and composer of pop music and musicals. He wrote Tommy Steele's *Rock with the Caveman* and was the sole creator of the musical *Oliver!* With *Oliver!* and his work alongside theatre director Joan Littlewood at Theatre Royal, Stratford East, he played an instrumental role in the 1960s birth of the British musical theatre scene, after an era when American musicals had dominated the West End. Best known for creating the book, music and lyrics for *Oliver!,* Lionel was described by Andrew Lloyd Webber as "the father of the modern British musical". In 1963 he won the Tony Award for Best Original Score for *Oliver!*. The 1968 film version of the musical won a total of six Academy Awards including the Academy Award for Best Picture. Some of his other compositions include the theme song to the James Bond film *From Russia with Love*, and the songs *Living Doll* by Cliff Richard, *Far Away* by Shirley Bassey, *Do You Mind?, Big Time, Easy Going Me* for Adam Faith, *Always You And Me* by Russ Conway, and several songs recorded by Tommy Steele. By the mid-1960s he was as well known for his outlandish lifestyle, his celebrity friends, his excesses and his parties as he was for his work. I wasn't invited to any of his parties.

Fan Club members filled the theatre one night unbeknown to the cast. After the interval, just as the curtain was due to rise, Jim Proby popped his head through the drapes and said, "I've worked it out. You lot are Todd Slaughter's mob. You're the bloody fan club!" which brought the audience to its feet in uncontrollable applause.

Just before Elvis died the Fan Club had grown to a very respectable 11,000 due to our trips to the States, loads of publicity, and public reawakening to the talent that Elvis possessed. Within six months of his passing that figure reached 29,000 and for us that meant a lot of magazines to pack. Our bookstall title *Elvis Monthly* was back to selling 60,000 copies again.

Fan Club branch activity flourished across the United Kingdom and Ireland. Film shows, discos, discussions and swap meets attracted hordes of younger fans who mixed in well with the fan club establishment. BBC Two, during the six week summer holiday, would screen Elvis movies back to back and the network would even end each presentation with the address of the Elvis Presley Fan Club. Such blatant product placement had never happened before or since on the BBC, but there was a general understanding in the media that our Fan Club was doing good things and raising enormous sums for charity.

Elvis in Concert, the CBS special, was transmitted in the USA on 3rd October 1977 and video copies recorded on North American NTSC equipment crossed the Atlantic, but they were not compatible with the European PAL system. Under cover of darkness, within the editing suites of the Natural History studios in BBC Bristol, clandestine converting did occur. David Attenborough was certainly not aware that his domain was utilised for piracy. BBC Bristol *officially* produced *Long Distance Information* in their "Play for Today" series which centred around a local radio DJ and Elvis fanatic who was on air the night that Elvis died. It was written by Neville Smith who also played the main character Christian Harvey, and broadcast in 1979.

Our second son, Geoffrey, was born on 29th July 1978. I was driving to Heanor and back to Loughborough every day, attending meetings around the country and travelling frequently to Luxembourg and life wasn't easy for my wife Vikki. To my shame I put my Elvis activities before family life. To add insult to injury I was off again to the southern USA to be spokesperson for the British fandom on what was the first anniversary of Elvis' death. I was wrapped up in my own self-importance which was unforgivable, but – well there's no but, because there wasn't any excuse.

The first Official Elvis Presley Fan Club Travel Service "Memorial Tour" to Memphis was planned for 1978 to coincide with the anniversary date of 16th August, visiting Memphis, Tupelo and finishing up in Fort Lauderdale, *where girls on the beaches commit a sin.* We had no idea how many would want to travel but were amazed that twice as many booked as when we were going to see Elvis in Las Vegas. The Fan Club had certainly captured the moment and the emotion of fans who wanted to pay their respects.

When we arrived in Tupelo it was as if the entire city had turned out to greet our eight-coach convoy. The streets were lined with people as police motorcycle outriders flanked our procession to the birthplace. It was hotter than Hades as RCA producer, Joan Deary, and Sun Studio manager, Marion Keisker, listened intently to my speech in response to a welcome given by the mayor.

The role of Marion in Elvis' life must never be underestimated. It was Marion Keisker who first laid eyes on Elvis. After Sun she joined the US Air Force. Elvis had not seen her for many years when on 1st March 1960 he spotted Captain Marion (Keisker) MacInnes at a press conference in West Germany. Elvis told her, "I don't know whether to kiss you or salute!.... We would not be having a press conference if it weren't for this lady."

In 1970, at the Jaycees Ten Outstanding Young Men of America Awards, Elvis was one of the recipients. Elvis saw Marion and invited her to his table. Introducing her to his wife, Priscilla, and his entourage, he told all and sundry, "she is the one who made it all possible. Without her I would not even be here." Years later, Elvis would be quick to remind anyone that it was in fact Marion Keisker, not Sam Phillips, who saw his potential. For me, it was certainly an honour to be in her presence in Tupelo. At events like this I always wondered how Elvis would have felt had he still been alive to experience the love and devotion of all those who still cared. I am convinced that Elvis Presley had no idea just how respected he was and that is so sad.

When we drove into Memphis the city was in lockdown. The National Guard were patrolling the streets in armoured vehicles to enforce a 9.00pm curfew because of a ten day strike by City Police and County Firefighters which was planned to impact on the first anniversary of Elvis' death. All bars across the city were closed. Fans had travelled from all over the world to take part in the first anniversary commemorations. We were based at the Ramada on

Union Avenue and we managed to get special dispensation from the authorities for our hotel to open its bar. By the evening of our first night at the hotel you could not walk down the corridors without stepping over TV camera equipment. The BBC and ITN were with our group, joined by a dozen or more others from as far afield as Japan and South America. Through the journalistic grapevine they heard that we had wine, beer and spirits – we were the only bar in town, so the world's media gravitated into our hideaway. Even the striking cops popped in for a pint of Bud.

On the morning of the 16th it was rumoured that a random Elvis fan had decided to become a human torch and perish in the flames at Elvis' grave. The urban myth of the day was that a reporter from the *Sun* newspaper had a cigarette lighter on hand just in case the suicidee's matches were damp.

Across the road all manner of tat was being hawked by unauthorised traders, and as expected Factors Etc Inc had a vast presence of T-Shirts, badges, books, posters and junk-jewellery amongst a myriad of other licenced souvenirs.

Thousands of fans made their way in a silent candlelit procession to the front door of Graceland. It was as if Elvis had never left the building.

The Elvis bubble was showing no signs of bursting and we took 300 members to the Scottish ski resort of Aviemore in the autumn. The pressure was always on to make a success of everything that I promoted, and with a doubling of membership we had to offer destinations to satisfy every taste.

Attending Fan Club events in different countries over long weekends was always an enjoyable diversion from the humdrum of our daily lives. Luxembourg provided us with the opportunity to be entertained by Tony Prince and the other guys, with Tony doing his headstands. An optional excursion to Bad Nauheim allowed us to follow in Elvis' footsteps, as did a drive to Frankfurt.

Hamburg was just an excuse to take a walk on the wild side of the Reeperbahn (The Ropewalk) and to see where the Beatles performed. The warnings are still legendary: *Leave the credit cards at home*: At sex shops and strip clubs do not pay by credit card. It is common for an establishment to get your PIN and then hike up your spend, say from €300 to €3000! The warnings were everywhere. Leave your credit cards in the hotel safe and consider using a money belt to conceal any extra cash that you may have. *Avoid Side Streets* Hamburg's Red Light District is home to many prostitutes, drug dealers, thieves, and muggers. Always travel in groups of two or more, stay alert, and never wander away from the main area, especially if someone is trying to lure you down a darkened alley. Avoid side streets. Despite our warnings those looking for trouble had certainly come to the right place. In our hotel there was a great Elvis impersonator to entertain us. Ali Aker performed his signature song "Zatz All Right Mamma."

Paris, Brussels, Torremolinos, Gibraltar, Dublin and Amsterdam (for more naughtiness) were popular destinations over the years. Having fun with members of fan clubs across the continent was, and still is, a wonderful experience.

Chapter Thirteen – You Don't Get Me, I'm Part of The Union – 'Til The Day I Die

Whenever the BBC has made documentaries about Elvis fans, they have often pointed a camera and waited for odd-bods to gravitate towards the lens. The annual Porthcawl Elvis Weekend attracts up to twenty thousand Elvis fans to watch wall-to-wall Elvis Tribute Artists. This happy gathering of nonsense will be forever tarnished by a 2018 BBC documentary. Since then Bridgend Borough County Council have threatened to cut their £20,000 funding for the event.

Julia Suddard, a researcher at Yorkshire Television in Leeds, was a big Elvis fan and was willing to discuss our proposition with Yorkshire for a TV film crew to travel with us to Graceland in August of 1979. Within weeks legendary TV programme host, Alan Whicker, had agreed to cover our Memphis trip for a *Whicker's World* Special.

During WWII Alan was one of the first journalists assigned to the Allied forces when they entered Milan. He took into custody an SS General who was guarding money that was to be used to pay stormtroopers. As a Pathé news reporter he discovered and filmed large amounts of cash in foreign currency, all contained within a large trunk. Alan later handed over the SS staff and the trunk of cash to the commander of an advancing US armoured column. He also shot footage of the body of fascist leader Benito Mussolini.

With his long-time partner, Valerie Kleeman, Alan travelled to Memphis in advance of our passengers and checked into the Peabody Hotel. When our charter aircraft, complete with eight YTV film crew, was halfway across the Atlantic news came through to producer David Green that ITV technicians had downed tools. Even Coronation Street went off-air during the strike, which took place from 10th August to the 24th October. The Yorkshire Television station, like the rest of the network, was off air for over two months (although appeals by the West Yorkshire Police in their search for the Yorkshire Ripper were periodically transmitted during the strike). Alan Whicker isolated himself with his girlfriend for a few days and, once it was known that the strike would last indefinitely, he flew to the UK without even saying "Hello." The crew and research team stayed with us for the duration but, in my heart of hearts, I guessed that the idea was now dead in the water.

World International Publishers in Manchester gave us notice that, although they would still publish our *Elvis Annual*, they were about to close their magazine distribution division. Ken Worsencroft was a sales rep for Paul Raymond Enterprises and he looked after the circulation of *Men Only* and *Club International,* two of our nation's most successful girly magazines. He was interested in adding *Elvis Monthly* to his distribution activities, already having contracts with WH Smith Wholesale. To make it economical we needed more titles.

Citizens Band Radio was big in the USA, particularly with truck drivers. There had been fuel shortages and "brother truckers" needed to contact each other to locate gas stations that had supplies. CB Radio was illegal in the UK but broadcast rigs and antenna mag mounts were entering the country in shed loads. We submitted our proposal to WH Smith for our forthcoming title, *CB News*. It took them a month to agree and, as soon as they did, we printed 50,000 copies. A week before we launched, the Exchange & Mart group published *Breaker* and there was the suspicion that there might have been a breach of confidentiality alerting E & M of our plans. *CB News* was successful despite the competition, so we cast a net to find cartoonists. I wanted a sister publication in the Marvel Comic mould and we launched *10-4 Action*. It featured a series of hairy-arsed truckdrivers with their big- busted, scantily dressed, Daisy Duked dames crossing the highways and byways of the USA spouting, “put your pedal to the metal and make your motor tota” jargon.

To stem the influx of illegal AM CB sets, the most powerful having a range of 200 miles, the government relented and agreed to license the production of sets operating on an FM frequency.

Amstrad was a British electronics company, founded in 1968 by a London East End 21 year-old entrepreneur. It produced a range of budget portable radios and telephonic equipment. During the 1970s they were at the forefront of low priced hi-fi, TV and car stereo cassette technologies. Lower prices were achieved by injection moulding plastic hi-fi turntable covers and undercutting competitors who used the vacuum forming process. The origin of the brand Amstrad was derived from the name of its founder’s initials. AMS Trading (Amstrad) Limited owned by Alan Michael Sugar. In the 1980s Amstrad was amongst the first to retail affordable home computers. Alan Sugar famously approached "someone who bashed out dustbin lids", to manufacture cheap satellite dishes. Amstrad was the only manufacturer producing Sky Satellite TV receiver boxes and dishes at the system's launch, and has continued to manufacture set top boxes for Sky, from analogue to digital and now including Sky's Sky+ digital video recorder. Lord Sugar is now host of the UK TV hit show "The Apprentice".

I was the only publisher who turned out for the launch of the new Amstrad CB Radio. I met Alan Sugar in the Dorchester in London's Park Lane and the demonstration began in a room overlooking Hyde Park. He attempted to contact an office junior parked in Hertford Street opposite the Radio Luxembourg offices. "Breaker Breaker this is "sugar-lump" do you copy?" Silence was golden. "Breaker Breaker this is sugar lump - f***in' answer will you?" CB etiquette went out of the window. After half an hour Alan gave up. Scowling he handed me a boxed Amstrad CB 901, "Take that f***er with you and ring me if you can get it to work."

Julia Suddard was in touch in January 1980 inviting me to YTV's Kirkstall Road studio in Leeds. I met researcher Barbara Twigg and production assistant Pat Brown. Both ladies had been on our Memphis trip the previous August and, although the filming was aborted because of the ITV strike, they had remained with our group undertaking a great deal of research, though Whicker had walked away from the project. "So, who is going to host it then?" An extremely nervous Pat Brown responded, "If we tell you we will have to kill you. Seriously Todd we have got the biggest name in television – someone who is a huge star in the USA, it's David Frost." I had no idea just how big a celebrity he was Stateside until we reached Memphis.

In the spring, I went with Davy Jones, one of our tour escorts and a brilliant photographer, to Florida. There was a massive CB Jamboree with special guest Bill Gross, a radio engineer who invented a handheld ground to air transmitter which the resistance could use to communicate with allied planes delivering food, ammunition and equipment by parachute during WWII. The Jamboree turnout was pitiful and confirmed to me that CB radio was a passing fad. With the Mitsubishi Roamer cell phone being tested by the Scottish Fire Service, CB radio was about to become an overnight antique.

Kid Jensen left Radio Luxembourg to support the launch of the Nottingham-based broadcaster Radio Trent in 1974. A year later he joined BBC Radio 1 staying there until the end of 1979, then leaving for Atlanta to take up a position as news anchor for WTBS The Superstation. Jonesy had to go to Georgia to check out the Peachtree Plaza Hotel in the state's capital. When we arrived at this luxurious lodging house we were greeted by Glen, the valet, who was perched on a lectern. Checking in at the same time were the Harlem Globetrotters basketball team. Being sport superstars and each at least seven feet tall, we allowed them to take priority with Glen. As he shuffled off his lectern perch, we could see that the hotel's valet was less than three feet tall, quite a sight being towered over by giants.

That evening I phoned Kid (now known as David), and Paul Burnett answered. Paul was over with his wife Nicole visiting Kid and his wife Gudrún. We all went out for a most unusual meal served in Aunt Fanny's Cabin, a Georgian plantation-themed restaurant that featured young African-American "menu girls" with signboards hung around their necks from a slavery styled yoke. The servers would dance and announce the menu items. Not at all PC in today's climate.

Kid said that there was a special event the following afternoon at the TV station's "dish farm", and we were all given VIP press passes to the happening. Greeted at the door by Ted Turner (in a sailor's cap having recently won the America's Cup), and his wife, actress Jane Fonda, we were there to celebrate the launch of Ted's new 24 hour news channel known then as "Cable News Network" (CNN).

Inspired by this new satellite delivered service, I called Colonel Parker, who invited me to Las Vegas six weeks later to attend a Satellite TV Exhibition in the Hilton's Conference Centre. Returning to the UK with arms full of photographs and literature, I set to work producing a magazine to replace *CB News*. To prevent any "industrial espionage" I printed the first edition before informing the distributor of our new title. When they agreed to take *Satellite TV News* I was able to deliver the first issue within 24 hours.

Although I had previously studied to become a mechanical engineer, I knew none of the science behind satellite broadcasting. My editorial was so technically inaccurate that the head of BBC engineering phoned offering his services, as too did his counterpart at ITV. The scientist who determined the geostationary position for 24-hour satellite coverage between Europe and the United States, Arthur C

Clarke, wrote for us too. The magazine became an industry sounding board publication for this new world of long-distance, real-time, domestically received broadcasting.

Steven Birkhill was a communications developer based in Sheffield. He contacted me as soon as he saw copies of our new title and I visited his "radio shack" behind his home. He had acquired a fire engine turntable upon which he had mounted a twelve feet diameter Marconi parabolic antenna, together with a system of pullies and wires. This enabled him to rotate the satellite dish seeking out a variety of telecommunication spacecraft. Arabsat, the Russian Gorizont, and a selection of US Intelsats carrying NBC, ABC and CBS feeds around the world. Steve too began writing for our magazine.

When our Capital Airways charter arrived at Memphis International, David Frost was VIP'd through immigration and customs. Unlike Whicker, David chose to accompany our 250 passengers, interviewing many during the flight. I took care of his baggage. It was bloody heavy and of encyclopaedic proportions. When I reached our hotel, again the Ramada on Union, I lost my ten-year-old son Gregory who was travelling with me. Panic set in only to evaporate when I found him in a pancake restaurant being treated to a giant stack by David Frost. Production assistant Pat Brown, who went on to produce *Heartbeat*, from then on kept an eye on my son and me whilst Barbara Twigg did all the fixing. Local media swarmed around Mr Frost and CNN sent Kid Jensen to meet the Yorkshire TV crew to get the scoop on the filming for his network. This was a big deal for the Official Elvis Presley Fan Club. We had always attracted attention whenever we travelled around the States but, having the world's biggest TV celebrity in tow, our story made all the major American networks. Even the BBC news team in Memphis for the anniversary carried details of his forthcoming ITV show.

David Frost did not isolate himself from our fan pack. He joined in with all the funny stuff. He was arrested when filming in the Graceland grounds without permission and, by slight-of-hand, my son Greg smuggled out cans of already-shot film that the police were about to confiscate. On hearing of the arrest, the governor, mayor and chief of police screamed up Elvis Presley Boulevard with sirens blaring and lights a flashin' issuing "bollockings" to the overzealous policemen and all was well. It appeared that one of the executors of the Elvis Presley Estate had sold the filming rights to Elvis' grave to *Good Morning America*. All our passengers were filmed, interviewed and featured in *Elvis: He Touched Their Lives*. The YTV team followed us to Tupelo and then to New Orleans. We were so fortunate to get such prestigious coverage, and we still are, to this day. Having David Frost front a documentary around our club gifted us with exceptional media credibility.

That same year in October, in association with the *Daily Mirror*, we filled Pontins Holiday Centre at Hemsby, a seaside village ten miles north of Great Yarmouth for a week with our first Elvis Festival. In 1946, Fred Pontin formed a syndicate to buy an old disused army camp at Brean Sands near Burnham-on-Sea, Somerset which was the start of the company known as Pontins. He gradually expanded his empire to thirty sites including the popular Southport, Camber Sands and Hemsby resorts, all three having played host to The Official Elvis Presley Fan Club. He opened up his holiday business into other parts of Europe, forming Pontinental in 1963 with seven holiday villages, including one which we still use in Torremolinos, Spain, now re-branded as Hotel Puente Real.

From the "get-go" our formula was right, the entertainment first class and from the States, Elvis' karate coach, Ed Parker held a Q & A. This was the blueprint for an event that has been successful over the following four decades.

Elvis was first exposed to karate in 1958 after he was drafted into the Army and stationed in Germany. His first instructor was a German Shotokan stylist named Juergen Seydel who taught Elvis at his off-base house in Nauheim. One nice thing about the military was that you had thirty days of paid vacation (leave) each year. During his vacation in Paris Elvis would take private lessons with Tetugio Murakami, one of Japan's top Shotokan stylists, who would help pioneer shotokan in Europe. At one point he spent nine straight days studying for several hours each day with Murakami.

With a lot of spare time on his hands Elvis would spend hours training with Rex Mansfield, another soldier stationed in Germany. It was during this time that Elvis would also start conditioning his hands for board breaking by banging his knuckles against hard surfaces.

In 1960, with Japanese style training under his belt, Elvis Presley met the Father of American Kenpo, Ed Parker, at the Beverly Hills Hotel after a karate demonstration. Parker introduced Elvis to Hank Slomanski, an instructor at Fort Campbell, to test for his black belt. It was Hank who promoted Elvis to Black Belt on 21st July 1960, giving Elvis his own black belt when he did so. He is said to have sent word back to Ed Parker "Your boy ain't pretty anymore, but he's a Black Belt".

Elvis trained from 1970 to 1974 under Master Kang Rhee in Memphis. He was advised that Master Rhee had a good reputation and came highly recommended by Ed Parker. During the four-year period under Master Rhee Elvis, like all the other students, selected an animal title by which to be addressed in the training area. After first choosing 'Mr. Panther', that name was later changed to 'Mr. Tiger' because of existing political implications associated with the name 'Panther'. Elvis trained with the other students in regular sessions. Classroom discipline was so strict that Elvis was able to train with the same freedom as ordinary students and without the usual press from adoring fans. Elvis was awarded 7th Degree Black Belt in 1973 by Master Rhee and on occasion, had the opportunity himself, to test and promote students of lower rank.

Elvis was an instructor in the Pasaryu Karate Association under Master Kang Rhee, serving with such karate greats as Master Rhee, who had been a Korean Grand Champion, and Bill Wallace, World Middleweight Karate Champion. During one training session he was instructing a female student in a breaking technique which called for the victim to scrape the shins of the assailant. After repeated attempts by Elvis to get her to perform properly, the exasperated student came down so hard against his shins that he collapsed in pain. She had learned. Younger students in the class were often overawed in the presence of Elvis. Upon learning of this problem Elvis called one 9-year-old boy aside to speak with him privately, and presented him with an 'Elvis Presley' engraved watch. Close friends call this period the Golden Years, the years of peace and spiritual contentment for Elvis.

It is safe to say that Bill 'Superfoot' Wallace was one of the biggest names in the world of martial arts in the 1970s and 80s but he also gained additional mystique as one of Elvis Presley's karate instructors. The King was an ardent fan, even once flying in an acupuncturist to treat Wallace at Graceland following an injury to his leg. On 4th June 1973, Elvis gave Kang Rhee a custom deluxe Eldorado Cadillac. This was no ordinary gift. Vernon Presley had purchased the white Cadillac, customized with the Continental rear-end and silver front-end grill, as a gift for Elvis. Elvis drove the car for ten months before bestowing it as a gift on Master Rhee.

What makes this gift so unique? Many friends of Elvis, such as Linda Thompson, his girlfriend at the time, say that he rarely gave away cars that had been personally customized. Elvis held his karate instructor in such high respect that this is how he wanted to express his feelings. We know that many fans want the opportunity to share all the wonderful memories which close friends, such as Kang Rhee, have stored in their hearts. Guests from America have always entertained our audiences in the UK. After Elvis died it was always possible to find friends and family members in Memphis and Las Vegas to talk to our group members about the personal and private side of Elvis' life.

"Elvis Presley was a legend, even in my homeland of Korea". When Master Rhee received a phone call from a man who identified himself as Elvis Presley and told him that he was interested in continuing his studies in the martial arts under his direction, it occurred to Master Rhee that this was most probably someone's idea of a joke; however, several hours later, he found himself seated behind his desk with the legend, Elvis Presley, seated across from him. In this meeting, Elvis explained that he had begun training in the martial arts because he was fascinated with the movements. He found the movements graceful as well as artistic and had the idea to incorporate them to make his stage performances more exciting. Elvis told Master Rhee that it was at Master Ed. Parker's suggestion that he contacted him. Master Rhee: "I was more than flattered, I was overwhelmed".

"Elvis was very humble. In many ways, Elvis taught me more than I taught him. He insisted on training and teaching in regular classes with other students and he quickly realized that students were watching him rather than paying attention in the class. He asked me to arrange a demonstration which would allow the students to view his technique and see that he was attending class as a martial artist, not as an entertainer. I selected a day when a promotion (rank advancement) test was already scheduled and combined the two events. I selected this day because Elvis particularly enjoyed working with children and the student to be tested was a boy”.

“Elvis, who normally trained in a traditional uniform, considered the demonstration a type of performance. Therefore, I designed for him a special uniform and belt, as a sort of costume. The uniform is trimmed in red satin, has the TCB patch which Elvis and I designed together, on the left chest and the crown fist patch on the left sleeve cuff. The belt is a black belt, embroidered with Elvis’ personal information, with all but the embroidered ends covered in the same red satin in which the uniform is trimmed”.

“In the early part of the demonstration, Elvis was demonstrating a kicking technique, when his pants ripped. Embarrassed, Elvis explained to me and the class that he did not wear any underwear, and asked me 'Now, what do I do?' Realizing that the demonstration of further kicking techniques was out, Elvis proceeded to demonstrate a variety of self-defence techniques, including defence against an attacker armed with a hand-gun. He demonstrated several defences at close range and then stepped back.”

“He pretended to demonstrate a defence against a gun technique from more than five feet away. He then dropped to his knees, explaining that the only defence from that distance is to 'pray'. This was very entertaining, the students and all spectators laughed and clapped. Elvis also demonstrated his fighting stance and jokingly challenged me to a fight, which everyone also found entertaining. As well as demonstrating, Elvis participated in the testing of the student by being part of the Black Belt judging panel.

Elvis watched intently as the student worked for his promotion and as others, me included, demonstrated."

Kang Rhee continued "Normally, in a traditional martial arts school, no one can train while wearing shoes or socks; however, on this particular day, I made an exception for Elvis. I made this exception because only a few days before Elvis had surgery to correct an ingrown toenail and I did not want his foot to become infected. Elvis also had an injury to his hand. A fan, in reaching out to touch him, had inadvertently scratched the back of his hand and Elvis had not gotten treatment for the scratch, which subsequently became infected. Elvis said that his hand looked 'much worse than it was'. Elvis was a deeply religious person, having presented me with a bible as a gift. Toward the end of the demonstration, I requested that Elvis offer a prayer for the students."

Elvis planned to make a full-length video documentary about his strengths and abilities in the art form sport of karate. Although the project was never completed, over 40 minutes of raw unedited material was assembled for a DVD programme that was originally released ten years ago. There is sound throughout but the participants were not "miked-up" so, at times, the dialogue is muffled. The footage is mostly filmed in two locations - at the Tennessee Karate Institute which resided above a drug store in Memphis and a smaller amount at Khan Rhee's own studio. First you see Al Hokum doing a 'demo', followed by Bill Wallace looking very, VERY impressive alongside Red West. Then Elvis appears with Dave Hebler and Red West. The most interesting footage is when Red West attempts to threaten Elvis with a handgun. All of these aficionados have wanted to be guests at our fan club events both in the UK and in the States.

Back in Heanor it was time to think of additional titles for our newly established Crofts Publishing business. An event in New York had me searching through the *Pop Weekly* and *Mods Monthly* archives for pictures of the Beatles. A local writer had produced copy to go in a John Lennon tribute magazine following his murder in the archway of the Dakota building. As a "one shot" magazine it enjoyed modest sales amongst 30 or so other tribute publications. We had the best pictures from the beginning of John's career with the Beatles. Another single-issue title that ended up in the best seller's list was a companion magazine that we published to coincide with the Christmas 1980 screening of *Elvis: He Touched Their Lives.* The Yorkshire TV programme made for ITV had an audience of 9,000,000.

Chapter 14 - Now Then, Now Then – As it 'appens!

1981 started with the launch of more Croft magazines including a series of quarterly Elvis fanzines titled *25 Years a King*, *Cannon & Ball* and *Little & Large* poster magazines, a Reggae music title *Rastamag,* and *Cliff with the Kids in America* recalling his first USA theatre tour and written by my secretary, Lorraine Cobb, who travelled with the fans. We published *Pump News,* a monthly free giveaway for a chain of petrol stations throughout the East Midlands.

I was also ghost-writing the *Brian Clough Book of Football* for Stafford Pemberton's publishing house. He also published our *10-4 Action* citizens band radio comic Christmas annual. Having only met Mr Clough for an hour at Notts Forest F.C., and knowing nothing about him, his team, or football, it surprised everyone by selling 100,000 copies the following Christmas. Peter Taylor his assistant manager was a great help, thank goodness.

I was working so hard and, having no time for a normal home-life, my marriage to Vikki failed. It was no consolation that I was doing well other than being able to support my estranged family.

Albert Harry Goldman (15th April 1927 - 28th March 1994) was an American academic and author. Goldman wrote about the culture and personalities of the American music industry both in books and as a contributor to magazines. He is best known for his bestselling biographies of Elvis Presley and John Lennon. He was Machiavellian in every sense, gaining the trust of friends of both Elvis and John and manipulated his sources to tell their personal recollections, combining fact with fiction and causing untold friction. BBC stalwart, Brian Matthew, hosted an arts and culture show and invited me to take part in a pre-recorded episode of his Radio 2 *Round Midnight* show to discuss the Goldman book.

I was waiting in the reception of Broadcasting House and in walked Jimmy Savile flanked by two uniformed air hostesses. “Now then, now then Doctor Todd, what are you doing sitting here in my territory? Do you like my fruit salad? This is pineapple number one, and this young lady is pineapple number two, both willing to make me a member of their airline’s mile-high club as it ‘appens.” I admitted that I was here on business and that I was waiting for Brian Matthew to talk about the new Goldman book. “I’ve read that – it’s terrible what he says about the King. Two things to say to my good friend Brian. Number one – there is no profit in telling the truth. Number two – wait and see what they say about me when I’m dead.” And off he went to record his *Old Record Club* programmes for Radio 1.

After Savile left, up walked John Peel. “Todd Slaughter isn’t it? Must be 25 years since we last met on the North Sea if I remember. Read a lot about you just recently, it really hit me when Elvis died. What are you doing talking to that blond-haired creep? Keep away from him – he is bad news.” And off he popped, no doubt into his perfumed garden, to record his *Peel Sessions* shows. I had only met John Peel once before, on my way back from Radio Caroline. Our tender, Offshore One, stopped at Big L to collect newsreader Paul Kaye and John – that had been a quarter of a century ago, and he still recognised me? That I could not believe. When he died in 2004 at the age of 65, on a working holiday in Peru, John Peel was BBC Radio 1's longest serving DJ. In an obituary in the Times it stated that he remembered the name and face of everyone he had ever met.

For six weeks I worked at Warner Brothers Pictures on Wardour Street in London's Soho district. Their offices were formerly the UK headquarters of Metro-Goldwyn-Mayer (MGM). I was there to promote the forthcoming release of *This Is Elvis*. Negotiated by Colonel Parker this was the only Elvis Presley movie produced and released by Warner Bros. Today they own other Elvis Presley films after purchasing Turner Entertainment, CNN, Turner Classic Movies, which includes all of Elvis Presley's MGM films, Allied Artists *Tickle Me* and National General Pictures' *Charro!*

The Fan Club had provided producer Andrew Solt with film footage of British fans, and early concert footage, filmed by the police, to identify possible lurid and sexually explicit movements by Elvis during his performances. This rockumentary film about the life of Elvis Presley was directed by Malcolm Leo. It combined archival footage with re-enactments and voice-over narration by pop singer Ral Donner, imitating Elvis' speaking voice. It was shown at the 1981 Cannes Film Festival and subsequently grossed $2 million at the box office in the US. My *raison d'être* was to invite celebrities and journalists to attend press screenings in Warner's private movie theatre. After each viewing the newspaper and magazine writers could collect one-liners to go in reviews in their publications ahead of the UK cinema release.

I invited every possible celebrity for an upmarket film and feed experience. Loads of DJs from Radio 1, Radio 2 and Radio Luxembourg; newsreaders from News at Ten and BBC Television News; stars Marty Wilde and his daughter Kim; Kirsty MacColl, best known for *There's a Guy Works Down the Chip Shop Swears He's Elvis* and *Fairytale of New York* with the Pogues, and her father Ewan MacColl, who wrote *The First Time Ever I Saw your Face*; plus David Bowie. I remember well an excitable Janet Street-Porter who beat my head with a rolled-up newspaper all the way through the screening. When the staff realised I was not a nutter I was invited into the projection box and asked to stand on a beer crate to achieve line of sight from the Warner window across the courtyard into a very large French window opposite. Just as I uttered the words, "What am I looking for?" into the bedroom walked a pot-bellied old bastard and a young naked nymphet that he attempted to bang the brains out of. It was a short stay of execution lasting no more than two minutes. The bondage battering he received after lasted longer. She was known as the Happy Hooker of Wardour Street. I had seen enough.

October 1981 and it was time for our second Pontins Elvis Week, this time we had moved to their Camber Sands Holiday Park on the beautiful Sussex coast. Up to 3,000 members filled the venue for a week-long party bash with fans from all over Europe adding to our numbers.

One of our crew, John Bryant, was a sound and concert-lighting rigger occasionally working for Paul

McCartney who lived just down the road. Curiosity got the better of Paul and he wandered into our event in disguise. Tony Prince came with Billy Fury, and we had a handful of 60s chart bands to entertain our excitable audience.

Vikki and I had separated at the end of 1980, and our divorce became “absolute” in April 1982. Our family home in West Hallam, Derbyshire, was part of the settlement, and our sons Gregory and Geoffrey remained with their mum weekdays and I looked after them every weekend. At the age of 11 Greg won a music scholarship to Trent College so I helped Vikki to move to Long Eaton, close to this fee-paying establishment. Six years later Geoff sat the same entrance exam and he gained a free place as well. We had our two children being educated at one of the country’s major public schools and it didn’t cost us a cent.

In the Spring of 1984 acclaimed Elvis photographer Sean Shaver, with Starla, his high school basketball champion girlfriend, was a much-appreciated guest at our Easter Special Festival Weekender at Pontins Southport. Crew member Andy Bacon was sent to the train station to pick up another guest. Armed with a picture of said guest, Andy had to identify Alan Freeman on the busy station platform. For the autumn it was a return to Camber for our Elvis Week with Tony Prince and Kid Jensen. Unless you had experienced the revelry, no words can describe the affinity of 3,000 likeminded souls who gathered to celebrate Elvis’ legacy and renew friendships cultivated within the love for the world’s greatest entertainer. Age, colour and creed were an irrelevance. It was a melting pot stirred and shaken with devotion.

Stoke Mandeville Hospital had a worldwide reputation for treating and rehabilitating patients with spinal injuries. Much of the aftercare was reliant on charitable donations. In September 1943 the government asked German expatriate and spinal injuries specialist, Ludwig Guttmann (a Jewish doctor who had fled persecution in Nazi Germany just before the start of the Second World War) to establish the National Spinal Injuries Centre at the hospital. The centre opened on 1st February 1944 and Guttmann was appointed its director, a position he held until 1946. He believed that sport was a major method of therapy for injured military personnel, helping them build up physical strength and self-respect. The Professor became a naturalised citizen of the United Kingdom in 1945. Guttmann organised the first Stoke Mandeville Games for disabled personnel on 28th July 1948, the same day as the start of the London Summer Olympics. The games were held at the same location again in 1952, and Dutch World War II veterans took part alongside the British making it the first international competition of its kind. These Stoke Mandeville Games have been described as the precursors of the Paralympics which were subsequently officialised as a quadrennial event tied to the Olympic Games. The first Paralympic Games, no longer open solely to war veterans, were held in Rome in 1960.

Jimmy Savile took on the challenge of raising £6 million for the hospital, and we collected donations from Elvis fans for a full year. We sent out donation cards to all members upon which could be affixed 20p coins in rows of five. A full card was equivalent to a fiver. We ended up with one hundred and seventy-five thousand 20p pieces which reluctant Barclays Bank staff exchanged for a £35,000 cheque. Jimmy Savile was a surprise guest at our Elvis Week now back at Pontins, Hemsby on Sea. He arrived in his Rolls Royce JS 247 to collect the cheque and agreed to be photographed individually with everyone present, providing each put a quid into a pot. At the end of the photograph session Savile was temporarily blind, and the on-site amusement arcade exchanged the pound coins for an additional cheque of £2,000 for the Stoke Mandeville Hospital Trust. By the end of the year we had collected a total of £50,000 for the hospital charity. My son Gregory and I were invited to Stoke Mandeville Hospital to present the additional £15,000 cheque. I still have a picture of my young son sitting on Jimmy Savile's knee - now then, now then!

Hemsby village is still the spiritual home of the Elvis Presley Fan Club "Elvis Week" and has been so for 40 years. Over those years our guests have included Elvis' musicians and vocalists D.J. Fontana, Scotty Moore, Charlie Hodge, James Burton, Glen D Hardin, Ronnie Tutt, Jerry Scheff, The Imperial Quartet, The Stamps, Kathy Westmoreland, and The Sweet Inspirations. We have also played host to members of Elvis' Memphis Mafia. Chart-topping British acts have also performed including Marty Wilde, Billy Fury, The Searchers, The Swinging Blue Jeans, Manfred Mann, Alvin Stardust, Suzi Quatro, Wayne Fontana, Joe Brown, Amen Corner, Union Gap, Pinkerton's Assorted Colours, John Leyton, Jess Conrad, The Tornados, PJ Proby, The Fortunes, Shakin' Stevens,

Showaddywaddy, Billy J Kramer, The Tremeloes, The Pacemakers, Herman's Hermits, and dozens of others. Freddie Starr arrived at Hemsby via helicopter, landing on the playing field in the middle of the camp. American fans are amazed to learn that pop stars who topped their Billboard Hot 100 regularly came to our Fan Club happenings in droves, yet Stateside, the only people who turn up at fan gatherings are withered and botoxed ex-girlfriends and Elvis' fair-weather "friends", anxious to turn a coin selling their "I was Elvis' Best Friend" autobiographies. Two thousand Elvis Presley Fan Club members bopping at the dance hall was a nightly sight to be seen, frequently featured in TV newscasts and archived today, courtesy of YouTube.

The wonderful D.J. Fontana, and I don't say that lightly because he was truly wonderful, was a regular guest; he loved our Hemsby Elvis Festival nonsense. He had the best of times. When he performed he was armed with accuracy, power, swing, dynamics and great timing - the best drummer ever. D.J. rocked the greatest singer ….. ELVIS!. He did it year after year, record after classic record. In a world of one trick ponies and lucky "Rock Stars," D.J. was the real deal. There was no edge with D.J. - he was a beautiful, gentle man who made friends with everyone and made every Elvis fan feel special. He was polite, funny, entertaining, compassionate, and always "game for a laugh". Being dressed up as a baby and being pushed around Hemsby in a bed collecting charity money in a bucket, he loved every minute of being in the company of Elvis' British fan club members. If our group was in Memphis he would come and find us. When we arrived at the airport, more often than no,t he was also at the baggage carousel picking up his own luggage and his eyes lit up when he saw hundreds of bedraggled Brits, and he helped them retrieve their bags. A real friend – a decent bloke – a diamond.

D.J. Fontana was the first drummer in Elvis Presley's band and played with him for 14 years, from Elvis' earliest days in the national spotlight through the 1968 television special, called simply *Elvis* that was widely hailed as Elvis Presley's return to form. It is important to know that it was never called *Elvis' 68 Comeback Special* (Colonel Parker strongly objected when NBC used that tag. This is no comeback special – Elvis has never been away!) D.J. backed Elvis on more than 450 recordings, including hits like *Hound Dog*, *All Shook Up*, *Blue Suede Shoes* and *It's Now or Never*, and was seen playing with him in the movies *Loving You, Jailhouse Rock* and *G.I. Blues*. He was later an in-demand studio musician in Nashville.

D.J. Fontana's entry into rock history came by way of his job as a member of the house band on *Louisiana Hayride,* a popular country music radio show broadcast from Shreveport, Louisiana. Elvis Presley, then at the beginning of his career, appeared on the show in October 1954 with his backing band, which at the time consisted of just two musicians: Scotty Moore on guitar and Bill Black on double bass. D.J. played with the band on that broadcast, and the next year he became a permanent member. Elvis' blend of country, blues and other elements was already distinctive. The addition of D.J.'s powerful drumming raised it to a new level.

"Elvis and Scotty and Bill were making good music," the drummer and singer Levon Helm said in an interview with The Associated Press in 2004, "but it wasn't rock 'n' roll until D.J. put the backbeat into it." In its early days the band played mostly the country music circuit where guitars, mandolins and fiddles dominated, and drummers were generally shunned. On early television appearances, including Elvis Presley's first on the television version of *Louisiana Hayride* in 1955 D.J. was hidden behind a curtain, his drums heard but not seen. By the time Elvis made his first appearance on *The Ed Sullivan Show*, in September 1956, a performance seen by 60 million viewers, the drums were in plain sight — and Elvis Presley was well on his way to becoming a worldwide phenomenon. While his star rose, his band remained on a fixed salary, causing increasing dissension. In a joint interview with *The Memphis Press-Scimitar* in late 1956, his three sidemen said they were each being paid $200 a week when on tour (the article called that "good money for sidemen") and $100 a week the rest of the time. They added that Colonel Tom Parker had permitted them to supplement their income by recording without Elvis.

Dominic Joseph Fontana was born in Shreveport on 15th March 1931 to Lena (Lewis) and Sam Fontana. His father owned a grocery store. D.J. Fontana's early influences were big-band drummers like Buddy Rich and Gene Krupa, and he played in local strip clubs and served in the Army in Korea before joining the "Hayride" band. "I heard Scotty and Bill and Elvis one night and knew that I couldn't mess up that sound," he said in recalling his introduction to Elvis Presley's music. "I think the simple approach comes from my hearing so much big-band music. I mixed it with rockabilly." D.J. Fontana worked with Elvis throughout his career until 1969 when Elvis started using increasingly bigger ensembles for his records and his appearances in Las Vegas. D.J. no longer felt he belonged, and the two parted ways. They never worked together again. D.J Fontana worked steadily after that as a session drummer in Nashville, recording with Waylon Jennings, Dolly Parton, Steve Earle and others. On occasions he reunited with Scotty Moore. In 1998 the two received a Nashville Music Award for the song *Going Back to Memphis* from their album *All the King's Men*; in 2001 they backed Paul McCartney on the Presley hit *That's All Right*, a track on the various-artists album *Good Rockin' Tonight*: *The Legacy of Sun Records.* (On one occasion Scotty came with D.J. to our Elvis week at Pontins in Hemsby).

One of the unexpected highlights was a cable TV service which was routed to all chalet accommodation. This service enabled the Pontins Yellow Coats to update holidaymakers with entertainment news during the season. When we were resident PTV was rebranded ETV, and we were on air with our own slapstick breakfast programme, a lunchtime special, a teatime update and Elvis movies throughout the day. Our occasional late-night programming was somewhat raunchy and often bloody inappropriate, attracting huge audiences.

The breakfast show was a must-watch, featuring roving camera reports from chalets, celebrity interviews and hourly news bulletins. I might not have cut the mustard reading the news on Radio Caroline in the 1960s, but I was in my element on ETV. I would diligently rob the news from the BBC in the early hours, just like we did on the boats, and read it to camera whilst being pelted with custard pies and assorted slime. A wet T-shirt competition was a must-see, but we also reported from the party-political conferences which always seemed to coincide with our event. The eight o'clock morning pan bang alerted those still asleep that we were on the air. By the end of the week most saucepans and frying pans were knackered. Pontins were not that bothered as the bar take during the week was greater than a month's sales during the height of their season.

During the 1980s there were an abundance of Fan Club sponsored one day events. The 25th anniversary of the fan club was celebrated in Wembley. The venue, originally dubbed as "Wembley Empire Pool", was constructed in 1933 for the Empire Games and later the Olympics. At the time it was the largest indoor swimming pool in the world. The swimming pool had a cantilevered hardwood structure that transformed the arena into a concert venue with a 12,000 capacity which was used throughout the 60s as the home for the annual NME Poll Winners Concert. By the time we used it in 1982 it had been renamed Wembley Arena. The guest list for our celebration was amazing. Actors Christopher Timothy and Norman Rossington were joined by Jess Conrad, Tony Prince, Mike Read and Billy Fury. Billy was such a lovely bloke. He was so drunk on champagne and kept thanking me repeatedly for such a wonderful day, at the same time trying to smoke two cigarettes at once.

Freddie Starr recreated an entire Las Vegas Elvis act backed by the BBC Northern Dance Orchestra. The show was to be filmed by ITV but, as a result of Freddie's derogatory comments about the network, Thames Television cancelled the filming. To say that Freddie was a loose cannon was an understatement. I had known him for many years – he was a fabulous bloke and his pranks were legendary. I was in the wings at the Britannia Pier Theatre in Great Yarmouth, watching the chorus girls strut their stuff to *Singing in the Rain* when Freddie clambered onto the gantry above the stage and pee'd all over them. I didn't escape the embarrassment either when watching his show at Blazers Night Club in Windsor. In the middle of his show he stopped his routine to welcome various local dignitaries, Bernie Clifton and Lorraine Chase, finishing by asking me to stand up and adding in his campest and limp-wristed persona, "And I would like to thank Todd Slaughter for last night!"

Freddie was born in Huyton in the county of Lancashire, England. One of seven children, he was the son of a bricklayer, who was often unemployed. According to Freddie, his mother Hilda was from Germany and was Jewish. His twin brother died at birth. As a young child, he was repeatedly beaten by his drunken father, also a part time bare-knuckled boxer. In one incident, he broke both of his son's legs. At the age of six, Freddie stopped speaking and was taken into care. As a result of these experiences he was teetotal for life. In the early 1960s he was the lead singer of the Merseybeat pop group, The Midniters, which was managed by Brian Epstein. The group recorded three singles, each produced by Joe Meek. The singles all failed to enter the charts.

Still relatively unknown to television audiences, Starr was discovered through the talent show, *Opportunity Knocks,* in 1967, where he appeared as part of comedy/beat act Freddie Starr and the Delmonts, winning the popular vote each time over six weeks. He appeared on the 1970 Royal Variety Performance during which he impersonated Mick Jagger of the Rolling Stones, Max Wall and Adolf Hitler in Wellington Boots. Freddie was the subject of one of the best known British tabloid newspaper headlines. On 13th March 1986 *The Sun* carried as its main headline: "Freddie Starr Ate My Hamster". In response Freddie said, "I have never eaten or even nibbled a live hamster, gerbil, guinea pig, mouse, shrew, vole or any other small mammal".

In 1985 my heart was broken. My father’s funeral took place on the day that BBC TV’s *Eastenders* was first broadcast. He was 76. My lovely dad had been diagnosed with Parkinson’s five years earlier and, although he coped with the disease for a couple of years, the last three were distressing and frightening for him. He had previously suffered two heart attacks, but generally throughout his life he was physically strong and incredibly wise. I never heard him swear, although he may have on the building site.

Dad was working on an extension and he needed some sand and cement to repair our garden wall. He used a few coin-bags emblazoned “Barclays” to hold the sand and cement, and tied them to the crossbar and handlebar of his pushbike. On his way home he was arrested and cautioned by a couple of bobbies in a Panda car. There had been a bank robbery in Leicester and they thought my little dad was the villain. They threw his bike into a hedge, cuffed my dad and put him in the back of their car along with the "loot". At the cop shop, they sliced open the bags on the desk sergeant's counter, covering the top and PC Plod in cement dust.

True Detective, along with *News of the World* were my dad's favourite weekly reads. He loved American gangster stories and I regret to this day that I was never able to take him to Chicago.

My Dad was a gentle and emotional man who sobbed like a baby when I discovered I had been adopted. I knew that he was getting ready to die when he said, "Brian, they say that the last mile is the longest. Well I can tell you it is, but I'm nearly there." When dad passed away his loss confirmed to me that there was no God, a belief that I resolutely hold to this day. (As Staff Sergeant Barry McGuire sang in *The Eve of Destruction,* "Hate your next-door neighbour, but don't forget to say grace" – such hypocrisy camouflaged behind a veil of religious hocus pocus.) Had there been one, He or She would not have allowed *my dad* to suffer so much. We might have been piss-poor, but love, kindness and dignity shone brightly from his heart and soul. I have never been able to aspire to his greatness.

Chapter Fifteen - The Empire Strikes Back

I launched a consumer magazine for collectors of pop music videos. *Rock Video* featured every music video title on sale in the UK. Stapled in the middle was an order form with a couple of articles and some editorial written by me under the pen name of Mark Stringfellow. We had a wholesale account with Golds, the best wholesaler for media product. I could buy Elvis-recorded product cheaper from them than RCA, and all the Elvis Presley video titles as a one-stop source. Pal Granlund (Flaming Star Elvis Presley Fan Club) had a chain of video shops across Oslo but there was one genre of material that he couldn't access in Norway. I don't need to tell you the content of these movies when I reveal that the company producing said properties was Electric BLUE. Pal bought hundreds of these skin flicks for his 12 stores.

Sales of *Rock Video* were sluggish so I made the next edition a pirate radio special, with a front-page illustration of the video programme "The Story of Radio Caroline", an East Anglia production. The Marine Offences Act had made it illegal to support pirate broadcasters but I arranged for a wedge of advertising on Radio Caroline to coincide with the publication date of *Rock Video* magazine. We printed 50,000 copies which were all sold in a week.

"This is the Department of Trade and Industry, can I speak to Mark Stringfellow, please?" I replied that he was not in the office. Within 24 hours I received a registered letter threatening unlimited fines and up to two years in prison. I rang the DTI, giving my name as Todd Slaughter and stating that Mr Stringfellow was no longer working for us as he had been given his cards. The customs officer asked, "Are you the guy that runs the Elvis Club, I'm a member. You are doing a great job Todd."

In 1984 Elvis' best friend and musician, Charlie Hodge, decided to move to England for a year to escape the torment of US fan politics. Graceland had by then been open to the general public for a couple of years. He was unimpressed by his fellow "Memphis Mafia" members who were competing for attention with those running the mansion. Charlie claimed that he was emotionally destroyed by Priscilla's "blanking" of him, ignoring his continued loyalty to Elvis, whilst others in favour were selling salacious kiss-and-tell stories to the tabloids. I can understand why Elvis loved him so much. Similar to Elvis in many ways he was highly intelligent and spent time reading a wide range of literature and considering different philosophies. Charlie was the most talented and entertaining court jester Elvis could have found in his life.

Born in Decatur, Alabama, Charlie Hodge began his musical career at age 17 in a gospel quartet, The Path Finders, with Bill Gaither. At 5'3", the tenor singer stood on an empty Coke crate as a comedy routine while singing with the quartet. Hodge then joined The Foggy River Boys, and first met Elvis in 1955 after the group performed in Memphis. Elvis came backstage while visiting to promote ABC-TV's *Ozark Jubilee.* Before Elvis became a national success, he told Charlie that he listened to The Foggy River Boys on the radio; at that time they were the number one gospel quartet in the country. During Army service they met again in

1958 at Fort Hood, Texas, travelled on the USS Randell to Germany together, and furloughed at the same time to visit Paris together. The two became friends and the guitar-picking tenor singer subsequently became part of Elvis' close entourage domestically, in the recording studio and on stage.

During his stay in England I took Charlie everywhere. He guested at our Fan Club events across Great Britain and Ireland, Germany, Norway, Denmark, Luxembourg, Belgium and behind the iron curtain to Hungary. It was so cold in Budapest that I had to borrow a pair of Charlie's long underwear, and because he was such a little sod we both referred to them as "short johns". Charlie also came with us to Torremolinos and was taken aback on seeing so many topless girls on the beach. He based himself in Norwich and acted as narrator in an Elvis musical which was written by local speedway driver, Barry White. The show was extremely popular in small theatres across East Anglia and also featured *Double Trouble* actress, Annette Day. (White was arrested having been charged with indecent assault on two under-age girls and committed suicide the day before his court hearing by tying his hands and legs together and tipping himself into the Norfolk Broads.)

Charlie Hodge was a great raconteur. All you had to do was wind him up, put a microphone in his hand and he would go the whole nine yards to express his love for Elvis. He was adored by fans and his conversation pieces were legendary. Charlie always wanted to be in a gospel quartet. He enrolled in the Stamps School of Music and met Bill Gaither when he graduated. They formed a quartet, sang together for about a year and then split. *"I went on network television and that's how I met Elvis. We played Memphis with Red Foley. And he came backstage and met Mr. Foley and then over to meet my quartet. And I didn't see him again until we both were drafted in the military"*. Charlie was standing on an old crate and singing when Elvis first saw him. The memory always made Charlie chuckle. Elvis liked people who knew how to bring laughter into his world. Every great person in history has had a kind of court jester, or a comedian around him. He always had someone who could make him laugh. 'The comic can get away with saying just about anything to him - and he can say anything he wants to his jester and the guy won't get mad at him.' That was to be part of Charlie's job for Elvis.

Throughout the 1980s our week-long Elvis Festivals in Hemsby were, and still are, a highlight of most UK fans' calendars. We augmented these events with one-dayers in the De Montfort Hall in Leicester and at venues in Bournemouth, Southend-on-Sea, Edinburgh, Norwich, Bristol, Newcastle, Blackpool, Birmingham and London. The formula for the day events involved Elvis' companions from the States, former chart-topping acts from the 60s and 70s, radio DJs and a variety of celebrities, all held together seamlessly by Ian (Major) Bailye, Bob Bacon and his brother Andy.

It was a real scoop when we had the star of ITN's News at Ten the day after he resigned from the programme. His appearance at our convention in Leicester attracted journalists from all corners of the UK. He was the UK's most famous newscaster, Reginald Bosanquet, who was reading the news the night that Elvis' died. Reggie was a staffer on ITN from its earliest days, initially as a sub-editor. He later reported from many parts of the world and was diplomatic correspondent for four years, before becoming one of its lead anchors during the late 1960s and 1970s, often working alongside Andrew Gardner, Leonard Parkin, Sandy Gall and, towards the end of his tenure, Alastair Burnet.

His partnership with the beautiful Anna Ford on News at Ten was popular with viewers in the late 1970s. Anna recalled, "Reggie was a dear. I mean, you wouldn't have chosen a man who had epilepsy, was an alcoholic, had had a stroke and wore a toupée to read the news, but the combination was absolute magic."

When I wrote a letter to invite him to our "do" at the De Mont, he phoned the office inviting me to lunch at his club. The club was the members' dining room at the Wimbledon Tennis ground. "Let's have well burnt bangers and mash old boy. The best nose-bag in the world." The saying is: never, never meet your heroes or you will be disappointed but that ain't true in my case. Reggie's fee was £300, which he refused to accept. "Stick it in the charity box old boy and here's another two hundred quid to make it up to a 'monkey'. I've had a bloody fantastic time – I've just met Marty Wilde." Marty's wife Joyce, a show business agent said, "How on earth did you get "Beaujolais?" I've been trying to book him for years. What did he charge – it must have been thousands?" I replied, "He paid us two hundred quid to be here." Her jaw dropped in amazement.

My magazine *Satellite TV News* joined forces with an exhibition company to stage a Satellite Television exhibition in London. Brian Haynes, formerly of Thames TV, had been using an orbiting test satellite to deliver two hours of music programming to those with cable telly in Europe. Rupert Murdoch, of News International, purchased the failing business for £5 million and continued to broadcast in Europe as Superstation Europe which was not licensed for reception in the UK. The exhibition featured satellite reception equipment of industrial proportions, potential international programming pilots, mostly game shows, and CNN. Radio Télé Luxembourg was also pioneering product. The conference was hosted by former prime minister, Sir Harold Wilson. This made him an enigma as he hated the prospect of commercial radio, closing offshore radio during his premiership, yet here he was championing the expansion of commercial television in his dotage. I don't use the word "dotage" lightly as he read the same speech twice when opening the conference, displaying the onset of Alzheimer's. When talking to me in the Gents the former prime minister turned towards me and pee'd all over my feet. There was a trend developing. First the brother of a US president, and now a former UK prime minister.

In 1985 it was Elvis Presley's 50th birthday, so we filled The Empire Ballroom in London's Leicester Square. Lots of star guests and celebrities appeared including Larry Geller from the USA, The Swinging Blue Jeans and Kim Wilde. We raised £15,000 for the Stuart Henry Multiple Sclerosis Appeal. The cheque was presented by actress Irene Handl.

Our August trip was no longer based in downtown Memphis but on Brooks Avenue, close to Graceland.

We started to promote our annual "Meet The Brits" Elvis disco parties in the massive function room of the Quality Inn. The 1,000 capacity venue attracted fans from all over the world, which in turn attracted Elvis' fair-weather friends who each had a book to peddle. Every member of the Memphis Mafia would roll up, even those who disliked me, and loads of staff from Graceland including Graceland CEO Jack Soden. I was standing at the entrance when this deeper than deep voice greeted me with an unexpected request. "Is there any one here that I can f***?" Our nearer-to-god-than-thee vocalist J.D Sumner had arrived "to party".

We had started a little T-Shirt business working with Factors Etc Inc., which later developed into industrial uniforms and clothing. The trading name was Maybe Baby Fashions and in later years became Uniforms to Go. When Juliet moved to Nottingham she worked for Speedo the swimwear and sports fashion company. Her family were farmers from Northowram in West Yorkshire. They lived in a farmhouse accessible from the top road, and overlooking a valley. On the other side was a secluded house which in the evening always seemed to be illuminated by spotlights. It only became apparent what was going on when the owner set light to a huge stack of magazines, and partially burnt pages were caught in the air by thermals and drifted across the undulating terrain towards the farm. Juliet's dad collected the airborne flotsam – porno pictures.

At the end of 1985 I married my second wife Juliet. Sten Berglind was my best man, who had been dating Anki, the former wife of celebrity busker Don Partridge who had a top ten hit with "Rosie". Don had moved to Barrow upon Soar (just 3 miles south of Loughborough), was living on a house boat and was a regular performer in the town's market place.

We had bought a house in Loughborough and by late summer our daughter Jennifer was born. Juliet has two brothers, Matthew and Charlie and a twin sister Sally who is a pharmacist.

In 1987 we returned to the Empire in London's Leicester Square and an even bigger audience as it was the tenth anniversary of Elvis' death. We branded the event "Elvis: Ten Years After" and our star visitors included Adam Woodyatt (Ian Beale), Susan Tully (Michelle Fowler) and Najdet Salhid (Ali Osman) - all from *Eastenders*, Chas & Dave, and the infamous Gary Glitter. At the time Glitter was a superstar from the glam rock era of the previous decade. His star was still shining though his "velcroed syrup" was beginning to look a little shabby. His piggy eyes resembled puppies fart holes.

Over the years there have been numerous attempts at assembling a posse of pop stars to pay tribute to Elvis and his legacy. Elvis Presley Enterprises announced that their "Big Show" at the Memphis Pyramid would include Tom Jones, Paul McCartney and Elton John, but ended up with Wet Wet Wet and a handful of country stars not known to the public outside of Tennessee.

I was thrilled to be asked to play a small part in a production by Central Television at their newly constructed studio complex in Nottingham.

More than 20 of the world's top rock stars gathered in the Midlands for a two-hour TV special to mark the anniversary of Elvis Presley's death and Fan Club members made up the audience for the recording of Central TV's rock spectacular *Love me Tender*, on 1st August 1987. We were in amongst pop and rock royalty and an Elvis tribute show doesn't get better than this line-up.

It was like a record store magically brought to life. You couldn't walk along a single corridor without bumping into a rock legend or a pop star. Turn a corner and you were chatting to Boy George; a few steps further and you met the mighty Meat Loaf; a stroll back and there was jovial Jaki Graham. They came from all round the world to gather at the giant Studio 7 in Central Television's Nottingham headquarters. They came to pay tribute to the King. Nona Hendryx, Ben E. King, Meat Loaf, Duane Eddy and Carl Perkins jetted in from the States; Dr. Robert rushed over from Paris, and Jaki Graham dashed from Malta.

Another limousine arrived offering up Elvis' original backing band - James Burton, Glen D Hardin, Jerry Scheff and Ronnie Tutt - direct from America. The foursome was teamed up for the first time since they had worked with Elvis and later stormed through a set with The Who star, Roger Daltrey.

Also appearing were Kim Wilde, Elkie Brooks, Dave Edmunds, Kiki Dee, Cozy Powell, PP Arnold - truly a star-studded supporting cast. As news spread fans began to arrive on the doorstep to catch a glimpse of the stars. Boy George fans, clutching teddy bears, were far outnumbered by Elvis Fan Club members, but everyone got on so well. Perhaps inspired by the fans, George later went on to add a version of *Teddy Bear* to his planned recording of *Are You Lonesome Tonight*.

Inside Studio 7 the stars were hard at work rehearsing. Birmingham soul queen, Ruby Turner, summed up the effort: "We all know Elvis songs - but how many people know the third or fourth verses?" Jaki Graham, Ruby's close friend, added: "All the hook-lines are there in your memory - but half the songs have to be learned all over again!"

In the dressing rooms there was organised chaos as the army of Central TV support staff looked after the needs of the superstar fan club. One make-up girl was dashing between two rooms to meet the vastly different demands of her charges, blonde bombshell Kim Wilde and soul singer Ruby Turner.

As recording began there was a "family" feel about the studios. In each corner clusters of stars gathered, renewing friendships and chatting about the old days.

"Remember the day we went to Graceland?" Boy George asked Ruby. "It was while we were on the Culture Club tour in the States. We went down there on the bus! It was nice to look round the place, but it was sad at the same time. I don't know how Elvis would have felt about it being turned into a museum."

Kim Wilde was talking family with guitar legend Duane Eddy. "I know your dad's work real well", said Duane, referring to British rock legend Marty Wilde. "You could say that rock and roll runs in my family", replied Kim. “Would you like to meet my dad?” Marty stepped onto the rostrum at the side of his daughter and Duane was really thrilled. Marty added, "In our house we’ve always been great fans of Elvis Presley. He really was the King of rock and roll."

Carl Perkins told friends: "Elvis and I went back a long way. We were poor boys together. He was a phenomenal guy - nobody swung guitar like him!"

The performances were all memorable with Kim Wilde's *One Night*, Elkie Brooks' *Love Letters* and Ben E King's *Suspicious Minds* particularly touching.

Roger Daltry sang *Hound Dog* with Carl Perkins, and Ruby Turner, Jaki Graham and Nona Hendryx teamed up for a version of *The Wonder Of You*. Pet Shop Boys star Neil Tennant said that he may go on to record one of the songs as a result. After recording *Always On My Mind* he said: "We may release it as a future B-side." (It topped the UK Christmas Charts in 1987 as an A-Side).

Equally moved was Meat Loaf after his emotional reworking of *American Trilogy*. "I may just record this for a single", he said, "I'd forgotten how good it was!"

Show director, Jon Scoffield said: "Other people are doing Elvis documentaries using archive film - Elvis in the army; Elvis on the Ed Sullivan Show. But surely showbiz is about the show going on, and the songs still being sung. If Elvis were still here, he'd still be singing. I think he'd be pleased with the show."

After the final sessions it was left to Roger Daltrey to sum up the historic occasion. "Quite simply, Elvis was the person who inspired me to become a rock star", he said. As you looked round, famous faces were all nodding in agreement.

If ITV gave us the best in live entertainment for Elvis' 10th anniversary then the BBC excelled themselves with the two-part mini-series *Elvis: I Don't Sing Like Nobody,* and *Cut Me And I Bleed.* Both were produced and directed by the delightful Anne Freer, also known for her 15 episode *The Rock & Roll Years*, and surprisingly *Antiques Roadshow*. Acknowledged as being the best television documentary about Elvis Presley, this was made by the BBC in 1987 for screening on the tenth anniversary of Elvis' passing. With the assistance of The Official Elvis Presley Fan Club of Great Britain, and Ger Rijff, this two-part mini-series used rare footage and remarkable interviews with Elvis' former girlfriends, family members, associates, songwriters, musicians, record producers, fellow actors and movie producers. This in-depth and very accurate programme was narrated by Suzi Quatro.

Anne E. Nixon and I wrote the book, *Ten Years After* which was printed in Budapest. It told the story of the Fan Club and our ten years after Elvis died. It was made into a radio documentary by Nottingham independent broadcaster Radio Trent. Managing Director and station manager Ron Coles, broadcaster David Lloyd, and myself were amongst those to travel to the Radio Academy Ceremony. This was held at the London Dorchester Hotel and was broadcast live on BBC Radio 2 by Terry Wogan and musician Steve Race. The *Elvis: Ten Years After* show won the acclaimed Sony Radio Award for Best Popular Music Programme. It was a rarity for Independent Local Radio (ILR) broadcasters to win any major gongs, with most going to seasoned broadcasters and producers within the BBC. It was unusual for an ILR station to include documentary items in their all-music schedules but our *Elvis: Ten Years After* show obviously hit the spot. We were thrilled as my narrative echoed around the venue. As I was sitting at our table something special happened. I could feel someone hold the back of my chair, and I heard that amazing, "the best a man can get" voice. "Mr Slaughter, how are you?" After a few minutes he had to go back to his group. Everyone at my table said, "Who was that?" I answered, "That man has the best radio voice in the world – it's Tommy Vance." In unison the question was, "How do you know him?" I explained that we met on Radio Caroline South. We had worked together at the British Film Institute. "I went to his wedding reception in the BBC Club when he married Sue Hanson from *Crossroads*. Tommy was the first person to give me a joint." A while later one of the girls from the Trent office cornered me and said, "We've been here two hours and whilst we recognise a few people we don't know anyone to talk to, but everybody knows you!" I smiled and said, "Well there's one person who works for you that I would love to talk to, and it's not Dale Winton. It's Neil Spence." "Why do you want to speak to him?" "Neil was a radio giant, he was Dave Dennis on the Big L." Looking puzzled she queried, "What's Big L?" I rest my case.

I do miss that amazing "TV on Radio" voice. Tommy Vance's delivery was so precise, so accurate and my first wife Vikki loved him. She met and swooned over him aboard Radio Caroline South.

Satellite TV News was becoming expensive to produce as we were not selling any advertising space. It was in danger of going under so I contacted Rodney Burbeck, the former press officer for RCA, for some advice.

Rod had left the "rough cut albums" office in Curzon Street, and had now become the managing director and editor of the UK trade journal *Music Week*. We had been asked if we might be interested in selling Satellite TV News, and that we had been offered £80,000. "Don't sell it Todd, let me get back to you in 24 hours."

Within 48 hours I had sold the magazine for £100,000 to *Spotlight Magazines*, owned by the Daily Express group. I was retained as a consultant meaning I would receive 10% of the profit. Spotlight changed the title to *Satellite & Cable TV News*, and kept it going for 14 months before calling it a day – two months before Rupert Murdoch announced the launch of SKY. However, I had £100,000 to invest in my pension plan which in today's money would pay me around forty grand a year.

Chapter Sixteen – The Eve of Destruction – Almost

On Boxing Day 1986 I received a call from Liverpool-based lawyer David Deacon, managing partner of Deacon Goldrein Green, a firm of legal practices scattered across Merseyside. He was a huge Jerry Lee Lewis fan with aspirations to open an Elvis exhibition in Blackpool. He asked if I would be interested in investing in the project but I declined, saying that I ran the Elvis Presley Fan Club not Alton Towers. I did add that he should meet with those who managed the Elvis Presley Estate if he wanted to proceed. Joseph Rascoff was the man he should talk to and was based in Beverly Hills. I was in LA on one occasion when Joe said to me and my kids, "I've got VIP tickets and backstage passes for you guys to see the Stones tomorrow night." We were travelling to London the following morning so I had to decline. "That's a shame, I bet you would love to meet the guys." I replied, "I already have, in 1965." A one-line response like that ticks all boxes.

Joseph "Joe" Rascoff was the legal affairs manager for Elvis Presley Enterprises Inc. which operated out of his West Coast Offices on Wilshire Boulevard. An accountant who showed little passion for rock 'n' roll, by default became the most powerful business manager and tour producer for a roster of powerhouse acts, including the Rolling Stones, U2 and Paul Simon. Mr. Rascoff was a partner at the Manhattan accounting firm Hurdman & Cranstoun in 1974, when he had a serendipitous encounter at an office urinal with Prince Rupert zu Loewenstein, the financial adviser for the

Rolling Stones. It is fascinating just how many business encounters take place in corporate "bogs". The Prince lamented that Hurdman & Cranstoun wouldn't take on the Stones as a client because they had a history of drug abuse and mismanagement. Joe took a leave of absence and became the Stones' road accountant and then their tour producer. He never returned to the firm, and also he never stopped being an accountant. His company pioneered tour management that oversaw nearly everything but the artistic side — from lighting and hotel bookings to arena scheduling, trucking, sponsorship and merchandising — thus taking the logistical details out of the artists' hands. He would contract out for all the services, and the artists just had to play. They would end up better financially while not having to run the tours. The merged company also represented David Bowie, Sting, the Allman Brothers Band and the Elvis Presley estate.

As the story goes Joe Rascoff pitched to the Elvis Presley estate with an analysis of record industry economics on a blackboard. He walked them through a lesson in royalties in records and music publishing, where the record companies had the edge. Two weeks later Joe got the job, beating two major accounting firms.

He sometimes tried to convince his rock-star clients that they did not need excessive perks. "He moaned like it was his money, if an artist wanted a two-bedroom suite, he'd say, 'But it's just *you* — you only need one room.' Or: 'Really, do you need audience lights? Why don't you turn on the house lights?

Mick Jagger and the Stones had a penchant for producing electrifying and extravagant shows befitting their brand as the world's greatest rock 'n' roll band.

Still, Joe could not help cringing at some of the lavish costs of their concerts. One day in Berlin in 1990, Spencer Rascoff was watching a Stones concert with his father "where there were these massive inflatable dolls that Mick punched and danced with as fireworks went off during *Honky Tonk Women*." Joseph Rascoff shook his head in disapproval because the fireworks had cost the tour $3 million and the "inflatable dragon woman Mick was gyrating on cost $100,000."

After Deacon gave him the business plan for a UK Elvis Presley Exhibition in Blackpool, there was one caveat that Joe insisted upon. That inclusion would damage my life, my health and eventually my marriage to Juliet. "I like Todd, I trust Todd, so I'll only do a deal with you Mr Deacon if he has a share of your business."

EPE wanted the exhibition in London as they had never heard of Blackpool. It didn't matter to them that Frank Sinatra had performed there when his career was in the doldrums. That said Frank also played the Boot and Shoe Working Men's Club in Leicester.

There was one venue in the centre of Soho that wasn't being used at the time, and it was certainly iconic. The Windmill Theatre in Great Windmill Street, London was for many years both a variety and revue theatre. It remains best known for its nude *tableaux vivants*, which began in 1932 and lasted until its reversion to a cinema in 1964. Many prominent British comedians of the post-war years started their careers working on this stage. I made an appointment to see the owner, Mr Paul Raymond – the publisher of *Men Only* and *Club International*. Having never seen inside the Windmill I was shocked to see how pokey it was and certainly not big enough to house an exhibition. I formed a most unsavoury impression of the gaff being full of old men in long raincoats with a Fagan-like Raymond sitting in the box office wearing knitted gloves without fingers.

As expected, there was nothing else in London within budget so Deacon pushed home the benefits of Blackpool, which EPE eventually agreed to. My participation in the project was to theme a visitor experience starting with a façade of a shack in Tupelo and concluding with a walk-through mini Graceland.

Accompanied by Anne Nixon, our appointed researcher who had been a regular columnist in Elvis Monthly since its conception in 1960, we flew to Memphis. As it was a Monday Graceland was closed to visitors. For me it was such a buzz to take a hire car up Elvis Presley Boulevard, wait for the music gates to open and to park outside of the Graceland front door. You have no idea just how special that was and we made that journey three times during our stay.

The curator, Todd Morgan, gave us a guided tour of those areas not accessible to the public, including Elvis' private quarters on the first floor and up into the attic. Todd (Morgan) explained that Graceland is a wooden-framed house with external stone cladding so public admission to the upstairs was both inadvisable and unacceptable. Inadvisable because the upper floor was not strong enough to take the traffic of 600,000 pairs of feet each year. Unacceptable because it would be deemed inappropriate to have an x-marks-the-spot indication of where Elvis died. There was nothing that Anne felt would be useful from the bedroom and bathroom areas. The attic, however, was a treasure trove. Daytime and stage clothing, personal effects, furnishings, boots, shoes, belts, scarves, ornaments, posters, records, pictures and jewellery. It was all there with steamer trunks crammed full of contracts, fan mail, fan magazines, gifts, police badges, books, bibles, toys, guitars and scripts. In one chest there were movie costumes and Anne discovered a moth-eaten Kid Galahad boxer's dressing-gown. Subsequently, the Graceland preservation people repaired the gown which is now on permanent display as part of the tour. There was a wardrobe of Gladys' clothing which Elvis had catalogued, with each garment perfectly preserved in individual zip-up plastic covers.

I was not privy to the deal that Deacon had negotiated with the Presley Estate, but it included the design and manufacture of UK-produced souvenirs to complement a range of Graceland giftware made in China. I assumed that Elvis Presley Enterprises would receive a share of the admission monies and a commission on souvenir sales. We arranged for the Blackpool confectioners to make several "boilings" of Elvis Rock – those pink coated, foot-long, mint flavoured sugar sticks on sale at every British seaside resort – ours having E L V I S in red lettering throughout.

Anne chose the chattels and FedEx delivered a hundred boxes to the exhibition site which was next door to the Blackpool Tower, above what was the old Woolworths Building. At the time "The Wonder of

Woolies" had become Pricebusters, a ghastly indoor market. Today it is a Wetherspoons and I bet "Spoons" is more profitable than any other business along the Golden Mile.

There were three of us "in the mix" when the Elvis Exhibition business was set up: myself, David Deacon and Terry McMaddy. I was told that Mr McMaddy was an investor, who would double up as the hired "heavy" to ward off local gangsters. Terry was ex-SAS who was "killed" during a covert action, black-bagged for the journey home to be laid to rest but inflight the bag moved. In civvy street he recruited a network of men who "ran the doors" at bars, pubs and nightclubs throughout Merseyside. To run the *Life and Times of Elvis Presley Exhibition* the company Park McMaddy Limited was formed, of which in accordance with Rascoff's demands I too was appointed a position of director. The business had a three-signature mandate with the Royal Bank of Scotland to prevent a payment being made by one person without the knowledge of the other two. RBS were also the bankers for the legal practice Deacon Goldrein Green.

A construction team was hired to build the exhibition area on the fourth floor of the building overlooking the promenade. The entrance shown to me by Deacon at the time of agreeing the site was an imposing corner feature, with highly polished handrails, leading to an elegant carpeted beadlight illuminated staircase. The entrance we ended up with was previously used as a hole-in-the-wall ice cream kiosk, adjacent to two iron gates leading to the Blackpool Tower Circus arena. The entrance had a peculiar smell, the source of which only became evident when I was making a 5.00am stock delivery. My early morning unloading, to avoid trams and traffic as it was a no-stopping zone, coincided with those iron gates opening.

Out into the dawn came a herd of elephants, llamas, zebras and camels which had been cooped up all night. They were all being taken across the quiet road and tram tracks onto the beach to relieve themselves, complete with bucket men to shovel up the shit. On their way past our Elvis exhibition entrance each creature decided to take a piss. Christ knows what it must have been like for the poor old ice cream man trying to sell a 99 with sprinkles amidst an aroma of ammonia. I can't guarantee that no animal was hurt during their lavatorial journey, but I am happy to confirm that no caged animals feature in the Tower Circus today.

Inside our exhibition, we had a café cum ice cream parlour with scenery showing the outside of Graceland, the Sun studios, movie sets, army barracks and the Tupelo shack. Occasionally singers would perform in the Sun exhibit, and there was Elvis music and documentary video screens throughout.

It took three months to build. On opening day, the council and fire service blessed the property as suitable for human occupation. We had all the public performance licences, food hygiene certificates and insurance papers in place, but, for some unknown reason the local authority wouldn't allow us to play music. McMaddy said to a random inspector, "We don't do brown paper bags [full of money] in this business." It took a visit from Terry's chum, renegade politician Derek Hatton, to calm the waters.

Two thousand Fan Club members rocked up on day one. We delayed the opening for an hour so that the local media could capture the Elvis fans' eagerness. Although the first day lacked music our members were thrilled to see over 150 of Elvis' personal possessions, costumes and clothing. The exhibition enjoyed several television spots including TVAM, BBC News, ITN, CNN, Sky and RTL. Radio One sent five feet small Bruno Brookes with seven feet tall Liz Kershaw (heights exaggerated to add to the descriptive impact) to broadcast live from our exhibition before having an Elvis-themed Radio One Road Show on the beach.

It was the hottest summer ever which meant that everyone wanted to get their kit off and stay on the beach and not venture up four flights of stairs to attend an exhibition in a greenhouse where the ice cream was liquidised. It was the year that SKY Television was launched in Europe and Atlantic 252 was broadcasting from the Irish Republic with a zillion watt long-wave transmitter owned by Radio Luxembourg to an eager British AOR audience. A fatwa was issued against Salman Rushdie by the Ayatollah Khomeini for his book *The Satanic Verses*, and the Berlin Wall was torn down as Communism collapsed across Eastern Europe. In the world of music Black Box with *Ride on Time* was the best-selling single of the year and spent 6 weeks at the top of the hit parade.

As the weeks trundled past our visitor numbers were only a third of our forecast. Daily, I would count the numbers in our venue at a specific time, then sprint down the stairs and leg it down the prom into the waxworks and take their head count. The results were worrying as their publicised attendance was five times greater than it appeared to be, and we had based our business plan on 50% of their annual achievement. It was no comfort that we were neck-a-neck when it was neck-a-neck of sod all.

Compounding the horror was the fact that Deacon had entered into a 25-year lease with a weekly rent of £2,000. At our current trading we would just break-even, but that was if we were trading for 52 weeks, not a thirty-week seaside summer season.

"Jock's Week", when all the Scots descend on Blackpool, wasn't particularly good that year because the weather was also "steaming" north of the border with no need to drive south. But the lights, the lights, the lights were only weeks away and during those ten weeks we were told that the streets were truly paved in gold.

The Blackpool Illuminations (known locally as The Lights) were first shown in 1879 when they were promoted as Artificial Sunshine, and consisted of just eight carbon lamps that bathed the Promenade in a flickering glow. The original event preceded Thomas Edison's patent of the electric light bulb by twelve months. The first display similar to the modern-day displays was held in May 1912 to mark the first British Royal family visit to Blackpool when Princess Louise opened a new section of the Promenade, Princess Parade. The Promenade was decorated with what was described as "festoons of garland lamps" using about 10,000 lightbulbs. The local Chamber of Trade, as well as other local businesses, requested Blackpool Council to stage the event in September of the same year. The subsequent event was such a success that in 1913 the council were again asked to stage the Princess Parade lights as an end of season event. With the outbreak of the First World War there were no further displays until 1925 when the lights were again on display and extended to run from Manchester Square to Cocker Square. In 1932 animated tableaux were erected, running along the cliffs from North Shore to Bispham, and the Illuminations were extended to their current length running from Starr Gate to Red Bank Road at Bispham.

The Illuminations were ready to shine in 1939 but the outbreak of the Second World War again interrupted the annual display and post-war austerity meant the lights were not switched on again until 1949.

Every year there is also the Festival of Light which features interactive installations, "a contemporary look at the concept of light and art working together to create entertainment". An *Elvis* was constructed as a “doff” to our exhibition and we paid for three of the famous trams to be emblazoned with our logo.

Illuminations traffic crawled along the seafront at a snail’s pace with the local firemen collecting donations from weary drivers. During weekdays we learnt that sightseers would drive in at the south end, exit at Cleveleys, and then drive home. At the weekend it was a mixture of Hen and Stag parties so there was no boost in revenue as expected, just the obstacle of evading pools of vomit on the pavement and the removal of lost stiletto-heeled shoes and frantically discarded knickers.

The following year it was more of the same. Elvis Presley Enterprises promised to refresh the exhibits and there was mention of a headline-attracting visit by Priscilla but it never happened. Terry and myself were horrified to find that the debts had escalated out of control, and that our backers were now looking for payback.

Our lawyers, Alsop Wilkinson, suggested that McMaddy and I take action against David Deacon on the grounds of a "fiduciary relationship". £20,000 later, and no more money in my corroded pipeline, meant the action collapsed.

Throughout this trauma we did have that unexpected publicity courtesy of Granada Television. In an episode of *Coronation Street* Rita Sullivan (Barbara Knox) was hiding out in a Blackpool B & B to avoid Alan Bradley (Mark Eden). Evil Alan tracked her down and Rita ran across the tramlines with Bradley in hot pursuit. He tripped and was killed by one of our Elvis Exhibition branded Blackpool trams.

It was a great exhibition but it almost destroyed me. Although the Royal Bank of Scotland passed cheques without honouring the three-signature mandate, they still called in the dogs and I lost our house and every penny I had in the bank.

However, I still had my pension fund now worth £250,000, or did I? My insurance broker evaporated into oblivion and I became a preferential creditor. The definition of a "preferential creditor" is that you are the first person to be told that you are going to get "sod all." Could things get any worse? Three years later they certainly did. In the meantime, the Somali Republic decided to publish a postage stamp with a picture of me with Elvis taken in Las Vegas in 1973. Melanie Coles, a BBC TV journalist and weather girl, and the daughter of radio station executive Ron Coles, came to record an interview me about the stamp for the news. Poor thing – she couldn't stop throwing up. "It's morning sickness, but don't tell my dad. I've not told him yet that he is going to be a grandad."

Chapter Seventeen – Hallmark of Quality?

Following almost 5 years of intensive work in York University, my eldest son Gregory successfully gained a position at British Aerospace. What he does there is a mystery, but in his leisure time he plays a variety of musical instruments.

In 1990 Juliet gave birth to our second child Tom, so I now had three sons and one daughter and we were skint. We moved into a rented property as RBS took our house and there were other debts that David Deacon had amassed by agreeing to leasing deals on equipment and fittings. A lawyer with 15 legal practices, he and McMaddy retained their homes but we lost everything. Being a fluent French speaker Juliet needed “Business French” if she was to find a position in multinational commerce. Athmane Lamoudi was a lecturer at Leicester University, and formerly captain, coach and manager for the Algerian National Football Team. He was also very much a businessman. His family owns the largest brick factory in the whole of Africa, and has land that boasts the only big hill in North Africa, on top of which was the world’s most powerful long-wave transmitter, now obsolete due to the proliferation of DAB cells all over the former French colony. At one time we thought it might be possible to lease the transmitter, get sponsorship from a tobacco company, create an English language oldies pop radio station and broadcast across the Mediterranean to the 3 million British ex-pats under the call sign of *Camel Radio*. There would be a daily Elvis Hour of course.

After enough tutelage she applied for a position in the Leicester office of an international company that planted and harvested jute, a natural, breathable fibre used in carpet backing and sacking. The company was based in the former French colony of Côte d'Ivoire, a country located on the south coast of West Africa. Ivory Coast's political centre is Yamoussoukro in the centre of the country, while its economic capital is the port city of Abidjan. It is one of the largest exporters of cocoa beans, and being a Francophile nation, most of the beans go to the Nestlé corporation. Ghana, formerly The Gold Coast, a British colony, exports its production to the Cadbury company. Juliet visited Abidjan and Ouagadougou, capital of the world's poorest nation Burkina Fasu. She worked for a charitable institution under the umbrella of HH The Aga Khan philanthropy. The Aga Khan is a business magnate with British and Portuguese citizenship, as well as a racehorse owner and breeder, but he did not buy Juliet a racehorse for Christmas.

I was asked to visit Jack Soden at Graceland at the end of September 1990. Elvis Presley Enterprises Inc wanted a post-mortem meeting to discuss the failure of the Blackpool exhibition. I was hoping to escape "pauper's prison", but that was not to be, so I thought I should get some advice.

I called Colonel Parker and he asked me to fly to Vegas. I got a $59.00 hopper and Colonel met me at the airport, Loanne Miller his assistant was driving. They first met in 1969 at the opening of the Las Vegas International Hotel, and when Elvis asked to go on the road again, Miss Miller became secretary of RCA Record Tours. We went to the Colonel's favourite,

Vickie's Diner on Las Vegas Boulevard South. It was a 50s style eatery complete with original furnishings and table tops housing jukebox controllers. We had chicken soup. Colonel sent his back because it didn't have enough meat. Loanne laughed, "He always does that, and they always serve him soup without any filling just so he can send it back." After the food fight I told him what had happened, how we lost our home because of the failure of the exhibition, and then he said something most unexpected. "Loanne and I were going to take a trip to London to see Freddy. If only I had known you were in trouble, I would have come to your exhibition. I'm sure everyone would like to come and say hello to the Colonel. You brought everyone to see me at the Hilton, and you got me Margaret Thatcher's signature on a photograph some years ago, and your boys bought me a shirt. See I'm still wearing it." I told them that the matter was in the hands of the lawyers but I wasn't holding my breath. Then he dropped another surprise into the conversation. "She is not Loanne Miller anymore, she's Mrs Colonel. We got married yesterday. Show him the ring wifey." That was strange to hear, as he always called her "nursey." He chose the term of endearment "nursey" from watching *Blackadder*. Elvis' favourite comedy was the BBC TV show *Monty Python*, and here was the Colonel who never missed an episode of *Blackadder*, also made by the Beeb.

After the "wedding breakfast" I was invited to their home at 2000 Plaza de Santa Fe, located in a walled community just off Highway 95, a mile west of Las Vegas Boulevard South. The Colonel moved into the complex in 1980, a modest home that at the time possibly cost $250,000. It was a three bedroom bungalow with a divided lounge full of cut glass elephants of all sizes that twinkled in the evening sunlight, projecting thousands of shards of light like a mirror ball all over the comfortably furnished room. A big TV dominated the lounge and in front of the screen was an even bigger electrically controlled recliner that Loanne called Colonel's Throne. Those who knew Colonel Parker referred to him as "Colonel" as if that was his forename.

I asked him about his childhood in Holland but he was more interested in talking about his "Great Escape". Loanne gave him his stick and he shuffled to the bathroom. Whilst he was sitting on his other throne, she asked me not to talk about his childhood, because it upset him for reasons previously explained.

He did talk about the canals and taking cheeses to the shipping lines. One of his uncles helped him to get work as a "lad" on a North Sea freighter out of Rotterdam. He travelled often to Harwich in Essex, and once or twice to Liverpool. It was from Liverpool that he missed the return sailing to Rotterdam, and booked in for one night at the Adelphi Hotel. He could only afford one night, but a bell boy found him an empty room and supplied him with uneaten food from the kitchens. Andreas Cornelis van Kuijk celebrated his 17th birthday at the Adelphi in 1926, then the following day jumped ship and landed in the port of Jacksonville in Florida. He returned home in time for his 18th birthday on 26th June 1927 – 50 years later he would be celebrating his 68th in Indianapolis just prior to Elvis' "final curtain".

I was about to leave when Colonel rang his lawyer in Memphis and arranged for me to meet him before I journeyed back to the UK. He then spoke about Elvis. "I didn't treat Elvis as my son, he was my friend. He lived his life the way he wanted to and I never interfered except when RCA became worried about his unmarried relationship with Priscilla. What he did was his business but the record bosses thought that any hint of immorality might harm his career." He then rubbed his thumb and forefinger together as if he was sprinkling something nasty, adding, "Elvis was a good man, an honest man but his family," he sprinkled furiously, "his family were shit!"

Quality Europe FM was a UK radio station transmitted across Europe via the Astra 1A satellite in the early 1990s. QEFM was one of the first European radio stations to use Direct to Home technology as its primary method of delivery, despite the use of the acronym FM (a reference to FM broadcasting) in its name.

The station first broadcast briefly from a half-finished house in Cheltenham (1991–1993). Quality Europe FM started when Roy Litchfield met Ray Pearson and suggested that they take up a short licence to cover the Cheltenham Festival of Music that year. They kitted out a caravan and sold local advertising. The idea was to create a new kind of radio station and go global by satellite. Ray had space on the top floor of an unfinished large house into which they installed two self-op radio studios. Local presenters and celebrities clambered up the unfinished staircase to find the studios. They played a full programme of music and covered many topics. QEFM had many on-air competitions which gained a terrific following all over Europe

On air QEFM had a very polished style and became home to some famous broadcasters. One such name was Dave Lee Travis who, after leaving the BBC following a much publicised spat, briefly presented his independent commercial show via the station. The President of the Official Elvis Presley Fan Club, that's me, also broadcast a very popular Elvis Show which I handed over to Mike Adams, ex-Radio One contributor and BBC Midlands presenter. QEFM closed down in 1994 after a series of financial and management-related problems. At its peak, QEFM boasted 23.8 million listeners a week from over 26 countries and became the number 1 satellite station after the demise of Radio Luxembourg in 1992.

As soon as my tenure with QEFM finished, I heard from Ron Coles that he was about to launch a new radio brand which would be owned by the SAGA group. The company had 6 regional stations, and one digital broadcaster Primetime Radio. Saga 106.6FM was the new independent radio station for the East Midlands, covering the counties of Derbyshire, Leicestershire, Lincolnshire, Nottinghamshire and Rutland. Part of the Saga Radio Group, the regional station was broadcast from the Riverside Business Park in Nottingham, close to the old ATV / Central / Carlton Television studios on Lenton Lane – the studios where our "Love Me Tender" tribute show was recorded in 1987. It was a quality service aimed at an audience aged fifty plus, and played familiar, melodic music covering most genres "from the last six decades and today". I continued my monthly Elvis Hour programme with Ron Coles on this new station, and although aimed predominately at the grey market, the outreach with named broadcasters was appreciated by all age groups. It certainly wasn't incontinence pads and stair lift radio.

Towards the end of 1993 I went to the dentist to have a crown fitted. Within 48 hours I had legs like Mike Tyson and feet resembling barrage balloons. I hobbled across to my medical practice to see the beautiful Doctor Susan Ford who asked me to go home from where an ambulance would pick me up and cart me off to Leicester Royal Infirmary. During the examination at Leicester Royal, the houseman who examined me asked if I drank a bottle of Scotch a day. "A few glasses of vodka on a good day but never whisky." Without hesitation he responded with the shocking revelation that I was going to have to go on the organ donor list as I needed a heart transplant. "I think you have cardiomyopathy Mr Slaughter."

Cardiomyopathy is a group of diseases that affect the heart muscle. Early on there may be few or no symptoms. As the disease worsens, shortness of breath, feeling tired and swelling of the legs may occur, due to the onset of heart failure, along with an irregular heart beat and fainting episodes. Those affected are at an increased risk of sudden cardiac death. That put the wind up me for sure!

In many cases the cause cannot be determined. Hypertrophic cardiomyopathy is usually inherited, whereas dilated cardiomyopathy is inherited in about one third of cases. Dilated cardiomyopathy may also result from alcohol, heavy metals, coronary artery disease, cocaine use and viral infections. Restrictive cardiomyopathy may be caused by amyloidosis, hemochromatosis and some cancer treatments. Broken heart syndrome is caused by extreme emotional or physical stress. Treatment depends on the type of cardiomyopathy and the severity of symptoms. Treatments may include lifestyle changes, medications or surgery.

In my case, in layman's terms, my heart was damaged by a viral infection most likely contracted by having a procedure from a "dirty" dentist. My heart muscle had expanded to two and a half times its normal size but the heart valves remained the original size so my heart was leaking like a sieve. There was no sticking plaster that could fix this, I needed a new heart, and to get one I had to wait for someone to die to save my life.

Chapter Eighteen – One Broken Heart for Sale

Being told that you need an organ transplant is bad enough, but a heart transplant to save your life is a big shock to the system. Everyone telling you that you are very brave is just not true. Bravery doesn't come into it when you are limited to a "do or die" decision. After waiting over a year for a donor organ to arrive, the "Do Not Resuscitate" notice at the foot of your hospital bed does concentrate the mind somewhat. During the waiting game, I came out of hospital from time to time to put together the next Fan Club magazine and to oversee what was happening in the Elvis world. I never told my mum that I needed a new heart and my absences were explained as frequent business meetings in London. Julie, Ian and Barbara took care of business in Leicester, with Alan and Gary at the Heanor end.

I had difficulty keeping warm so I would drive hundreds of miles with the car heater at full blast to remain comfortable.

Because my leaking heart had regulated itself with an extra beat, every student doctor and nurse were instructed to have a listen without first being made aware of the anomaly. Those that spotted it were awarded a Brownie point. Those that missed it were "bollocked" good-style by Prof. Anthony H Gershlick.

On the morning of 14th November 1994 I was woken with a kiss. An excited nurse said, "Wake up Brian, we're going for a ride in an ambulance – Papworth have a heart with your name on it."

I sat in the front next to the driver, with my nurse behind me monitoring my "sats". My driver didn't know the way and, having been there many times before, I guided him to the M1 South, leaving at junction 19 onto the A14 in the direction of Felixstowe. I was later told that I was unconscious upon arrival, and my heart stopped whilst being pushed into the hospital. I was immediately piped up to a bypass pump and the seven hour operation began. The staff referred to my surgeon as "Sam The Chef", as he was nifty with a carving knife. Mr Samer Nashef qualified as a doctor at the University of Bristol in 1980 and trained in general surgery in London and Exeter. His specialist training in cardiac surgery was in Glasgow, Sheffield, Manchester and Bordeaux in France. He was appointed consultant surgeon at Royal Papworth Hospital in 1992. He practises all types of cardiac surgery, with a special interest in minimally invasive coronary bypass, mitral repair, and surgery for atrial fibrillation. He is also interested in surgery of the aortic root. He has many research interests, a major one being measuring and monitoring the quality of surgical treatment and has led national and international projects in this field. He is the author of the *Naked Surgeon*, a book which deals with the issues of transparency in medicine, and how to operate in the buff.

I was told to bring a box of ice pops so I had something to suck on in intensive care but I wasn't *compos mentis* until I was transferred onto a ward, and even then "Sam the Chef" had to keep slapping my face to bring me back into the land of the living. When I was fully conscious, I could hear my heartbeat, *It feels like, It feels like I'm in love, My knees shake, My heart beats like a drum boom boom* - The Kelly Marie hit written by my friend Ray Dorset (Mungo Jerry) who lives near me.

Every time I see you lookin' my way Baby, baby, can't you hear my heartbeat? In the car or walkin' down the highway Baby, baby, can't you hear my heartbeat? When you move up closer to me I get a feeling that's ooo-wee Can't you hear the poundin' of my heartbeat? 'Cause you're the one I love You're the one I love the Herman's Hermits hit written by John Carter who doesn't live near me.

Within two days I am out of bed and in a bloody gym. Never been in a gym in my life, and there were eight of us – all transplanted at the same time – a fog on the A14 I'm told, and eight organs "harvested" due to a massive pile-up. What a gentle term "harvesting", describing the removal of a donor heart from a loved one.

In a bed next to me was an American guy who was recovering from a quadruple heart bypass. He had been attending the marriage of his son to a local girl, his son being based at the US Alconbury Air Force base near Huntingdon. (Adjacent to the base was a McDonalds, housed in the Megatron Flying Saucer restaurant and frequented daily by USAF personnel). Just as the patient was about to be discharged, I asked what the NHS bill was, he being a visitor. "There was no charge," he said with a big smile on his face adding, "possibly because they didn't have a credit card machine to take payment." (That saved him $150,000)

I had not eaten any solid food for months and I was looking forward to my first meal. The hospital food was amazing. All patients sat around a dining room table in the ward, and we enjoyed a choice of foods which were "waitress" served.

In the middle of the night I would get out of bed to go pee-pee. On the way back to my pit, as I had a craving of salt, I would wander around looking for nibbles. Everyone seemed to have a tube of the recently launched Pringles snack, yet I didn't have any. I would steal a few crisps from every pack, for medical reasons of course, to redress my salt deficiency.

One of the procedures that I had to undergo was a biopsy.

This procedure is done in a cardiac "cath lab" and takes about 30 minutes. A doctor gives a local anaesthetic to numb an area around the neck. A long tube (catheter) called a bioptome is passed through a small incision on the right side of the neck then down into the transplanted heart. A type of X-ray, called fluoroscopy, helps the doctors guide the bioptome through the jugular vein and into the right ventricular chamber of the heart. The jaws of the instrument, like a small pair of pliers, are opened and closed, and a small piece of tissue is snipped off and removed. A few samples are taken, and I remember seeing them bouncing around in a test tube as if they were minuscule Mexican jumping beans. In the "path lab" the technicians look at the white blood cells to determine if there is any rejection. The biopsy results are generally available in a few hours. This procedure was done by an amazing cardiologist, Doctor Jayan Parameshwar, and during this barbaric practice I would sing the Erma Franklin song *Take another little piece of my heart now baby.* I wasn't the only person to do that. I have since heard that comedian Eddie Large did the same when he had a new heart at Papworth in 2003. Eddie, of the "Little & Large" duo, died on 20th April 2020 from Coronavirus.

Within 19 days I was back home, returning to Papworth every other week for the first three months, then every six months thereafter for an MOT. I still see the same nurses and Jayan has become a good friend. I find it an emotional experience even now that the old Papworth Hospital in the village of Papworth Everard closed in 2018. My clinicians are now housed in the vicinity of Addenbrookes University Hospital on the Cambridge Biomedical Campus. The Royal Papworth is the world's leading organ transplant facility, even though its state-of-the-art reception areas resemble a Stansted Airport departure lounge. It is a fabulous institution. I was, and still am, so lucky.

When I got home, I needed to return to work and local Elvis Presley Fan Club branch leader, Michael Haywood, offered to drive me. "Mad Mick" lived in a terrace property that he named "The House of Elvis", just across the road from our Empire Road office. It was festooned with Elvis pictures, posters, memorabilia, records, books, CDs and video tapes which he swapped, traded and sold. Mick operated another venture which only came to light after he died. Tony Wadsworth and his wife, Julie, were producers and presenters on BBC Radio Leicester, and over the years I had often been invited to speak about Elvis on Tony W's programmes. This husband and wife team were Mick's biggest customers for pornography which Mr Haywood would duplicate on a bank of video tape recorders. Tony and Julie Wadsworth were a well-known double act in the Midlands, presenting together for more than two decades for BBC local radio in Leicester and in Birmingham. The couple were known for their double-entendres and "Carry On" sense of humour - and played up to it on camera and for publicity.

Then in 2017 they were found guilty by a majority verdict of encouraging six boys to take part in sexual activities in 1996. The couple were also convicted at Warwick Crown Court of outraging public decency by having sex in woodlands. Following a three-week trial, Julie Wadsworth, then age 60, was convicted by a majority of 10-2 verdicts of nine indecent assaults against boys and five counts of outraging public decency. Her spouse, 69, who acted as a look-out, was found guilty of the same charges, also by majority verdicts. Some victims, who were aged 11 to 15 at the time of the offences, told the court Julie Wadsworth was variously dressed in a "flasher's mac" trench coat, white high-heels, stockings, suspenders and a split-skirt.

Prosecutors said the abuse took place at several locations, including the couple's then home in Atherstone, Warwickshire, as well as on a nearby golf course and surrounding woodland.

I had been interviewed by this perverse pair after my heart transplant operation and although Julie was well known for her plaid pelmet-length mini-skirts there were never any rumours of their deviant "out of school" behaviour. In an attempt to raise a few quid for the Papworth Hospital trust charity I recorded the track *Take Another Little Piece of My Heart* which was released as a single, reaching the dizzy heights of 176 in the charts and my record was played on the BBC by the dirty dastardly duo.

In January 1995, the Fan Club staged a Diamond Jubilee Elvis 60th Birthday Party at the Birmingham Locarno Mecca Ballroom with Tony Prince and a whole bunch of local celebrities attending which doubled up as a celebration of my successful heart operation. Still “cathetered-up” I was given the most resounding and heartfelt reception from almost fifteen hundred fans.

Julie and Ian, from the Elvis Exhibition, moved from Blackpool to Leicester to help with the Fan Club mail order fulfilment which was especially important during the time I was waiting for a donor heart and the months of recuperation after. I was invited by Jack Soden to attend a licensing conference in Memphis and speak to would-be-licensors about fan club networks across Europe. Unable to travel on my own, Julie came with me and realised her dream of meeting country star Hal Ketcham, who has recently been diagnosed with Alzheimer’s disease.

My meetings at Graceland were interesting and the sales pitching to potential licensors was evangelical. Priscilla Presley, who addressed the multitude, would have put American radio preacher Garner Ted Armstrong to shame. At a reception afterwards she singled me out to talk about her *Dallas* co-star Larry Hagman. At the time he was waiting for a liver transplant, and she had mentioned to him that she knew someone who had recently had a new heart. Larry, who played the part of J.R. Ewing, asked Priscilla if I could talk him through the procedure. The following day he phoned me and I reassured him, adding that he should make sure that his surgeon was good at cross-stitch. "For me it was free on the NHS! For you, however, you will end up with a bill for half a million dollars."

Juliet had been asked to set up an office in the USA for her Ivorian employees, so that they could ship equipment which was manufactured in America direct to Africa without going through local agents. The producer of Elvis' American Sound Studio sessions, Chips Moman, found her a serviced office on Music Row in Nashville. Record company executives, Roger Semon and Ernst Jorgensen, needed to have the use of US premises for their forthcoming collector's label and agreed to share the lease. The plan was to release four officially licensed Elvis CDs each year which would be exclusive to fan clubs, and which at the same time would thwart bootleggers. The CDs would carry material which would be of little interest to the general record buying public, yet for Elvis fans would be highly collectable. The style would replicate that of the Fort Baxter label illicitly produced by Ger Rijff from tapes spirited out of RCAs own vaults, with the connivance of record company executives.

Roger and Ernst decided that they did not need an office in Nashville after we had signed and guaranteed the lease. We ended up using the offices as a drop-off point for security officer uniforms, and logo artwork from the CIA, the FBI and the White House.

Half a mile from the Leicester Fan Club office a new exhibition experience was being constructed. The National Space Centre needed staff uniforms. Heightened security levels also called for a new breed of security guards, all of whom needed kitting out with American-style uniforms. Juliet's twin sister, Sally, was then living in Washington with her husband who was a three-star general in the US Air Force. Sister Sal was mixing with the Washington elite, including the President's wife, Barbara Bush, and a few national security heavyweights. Just like our Houses of Parliament, their White House, the FBI Offices and those of the CIA all have gift shops full of branded government bric-a-brac made in China but they did not have any pottery. Our Staffordshire Elvis Fan Club branch leader, Vicky Molloy, was a ceramic artist working for the Beswick brand of the Royal Dalton group and she knew where to get good china. So, our Leicester office ended up selling suits, frocks, and pots.

My cousin Doreen visited from Australia and made a surprise call to see my mum. It was an emotional reunion with my mum, on hearing her voice, turning to see her and saying, "Hello Doreen, what are you doing here?" They had not seen each other for 40 years. Lots of relatives came to the party, including a little old lady in a wheelchair. Her toothless grin said it all for she was my "summer the first time" after we met at my cousin's emigration party when I was 14 and she 36.

During my convalescence, Julie Munday, our Milton Keynes Fan Club branch leader, took over the production of the magazine, upgrading the design and making it suitable for both retail and membership subscription. Distributed to the newstrade through Virgin it faltered badly and ended up being a financial disaster.

Colonel Parker made his last public appearance for our Fan Club in 1994. By this point he was a very sick man stricken with diabetes, gout and other health problems and barely able to leave his own house. On 20th January 1997, Loanne Parker, his wife, heard a crashing sound from the living room. When there was no response to her calls, she went in to find him slumped over in his chair. He had suffered a stroke.

Colonel died the following morning at a hospital in Las Vegas, Nevada, from complications to the stroke at the age of 87. His death certificate lists his birth name as Andreas Cornelis van Kuijk, his country of birth as the Netherlands, and his citizenship as American, proving once and for all that he was a naturalised American. His funeral was held at the Hilton Hotel and was attended by a handful of friends and former associates, including Eddy Arnold and Sam Phillips. Priscilla Presley attended the funeral to represent the Elvis Presley Estate and gave a eulogy that, to many in the room, summed him up perfectly: "Elvis and the Colonel made history together, and the world is richer, better and far more interesting because of their collaboration. And now I need to locate my wallet, because I noticed there was no ticket booth on the way in here but I'm sure that the Colonel must have arranged for some toll on the way out."

The Elvis Presley Estate and their lawyers had made many attempts to claim that Parker had misappropriated Elvis' income. This was never proven and EPE paid the Colonel a considerable sum of money and in return he gave them unfettered access to his archive which is now stored at Graceland.

What is without doubt is that Elvis Presley is the single most important figure in American 20th century popular music. He is simply the best, no one could argue with the fact that he was the musician most responsible for popularizing rock and roll on an international level. Viewed in cold sales figures, his impact was phenomenal. Dozens upon dozens of international smashes from the mid 50s to the 70s, as well as the steady sales of his catalogue and reissues since his death in 1977, make him the single highest-selling performer in music history.

RCA Records owned all of Elvis' music recordings. The RCA Records Label was bought by BMG in the 1980s and in 2004 BMG merged with Sony Music Entertainment to become Sony BMG. Sony owns Elvis' recordings and they continue to use the RCA Records label for issuing Elvis releases. The various composers/publishers own the songs themselves. People are confused about the ownership of the recordings and that of the songs. They do not understand a deal Elvis and his manager made with RCA in 1973. Elvis began his recording career with Sun Records in Memphis in the summer of 1954. Sun Records owner/producer Sam Phillips sold Elvis' recording contract and the catalogue of Elvis' Sun recordings to RCA in the fall of 1955. Elvis began recording for RCA in January 1956 and continued under contract with RCA for the rest of his life. Elvis never had ownership of his Sun or RCA recordings. Elvis received an artist's royalty on record sales as per the terms of his contracts with the record company. Typically, that is how it is done.

In March 1973, Elvis and Colonel Tom Parker approached the record company proposing that Elvis be paid a large lump sum payment in lieu of all his future artist's royalties for ongoing sales of anything he had recorded up to that time. The deal was made. RCA paid $5.4 million which Elvis and the Colonel split 50-50. That meant Elvis, and therefore EPE, no longer received his artist's royalties for the ongoing sales of any recordings created before the March 1973 deal. However, Elvis did continue, as does EPE, to get his artist's royalties on sales of recordings created after the March 1973 deal. Some people think that Elvis had a share in the ownership of his recordings and that this is what he sold to RCA. He did not.

Totally separate from the ownership of Elvis' recordings is the ownership of the songs themselves. Elvis recorded over 800 songs. Elvis, through his own publishing companies (Elvis Presley Music, Gladys Music, Whitehaven Music and Elvis Music, Inc.), was part owner (typically half or third) of many of the songs he recorded and even some he did not record. Hill & Range Music, owned by brothers Julian and Jean Aberbach, was his publishing partner for the most part. Typically, in the deals made with the publishing companies, the composers retain a share. The publishing companies manage the material.

Elvis did not sell his publishing interests. EPE still holds those interests and these are one of their major assets. Thus, the 1973 deal regarding Elvis' artist's royalties had no effect on his publisher's royalties. Elvis continued to get (EPE still gets) his publisher's royalties on sales of recordings of songs he had publishing interest in, no matter what date they were recorded. Elvis also recorded many songs that he did not have publishing interest in. Occasionally, as per the contracts signed in Elvis' lifetime, his publishing interests expire on some songs

The *Follow That Dream* label pays royalties for music publishing, and to EPE on the release of previously unpublished musically vocal materials, excluding the spoken word. Eventually, without the need of an American office Roger Semon and Ernst Jorgensen created the *Follow That Dream* Elvis fan club collectors' label. It was launched by the British Fan Club in 1999 with fan clubs all over Europe and the Far East becoming authorised distributors. It worked like a dream. Four releases each year was an investment well within the means of the average fan. Within the fan community, however, many believe that the product frequency has become excessive. Four CDs became six then eight releases each year. Then three books and CDs each accompanied by five gatefold double LP sets, mastered at Abbey Road Studios and pressed on 180-gram fine vinyl which increased the spend tenfold. What started out at £60 a year has now ramped up to £600+ and put the brand out of reach of the average Elvis collector.

When EPE was planning to tour "Elvis The Concert", Todd Morgan asked who he should contact in London to promote their first outing of this virtual show. A world tour for their audio-visual production with Elvis on the big screen behind assembled musicians, including Elvis' original bandmates. I suggested the people behind "Elvis The Musical" but because that show hadn't been approved by EPE Todd Morgan said such a relationship would be inappropriate. The biggest theatre owner in London at that time was Paul Raymond, but I thought if EPE wouldn't want to do business with Lord Brian Rix's company, then Mr Tit & Bum Raymond wouldn't sit well with the puritanical Memphis mob. So, it had to be Bill Kenwright CBE.

As a young man Bill Kenwright became an actor. His early successes included a role in *Coronation Street* as Gordon Clegg, who was introduced in April 1968. Kenwright left the show after a year to pursue his producing career, although he did return to the show on occasion throughout the 1970s for guest appearances. He continued to appear in *Coronation Street* occasionally until 2012. He had brief stints in other shows, such as *The Villains* and *The Liver Birds*, and had cameo parts in the films *Carry On Matron* (1972) as a reporter, and *England, My England* (1995). Since 1997 he has managed the Theatre Royal in Windsor. Kenwright is one of the UK's most successful theatre producers, best known for the long-running West End hit *Blood Brothers* and the record-breaking UK tour of *Joseph and the Amazing Technicolor Dreamcoat*. Other productions have included West End runs of *Whistle Down the Wind* at the Palace Theatre, *Festen* in London, on a UK tour and on Broadway, *The Big Life*, *Elmina's Kitchen*, *Scrooge – The Musical*, *The Night of the Iguana*, *A Few Good Men*, *A Man For All Seasons* alongside UK tours of *Jesus Christ Superstar*, *Tommy*, *Tell Me on a Sunday* and *This is Elvis*. He produced the London revival of *Cabaret* at the Lyric Theatre in September 2006, starring Anna Maxwell Martin, James Dreyfus and Sheila Hancock. It must follow that it was somewhat of a surprise that this doyen of the West End was knocking on my door asking for assistance.

I had a meeting with Bill Kenwright - Wembley was the ideal venue, 23rd January 1999 was the chosen date and we started to sell tickets. It was a 12,000 seater sell-out. BBC Radio 2 presenter and former Conservative MP, Edwina Currie, interviewed Bill and I on her programme following the concert. "I didn't see much advertising for the show Bill," Kenwright replied, "I didn't have to, Todd Slaughter's Elvis Fan Club members bought most of the tickets." After the show we hosted a *meet and greet* party for the TCB Band, The Sweets, the Stamps and The Imperials. Jack Soden and Todd Morgan from Graceland, together with others from Memphis, came over on a jolly. A fitting end to a successful day. The Fan Club did the same the following year.

After 40 years of uninterrupted publication, *Elvis Monthly* was closed, not by the Fan Club but by WH Smith. In the year 2000 the wholesale arm of the magazine retailer culled all titles with a circulation below 35,000. In today's market a magazine with a print figure of more than 10,000 is judged to be viable, but not so two decades ago. At the same time, Sony BMG approached the British and Norwegian Fan Club to see if it might be possible to produce a global Elvis periodical. The Flaming Star EPFC of Norway headed by Pal Granlund produced a "perfect bound" members mag, with the best quality printing and access to an archive of beautiful pictures. Pal's picture library was, and still is, the best in the world outside of Graceland. He invested tens of thousands of pounds in buying former picture agency prints as hard copies had been converted into digital formats alleviating the necessity for costly storage.

It is much easier to supply pictures electronically in milliseconds than having the cumbersome job of sifting and sorting, packing and posting, and ensuring that those precious prints are returned in good order. I have supplied hundreds of 8" x 10"s to RCA over the years, never to have them returned to the Fan Club. I bet the record label has "borrowed" tens of thousands of pounds worth of our Elvis prints.

Not long after I had my heart transplant, I struggled to London with a car full of Elvis Las Vegas Hilton posters, banners, pennants, bench transfers, pictures, stencilled 32 sheet billboard advertisement art, menus, event cards and badges given to me in 1972 by Colonel Parker. Today this stash would attract an auction value of around £100,000. The record company wanted them for a promotional video project. I've never seen them since, yet from time to time I have seen what I believe to be the very same items on sale on eBay.

Pal and I created *Elvis Today*. It looked classy but suffered from extremely poor English. Pal produced the content and the print, and we handled the subscription and publicity logistics. So that this subscription-only magazine could be distributed in the States "Blackpool Julie" and her then-husband opened an office from their home in Paducah, Kentucky. Initially it was extraordinarily successful but, like most subscription-only magazines without a pedigree, the renewal take-up was minimal. The promise of ongoing promotion from RCA evaporated and this beautiful magazine withered on the vine.

My mum, Ada, had always been a very independent woman. In her mid eighties, after my dad, John, had passed away ten years earlier, she went on a European cruise which also sailed down the West African coast. Juliet and I accompanied my mum on holidays to Spain and the low countries, and along with her brother, my Uncle Fred, I took them to an Elvis week in Torremolinos.

From time to time Mum went to a Skegness care home for respite. At the age of 89 she decided she wanted to stay in Skeggy and gave up her council-owned bungalow in Leicester. We would go and visit her every two or three weeks and take the kids around the amusements - I'm addicted to the "grabbers". When she was 92, over the August Bank Holiday, she fell and ended up in the Pilgrim Hospital in Lincolnshire. Young Tom and I went to the hospital in Boston but she had been discharged back to the care home. On the journey in the hospital mini-bus she died, but no one knew where she had been taken. The care home didn't know, neither did the hospital or the police. The hospital bus driver could not be found and it wasn't until the following day that the police located the funeral home. It was the saddest funeral ever with me, my wife, Uncle Fred and three care home staff. All her friends and other family members had previously died.

Chapter 19 – A New Dawning

At one minute past midnight on 1st January 2000 computers didn't fail, clocks didn't stop and electricity-generating plants didn't implode. Bit of a happy anti-climax as it turned out. We were not on the verge of the eve of destruction.

Due to financial irregularities by one of the Fan Club staff members, I closed the office in Leicestershire, and moved the operation to Uttoxeter in Staffordshire, purchasing a shop and office complex. Vicky Molloy, the Staffordshire Fan Club leader who had helped Juliet with bespoke pottery, lived locally. She joined as office manager, controlling the membership subscriptions and organising the social side of our national events, both here and in Memphis. Vicky also handled the logistics and licensing for our theatre tours. We had a considerable amount of help from her family members - mum Ivy, father John, brother Andrew, niece Charlotte, sister-in-law Alison, daughter Sally and Vicky's husband Duncan. Dunc remains one of my best friends.

My daughter, Jennifer, had won a scholarship at Ratcliffe College, and by 2001 Tom was attending the same school. Jenny eventually went to university in Birmingham, became a teacher and today works in Australia. Tom went to Sports College on the Loughborough University campus, leaving to become an electrician. He moved to Bournemouth working for the luxury yacht maker Sunseekers, then to Taylor Wimpey as a site manager, and has now become an executive of a Dorset based house-building company.

I had done a little bit of work for the British breakfast broadcaster TV-am when it first started in the 1980s. I had to talk about pop music, and Elvis in particular, with MP Shirley Williams. Their silver-service breakfast was amazing. When GMTV took over the ITV breakfast franchise in 1993, I was on an early show with Carl Perkins who was talking about a show he was about perform with Paul McCartney. *Grotbags* actress Carol Lee Scott, whose TV show was being axed by Central Television, was also on the couch. For a children's entertainer she was the most foul-mouthed witch I had ever met and complained bitterly about the after-show sustenance being just a donut and a cup of coffee.

At the end of 2000 I was back in the South Bank Television Centre to discuss a *Search For Britain's Best Elvis* competition that was being promoted by impresario Jonathan Shirlaw. On the judging panel were TV presenter Richard Arnold, vocal coach Jane Pegler and me.

There had been a few Elvis tribute singers performing in Working Men's Clubs, end of pier shows, and in the odd rock and pop musical, but GMTV with their three-month long contest were raising the Elvis Tribute Act bar big time. From a shaky start in 1993, GMTV was winning the viewing battle over BBC Breakfast having anchor Eamonn Holmes, and presenters Penny Smith, Jenni Falconer, Kate Garraway, Lorraine Kelly and Ross King. Hundreds of wannabe Elvii flooded the production office with applications and we travelled around Great Britain auditioning up to 50 in every ITV region. The heats were pre-recorded in shopping centres, hotels and attractions. The contestants varied from the sublime to the ridiculous. It was a lot of fun and raised the profile of the Fan Club and interest in Elvis immensely. I was told that Elvis Presley Enterprises decided to fire a couple of "cease and desist" salvos at the broadcaster for using the name "Elvis" in the contest. EPE had just done a deal with Disney, but they were not aware that the Disney Corporation was a big stakeholder in GMTV, so ITV's breakfast station was thankfully able to bypass the legal challenge.

The final took place in a sound stage of the South Bank Television centre with guests that day including Danny Foster, Myleene Klass, Kym Marsh, Suzanne Shaw and Noel Sullivan – all members of the newly formed pop band Hear'Say.

The next time I was with Kym Marsh was December 2005 when Vicky Molloy's daughter, Sally, was in the cast of Mother Goose at the Regent Theatre in Stoke-on-Trent along with pantomime dame and playwright, Eric Potts formally Diggory Compton, the eccentric baker in *Coronation Street.* Soon after, Kym joined "The Street" playing the part of Michelle Connor for 13 years.

The winner of the *Search for Britain's Best Elvis* was Heath Ashton from Devon. His competition prize didn't materialise as expected, so the Fan Club, in association with Handshake Productions, put on a *One Night with Elvis* tour in 2007. GMTV soft-peddled their support for Heath upon hearing that he sired his first child before he was 14 and were concerned about any negative publicity that might tarnish the station's family image. Heath Ashton is a fantastic guy, a great performer and one of the funniest Elvis Tribute acts that I have ever encountered. He had all the GMTV presenters in hysterics. Another outstanding contestant was Cypriot Mario Kombou who had trained in musical theatre, was an actor and already had a stage act that enjoyed a loyal following. He went that extra mile to help other contestants against who he was competing, going as far as lending his professionally tailored costumes to those who were turned out wearing something that their mothers had run up on a treadle Singer sewing machine. Mario went on to star as the lead in the 2004 West End production of *Jailhouse Rock* the musical.

For me the year 2001 saw the resurrection of my Elvis Hour when the offshore radio brand Wonderful Radio London, The Big L, was born again three miles away from the pirate radio station's original anchorage in the North Sea. This time it was on *terra firma* in the sleepy Essex seaside town of Frinton-on-Sea. Ray Anderson of East Anglia Productions, onetime owner of Laser Hot Hits and television programme maker, established Big L which could be heard on Sky Satellite as a radio channel, and from a 1395 AM transmitter on the Dutch Coast. With Mike Read and David Hamilton as the main presenters, the new station enjoyed massive publicity, especially when Sir Cliff Richard launched Big L by driving a vintage London Routemaster double decker red bus from the centre of London to the new Frinton studio complex a la *Summer Holiday*.

Even to this day, some of our more fanatical and totally out-of-touch fans write, phone and petition the Fan Club for RCA (Sony) to release another Elvis single. Oblivious to the fact that there are no singles by any artist released any more, streaming of previously released material only works when a specific song captures the spirit of the nation such as *We'll Meet Again* by the late Dame Vera Lynn.

This wasn't the case almost two decades ago when, in 2002, a JXL remix of *A Little Less Conversation* was used in a Nike commercial for the World Cup. It shot to the top of all European charts, sold a couple of million, but didn't sell a massive amount of copies Stateside. Jack Soden said that EPE were a bit miffed because they were not involved or consulted about this project. Football had never been a massive crowd puller in the USA. A good example of just how politically entrenched Americans are, I gave Jack Soden a *Spitting Image* latex head of Margaret Thatcher. He thought the caricature of Maggie was hysterically funny. I told him that it was part of a pair, magicking a rubber Ronald Reagan out of my bag. I am convinced to this day that he wanted to have me shot for defiling his president. As we know of late, American politics can be dangerously divisive.

After this success we suggested to Sony BMG that they re-release Elvis' former number ones as a CD box set, with the Fan Club shipping out the saver-boxes complete with the first single in the series, which they agreed to do in 2004. For a further 17 weeks queues at most HMV shops around the UK and Eire witnessed a buying frenzy with fans anxious to get the precious limited and numbered CD singles and the 10-inch vinyl versions. All these re-releases made it into the top 10, with three occupying the top placing, giving Elvis Presley a total of 21 number ones – more than any other act. Once again EPE played "silly buggers" by refusing to allow *Top of the Pops* to screen a clip from the movie of Elvis singing *Jailhouse Rock.* MGM had already supplied the clip to the BBC as it would promote their DVD release, but Elvis Presley Enterprises refused to let them air it. It was reported that EPE would relent if the Beeb paid big money to use the two minute promotional clip.

This avarice defies logic. For years, the Visit Tennessee tourist office people have used the same picture of Elvis standing outside Graceland in their promotion of Memphis' biggest visitor attraction. When the Authentic Brands Group purchased EPE, they approved the free publicity they were receiving in a proof copy of the brochure, whilst attempting to charge the tourist office for the use of the Elvis picture.

Local radio entrepreneur and former Radio Trent boss, Ron Coles, had gravitated from Radio Trent to GEM AM (an extremely popular oldies AM station with a footprint covering Leicestershire, Derbyshire, Lincolnshire, and Nottinghamshire – the *Great East Midlands*). Later he was to manage Century 106 FM covering roughly the same counties as GEM, but his biggest success was with SAGA. The Saga Radio Group was a British radio network owned and operated by Saga Services Ltd, and aimed at an audience aged 50 and over. The first Saga station was launched in the West Midlands in October 2001 and was subsequently followed by two others based in the East Midlands and Glasgow. The network won a fourth licence for the northeast in 2006, but was sold in December of that year to Guardian Media Group, which decided to relaunch Saga along with its Smooth FM stations as Smooth Radio. All Saga stations were closed on Friday

23 March 2007, and Smooth Radio was launched the following Monday. During the Saga days I co-hosted my Elvis Hour with Ron and we enjoyed a very loyal audience. The show also appeared from time to time on Saga's digital national station Primetime Radio. David Hamilton and I moved from the faltering Big L operation and together we teamed up with Saga. When the station was re-branded as Smooth, we were asked to leave after six months as we were deemed to be too old for the new network.

When I left Wonderful Radio London (Big L) I jumped ship and transferred my weekly Elvis Hour to Radio Caroline which in 2000 was broadcasting on the Sky radio platform and online. After years of campaigning Radio Caroline, in 2017, was "gifted" by its former arch enemy Ofcom with a disused BBC transmitter tower and World Service frequency of 648 AM together with a licence to broadcast. Today Radio Caroline, the original pirate from 1964, gets its programmes out to a worldwide audience online, on smart speakers, on eight UK digital radio platforms, all over East Anglia and across the North Sea to the continental Low Countries on good old medium wave. The radio ship The Ross Revenge is now a working broadcast studio anchored in the Blackwater River estuary leading into the North Sea, and each month squirts its transmissions up to the northern counties courtesy of Manx Radio under the brand Radio Caroline North. Caroline FM is now a new kid on the block with an East of England footprint. Former Postmaster General, Tony Benn, who scuppered the offshore broadcasters with 1967 legislation, would be spinning in his grave.

In addition to Elvis related radio work, I was getting more television including a piece for the History Channel, frequent news pieces for all networks, and a few guest appearances on the home shopping channel. QVC hosts are skilled presenters who must pass a stringent auditioning process including being able to talk about a pencil for ten minutes.

In the spring of 2007, our One Night of Elvis Competition tour played 15 venues, finishing with a grand finale in Blackpool in June. The star of our tour was GMTV contest winner Heath Ashton along with his band Midnight America. The USP of the show in each of the 15 locations across the country was to have our audience vote for the best Elvis Tribute Act. Would-be contestants would arrive for auditions in the morning and an independent judging panel would select the three best to go into the main body of the show. The winner from each location would then appear in the Blackpool final. To make the performance feel like a "seaside" special we had a dance troupe who were professionally choreographed by Toni-Marie. "Miss Toni" devised world-class routines set to Elvis recordings and the girls practiced for a hundred hours at the renowned Vivienne Shelley Theatre School in Cheadle. All our hoofers - Rose, Katie, Jess, Sinitta and Chelsea, although only in their late teens, were highly proficient including the cheeky "kid" Sally Molloy who added humour to the routines. We had our own roadie Mick who drove the mini-bus and Miss Toni's mum, Janet, who provided the "sarnies", sausage rolls, pop and most importantly the Pom-Bears.

The marketing across all local media outlets had to work, as we factored in no advertising budget. The strength of Elvis, the competition and the ultimate prize of appearing in Memphis was more than sufficient. Regional television covered the daytime auditions using vox pops from the local ETA wannabees. Come the evening of each show we were sold out for every performance. The counting of the votes to select the local winner was never without controversy, occasionally resulting in a recount, and the local rivalry certainly added to the entertainment mix.

The Final attracted a variety of celebrities who acted as judges. Robin Duke, the entertainments editor of the Blackpool Gazette, ensured pre-event publicity. Other judges included Tony Prince, Mike Read, Darren Day and Rolf Harris. Rolf had at that time just painted a portrait of Elvis Presley and appeared on stage with a didgeridoo, together with a big guy known only by the name The Bear (also a 'doo blower). Including those in the Winter Gardens the total audience for our tour was over 35,000, a record for 15 one-nighter provincial theatre gigs.

Simon Patrick was our winner and he came with us to Memphis in August 2007. The same year EPE announced their inaugural event in which they were looking for the "best representation of the legacy of Elvis Presley." Simon was entered straight into their contest. Twenty-four of the best ETAs from around the world travelled to Memphis during Elvis Week 2007, with Shawn Klush of Pennsylvania winning the first "Ultimate" title.

In response to the excitement generated by the 2007 contest, Elvis Presley Enterprises has brought the contest back every year since. Brandon Bennett from Louisiana won the ultimate title during Elvis Week 2008, Bill Cherry from Illinois won in 2009, Justin Shandor from Michigan won in 2010, Cody Slaughter of Arkansas took home the 2011 title (no kin of mine), Ben Portsmouth from England was crowned the 2012 winner, Dean Z of Missouri took home the 2013 title, Louisiana native Jay Dupuis was the 2014 champion, David Lee of Alabama was EPE's 2015 winner, and in 2016, Dwight Icenhower from Florida took home the title. Gordon Hendricks from England won the contest in 2017, and Ben Thompson, also from England, won the 2018 contest. Taylor Rodriguez of Virginia won the 2019 contest. Due to the Covid-19 there was no 2020 competition as regional heats were cancelled due to the global virus, and live entertainment was banned in Memphis.

The 30th anniversary of Elvis' death in 2007 was a major event in the Elvis calendar. One thousand British Fan Club members travelled to Memphis. The Elvis Presley Fan Club Travel Service planned a tour that started in Atlanta, journeyed to Chattanooga, to Dollywood and Gatlinburg in the Great Smokey Mountains. Then on to Nashville via Knoxville, the Tennessee State Capital. After the delights of the country music capital we dropped down into Tupelo, Mississippi for a civic reception, then back into Tennessee and Memphis basing ourselves once again in the Peabody. Our "staff" had to get to each stopover in advance of the main group of 20 buses so we all piled in a stretch minibus that I elected to drive.

Duncan, Vicky and Sal, my son Tom, Miss Toni and our producer, Jon Aldersea, were always on duty.

Being once again based at the Peabody our wonderful Tony Prince used the splendid ante-rooms in the hotel to capture celebrity interviews. He was filming a *Marrying Elvis* documentary for his new Sky TV station *Wedding Television*, produced by ITV's *It'll be Alright on the Night* Simon Withington, in between standing on his head and singing *What'd I Say* at every opportunity. He spoke to Priscilla in private about her wedding day and there were a few, not so young starlets in town eager for airtime to promote their books. One special outtake doing the rounds sees Tony asking Suzanna Leigh if Elvis had a big willy!

Over the years we have booked many famous acts and Elvis-related personalities to appear at our functions. For the most part, when it comes to interviewing celebrities, I have nominated those who are more proficient in public speaking to do the honours. In 1999 Red West attended our East Coast week-long autumn bash in Mablethorpe, but none of the crew volunteered to do the dirty work. I wouldn't have booked Red in a fit, as he was one of the most despised "Memphis Mafia" members. I was not fazed at the prospect of having to confront him, I just did the business. I was aware that when cornered he would suffer from verbal diarrhoea, wanting to defend himself against every criticism levelled at him for writing the book *Elvis, What Happened?* His catalogue of excuses meant neither "arsehole nor watercress" to me. I was convinced that the West Brothers would realise on their death beds that their writings accelerated Elvis Presley's death. I was pleased when he admitted that that he wrote the book for money. (To be honest I could not believe the outpouring of grief when the man who contributed to Elvis' distress and subsequent early death, himself died in 2017.) Celebrities that I deliberately positioned myself to interview included Sir Tim Rice, Lord Michael Grade, Tony Prince, Mark Wesley, Marty Wilde, Suzanna Leigh, Charlie Hodge, Annette Day, Guy Fletcher, Reginald Bosanquet, Ken Howard, Ray Dorset and John Leyton.

One of our most interesting live guests was John Leyton. Not only did he perform a fantastic rock 'n' roll show but he spoke about his amazing acting career. Born in 1936 in Frinton-on-Sea John Leyton went to Highgate School and after completing his national service he studied drama, paying his way through drama school with bit-part roles in films and on television. His first major acting role was his portrayal of Ginger in a 1960 Granada TV adaptation of *Biggles*, which earned him a large following of young female fans and led to the formation of a John Leyton fan club. Following the success of *Biggles* Leyton was persuaded by his manager, joint owner of *Pop Weekly*, Robert Stigwood, to audition as a singer for record producer Joe Meek, and subsequently recorded a cover version of *Tell Laura I Love Her*, which was released on the Top Rank label. In 1961 though, the Top Rank label was taken over by EMI who then issued Leyton's records on their HMV label. EMI had already released Ricky Valance's version of the same song and Leyton's recording was withdrawn from sale, whilst Valance's version reached number one in the UK chart.

A second single, *The Girl on the Floor Above*, was released on the HMV label, but was not a success. His first big hit, *Johnny Remember Me*, coincided with his appearance as an actor in the popular ATV television series *Harpers West One*, in which he played a singer named Johnny Saint Cyr. Leyton performed *Johnny Remember Me* during the show (backed by the Outlaws), and the single subsequently charted at Number One. His next single, *Wild Wind*, reached Number Two in the UK Singles Chart, and his later 45s also achieved lower chart positions. In that same year, John Leyton headlined a tour with up and coming support act the Rolling Stones. Very quickly, it became apparent that the Stones were more popular than the headline act and Leyton, with great dignity, abandoned his pop career on the spot to concentrate on acting.

He became a familiar face in film and television during the 1960s. He played himself in the 1962 Dick Lester film *It's Trad, Dad!*, performing his latest single *Lonely City* in a radio studio. In *The Great Escape* (1963) he played tunnel designer Willie Dickes, one of the only three characters who successfully make it to freedom. Leyton also cut a single with lyrics to Elmer Bernstein's theme to the film. He also appeared in *Guns at Batasi* in 1964; *Every Day's a Holiday* (aka Seaside Swingers in the United States) and *Von Ryan's Express* starring Frank Sinatra and Trevor Howard in 1965. In *Krakatoa, East of Java*, in 1969 he played the designer of a diving bell.

From 1966 to 1967, Leyton played the lead role as SOE Royal Navy Lieutenant Nicholas Gage, an expert in demolitions, in *Jericho*, an American TV series about espionage in the Second World War.

I interviewed John Leyton about the time he spent with Elvis at MGM filming *Spinout* produced by Emperor Rosko's father Joe Pasternak, when John was working on his American TV series *Jericho*. I also asked him how much he got paid every time *The Great Escape* and *Von Ryan's Express* is screened by the BBC. His answer, "Nothing, there were no residual fees in my contract. Frank Sinatra, Trevor Howard, Steve McQueen, Charles Bronson and Richard Attenborough got the big bucks."

Chapter 20 – They Tear Your Heart Out, Don't They?

In March 2011 my pet miniature dachshund, Harvey, died. I went to Oslo in 1998 with my daughter Jennifer and son Tom to see Pal Granlund. His Alsatian dog, Lady, had died the previous year and now he had a new Lady, a large sausage dog. In Norway they are called "Pipe dogs". She was a cutie and when we got back, for two years my kids kept repeating, "We want a dog", "We want a dog", "We want a dog." Eventually Juliet and I surrendered to their demands and into our home came Harvey – and he was "double cute". I will say now that these attractive creatures are bred to be cute, yet they are prone to health problems. I've yet to come across an owner whose dachshund has never suffered with back issues. Harvey had two back ops each costing in excess of £2,000. I guess these days such operations would cost £4K. Obviously you can buy pet insurance though you pay the first 20%. In the end my little man died of cancer of the spine. When I moved to Uttoxeter he became the office dog. Mini dachs are vicious little buggers, and Harvey was no exception having bitten the delivery men from Parcel Force, DHL, FedEx, Wells Fargo, UPS, DVS and Royal Mail. We walked miles with Duncan's border collies, Bess and Buster. Harvey went camping all over Scotland. One irate camper said that little Harvey had cocked his leg and pee'd all over his tent. If Harvey tried to cock his leg up he would fall over. Dachs squat when they have a whiz. It would be two years before I would let another dog into my life because when they get their wings they tear your heart out.

Throughout the 1960s one of the most popular shows on Radio Luxembourg was *Battle of the Giants* where two acts competed against each other each week. It could be Brenda Lee against Dusty Springfield, the Beatles vs The Stones or Cliff up against Elvis. At the end of each series, there would be a winning girl, a winning guy and a winning group. Elvis would always win the male section and his Battle of the Giants award was presented to him on stage in Las Vegas during his December season in 1976. I thought the idea would make a great proactive musical with the audience voting for their favourite. For nine months we rehearsed with a 15-strong cast of singers who could also dance, and musicians. Our back screen showed films of DJs, radio stations both on land and at sea, adverts of the time, vox pops with the Beatles, Stones, Cliff and others and several links from Jimmy Savile. The pre-launch played to a full house at Staffordshire Gatehouse, attracting last minute sales following the death of Sir Jimmy Savile OBE KCSG five days before the show. The London premiere took place at the Shaw Theatre on 3rd November and Sony released a soundtrack CD of original artists to coincide with the 2011 tour.

When our cast was about to reconvene the following year for our theatre tour, it had to be canned as no one would wish to listen to an evil man's narration on the big screen behind our cast and crew. Everyone was shocked by the revelations that Jimmy Savile's £40 million fundraising had turned out to be camouflage to cover up his perversions. Dubbed as "the world's most prolific paedophile" the name Jimmy Savile was soon to be erased from everyone's memories of the swinging 60s. I recall the words of the pretty studio assistant at the BBC when we tethered Savile by his ankles and hoisted him upside down by a rope draped over the rafters. I tugged the other end of the rope, assisted by the young BBC trainee, as he did his piece to camera announcing the acts due to appear on the following week's Top of the Pops, and she whispered in my ear, "We've made a mistake Todd, this rope should be 'round his f***ing neck!!"

For many years I went camping in Scotland with Vicky, Duncan and Sally, plus our collection of pooches. Ten years ago Duncan and I made many sorties into the Irish Republic, tracing the activities of the rebel fighters, drinking the local brew and listening to the fiddly-diddly music in and around the Dingle Peninsula overlooking the wild Atlantic coast. There are 40 million members of the Irish diaspora living in the northeast portion of the United States, whereas there are just a little over 4 million Irish living in the Republic. For most of the year hotels, bars and cafes in Dublin, Dingle, Galway, Cork and Killarney are heaving with Americans retracing their Irish roots.

One of Killarney's most famous sons was Hugh O'Flaherty and that city pays due reverence to one of its own. Monsignor O'Flaherty lived in Italy during the darkest years of World War II, during which time he held a secretarial position in the Vatican. But he was no airy dilettante prepared to wait indifferently for one side to finally hammer the other. As the everyday reality of Nazi atrocities became irrefutable O'Flaherty used his status as a priest and the safety of the Vatican to rescue over 4,000 Allied prisoners of war and an untold number of Jews and other refugees from the hands of the fanatical Gestapo. His was deeply hazardous, requiring frequent trips out of the Vatican to secure food and shelter. Disguised as a beggar, a postman, a nun and once even as a Nazi, the daring Monsignor operated an effective escape route for refugees without the knowledge or permission of his church superiors and in the face of constant death threats.

Very quickly the chief of SS forces in Rome, Colonel Herbert Kappler, gave top priority to killing every member of O'Flaherty's network, but they could not capture the man that author Ian Fleming called the Vatican Pimpernel. When the Allies entered Rome in June 1944, more than 3,900 refugees rescued by O'Flaherty were still alive thanks to his efforts. The story of the Monsignor is immortalised in the film *The Scarlet and The Black* with Gregory Peck playing the good priest and Christopher Plummer the bad colonel. I felt an affinity to Killarney as I had heard that my birth mother was a 14 year old County Kerry girl who had worked in servitude in Leicestershire during WWII. That urban myth turned out not to be the case.

Since 1965 the Official Elvis Presley Fan Club of Great Britain had been operating exclusive affinity group travel opportunities for our membership. Initially these enabled us Brits to meet with our European friends and affiliated official fan clubs. In 1972 we started to take fans to see Elvis in concert and, after Elvis died, our tours became more of a pilgrimage to experience the sights, sounds and various cultures in the different parts of the USA where Elvis lived and worked. Our occasional trips to Spain, France,

Germany, Luxembourg, Belgium and Holland continued to operate.

The revenue that we received as commission covered the cost of sending out brochures, marketing our holidays, postage, printing and advertising. This additional income assisted the Fan Club in expanding our social media activities, radio production, publishing and promotion. In 2010 our relationship with our former tour operator soured due to a variety of issues, so much so that I found our arrangements had become untenable.

We operated two remarkably successful out of season trips to Memphis with Co-op Travel before engaging with Kelvin Ford's Yesterday Once More, this country's largest and most successful operator of music-themed holidays, weekends and concerts.

Not long after my little sausage dog died I had another house guest. I had moved from Uttoxeter to the village of Tean and, always being skint, I decided to advertise for a lodger. Zach moved in, complete with a sound system that would clear wax out of your ears. He became a good friend and somewhat of an entrepreneur, opening one of the first vape shops in the county.

In 2013 another creature entered my life. From the local dog pound I picked up Jack, a demure timid border terrier cross. Timid, that is, until he found his feet, then he became a "terror terrier" wanting to attack every dog apart from the ones he got to know. He hasn't mellowed with age. When my lodger Zach appeared with girlfriend Cassie she was joined at the hip to a lovable but sturdy Staffie. Jack had met his match as Rocky retaliated. Apart from a couple of stitches there were no broken bones, and now when together they are “polite” to each other.

Tom, who had relocated to Bournemouth, also brought a dog into his life. A stunning liver-coloured “working” Cocker Spaniel called Chino, as in cappuccino, though more often than not now known as “cheese-beans”. An accident at work meant that Tom for almost a year could no longer take care of Chino so she came to live with me and Jack.

My eldest son, Greg, met a girl called Joanne who was travelling with her mum, Gladys, on one of our Memphis trips. After the holiday Greg and Joanne met again and their romance started to flourish. In 2012 they married in Joanne’s hometown of Oldham, and they have lived together since in Lytham St Annes close to my son’s work place. Dadly, Zulu, Joanne’s beautiful Blue Merle dog passed away a year ago.

When Greg was young and living with his mum Vikki, his brother Geoff was being bullied at school, and was held under the water on one occasion during a swimming lesson. When the headmaster refused to take any action against the bully, Vikki waited for the brat in question to be reunited with his mum at the school gate. An altercation took place between the two mums and Vikki was carted off to the cop-shop. She was about to be cautioned when a stray Pekingese was handed in to the desk sergeant who had no idea what to do. Vikki stepped in and offered to foster the mutt. Relieved not to have the responsibility of a pooch patrol the caution was dismissed and Mr Ying-Yang had a new home. A house is not a home without a dog.

When Vicky and Duncan’s dog Bess died their other border collie Buster was on her own. Most nights

Duncan and I would walk Jack, Buster and Chino in the fields, planning our next adventure to the Emerald Isle, while trying to avoid the cowpat traps farmers would set to discourage dog walkers. I often slipped into the shitty slurry ending up stinking like a badger's arse.

The following year my son Geoff married his fiancée Paula and they live in Hampshire. In August 2014, my granddaughter Sophie was born. Geoff decided it was time to increase his life insurance.

Chapter 21 – Somewhere In Belgium

Somewhere in Belgium we landed one day,
We saw Ostend and Aalst, and right here we had to stay,
It isn't a village, it isn't a town,
It's just a gun-site where we settled down.
It's just a gun-site with gunners and guns,
And Number 10 and 584 all help to fool the Hun,
But we never grumble, just say it's a pest,
When doodle bugs pass us, and "Jim" gives us rest.
And we curse when our sergeant says "water",
For we know what that means from the start,
Then we fill all the cans in our quarters,
And then we empty the water cart.
Somewhere in Belgium we are thinking of you,
And there by candlelight we try to write a line or two,
And then when we're manning our thoughts ever stray,
Over the water, down old Blighty way

Betty Doreen Gitsham 1944

Geoff filled in a form to increase the parameters of his life insurance cover. He declared that his dad had had a heart transplant. In a heartbeat, literally, he was no longer insured. Geoff's insurers said that he would remain uninsurable until they had seen my parents' medical records. Ada and John were my mum and dad and I had no interest in spending money with the Mormons who own *Ancestry.com* - a privately held online company based in Lehi, Utah with links to the Church of the Latter Day Saints.

The largest for-profit genealogy company in the world operates a network of genealogical, historical records, and related genetic genealogy websites. As of

November 2018, the company claimed to provide access to approximately 10 billion historical records, to have 3 million paying subscribers, and to have sold 14 million DNA kits to customers. In 2019 Ancestry.com received the German *Big Brother Award*, a negative recognition "for exploiting an interest in genealogy to entice people into submitting saliva samples" - in other words to pile up a treasure trove of genome data for commercial research, because that is their actual business model.

I had understood that my birth mother was a 14 year old Irish girl and my biological father was a GI. Rubbing my hands with glee, I thought that this would enable me to get my hands upon an Irish passport, if not a “green card”.

A couple of emails to my local authority, a meeting with a councillor and I am informed that my birth mother was Betty Doreen Gitsham of Totnes in Devon. I was born in a “waifs and strays” home in Southport so I am not Irish, I am almost a “scouser”.

The heart-wrenching part of this procedure was not finding the details of my biological parentage but reading the court applications for my adoption by my mum and dad. “A non-parlour type of house, clean and comfortable. Male applicant is a bricklayer on £6 a week, rent and rates 15/1d – owner tenants. Infant has been in custody of applicants for 6 months.”

That was the easy part, tracing my birth family was a little more difficult, in which I was assisted by the good offices of Andrew Woolliscroft, Vicky Molloy’s brother.

Betty had moved from Southport to Loughborough to be close to a friend, and my mum and dad went on the bus from Leicester to Loughborough to collect me. That must have been a mixture of emotions for all concerned.

Learning that Betty, who had died in 1995, had married a hairdresser, I traced their former home to the village of Wymeswold, not far from where my good friends, George & Goska Jaroszkiewicz, live. I went a knocking and was directed to the home of Ruth, a fully paid-up Elvis fan and next-door neighbour to Mr and Mrs Clarke. "Did they have any children?" I asked, curious to know if there might be any half-siblings. "No, not whilst they were living here", replied Ruth, "but there was a rumour." I revealed that I *was* that rumour. We then went to find another neighbour who was the font of all knowledge concerning the Clarke family. She wasn't talking and couldn't wait to close her front door ending a ten-word conversation.

My given name at birth was Brian William Gitsham. Betty married William Clarke. My adopted name at the time of my christening became Brian John Slaughter, John being my dad's name. Mind you Dad had two names - John George Slaughter and Jack Weeks which is still a mystery.

Ruth had an address for Betty's youngest sister so I went to meet my Auntie Sheila who now lives in Exeter, and since then I have been thrilled to meet my new family, who all assembled one afternoon to see the return of the "prodigal son." I visit Auntie Sheila as often as I can which for me is a heart-warming experience. Elsewhere in the county, almost at the same time as my "knocking", appeared a "prodigal daughter" born to another sister, who was also put up for adoption. US Soldiers were very athletic in 1945.

Betty, my birth mother, was in the women's army during the Second World War. Private Gitsham was based not far from Ostend and was listed as being an anti-aircraft gunner. True to rumour, my biological father was a GI in the US Army, so I was conceived in Belgium. He is not named on my birth certificate, possibly because it was protocol for the US military not to admit to having sired children whilst operating within a theatre of war. I am classed as "spoils of war" by the American government, or more commonly referred to in the UK as a "bastard".

As for my son's life insurance, not being able to supply details of G.I. Joe, they had to accept the letter supplied by my Papworth Hospital cardiologist.

Also, in 2014 our Fan Club held an event at Sachas Hotel in Manchester to commemorate the 60th anniversary of Elvis recording *That's All Right* at Sun Studios which attracted huge publicity. I recognized the area as the hotel was located just around the corner from Fountain Street, the location of the former nightclub "The Three Coins" that I had first visited some 40 years earlier. We wanted our "bash" to be special because the 50th anniversary was a total Elvis Presley Enterprises screw-up. They planned to have *That's All Right* played in Sun Studios and relayed by satellite around the world at precisely 12 noon on October 16th 2004. The powers that be had thought that every radio station would take the feed but none did! At the top of the hour on every radio station around the world it is time for the news. I could not believe that the media people within EPE couldn't work that out, but where the obvious is concerned they are more often inept. So, we put on our own big bash for the 60th anniversary attracting TV, radio, and an incredibly special guest, Annette Day, the English actress who co-starred with Elvis in *Double Trouble.*

We were back in Sachas two years later to celebrate the Diamond Jubilee of Elvis' first release with RCA, and we had one hell of a party with a special performance of the musical *Memphis Son,* written and presented by actor/singer Daniel Constantinou, with Dominic Halpin and The Honey Bees. Phil Shakespeare spun the records and Tony Prince performed *What'd I Say*. We enjoyed a great deal of media coverage and there was a plethora of paparazzi outside as television actress, Michelle Keegan, put in a surprise appearance. Everyone who was anyone from the Manchester scene was present. The no-show was RCA - the record label (Sony) that couldn't be bothered to attend the anniversary party they asked us to organise and which they wanted in *Manc Land* because the new "Media City" was based in Salford.

Having sold my house in Staffordshire, I relocated to Dorset to live with my son Tom, leaving Vicky, her daughter Sally, best friend Poppy and Henry Nicholls to take care of business. Our Cheadle office, opposite the Staffordshire Oatcake Shop, was in a dilapidated retail property. Leaky ceilings, leaky floors and mouldy walls – it was an allergy sufferer's nightmare. In its favour it was a "cock-stride" to Wetherspoons.

DEAR MR PRESIDENT

In April 2017 I wrote the following letter to President Trump

This year I have been President of the Official Elvis Presley Fan Club of Great Britain for 50 years! As a

Fan Club we have collectively achieved some remarkable successes, as well as empowering 100,000s of UK fans to visit Graceland and beyond, and 2017 being the 40th anniversary of Presley's death we will have the largest international affinity group in Memphis.

Sir Paul McCartney, Sir Mick Jagger, Sir Elton John, Sir Bob Geldof, Sir Rod Stewart, Sir Van Morrison, Sir Ray Davies, Sir Tim Rice, Sir Cliff Richard, Sir Tom Jones and dozens of other British entertainers possibly not known to you have all been influenced by the music of Elvis Presley, and have received Knighthoods by HM Queen Elizabeth II. Female singers such as Dame Vera Lynn, Dame Shirley Bassey and Dame Julie Andrews are awarded Damehoods and such awards are gifted for both their services to entertainment and charitable acts. (Politicians too receive awards, the most notable being Sir Winston Churchill, and it goes without saying that if you were a Brit, then at the end of your tenure you could possibly have been knighted and thereafter known as Sir Donald Trump).

As it is in your power to bestow awards to your fellow Americans, this year Elvis Presley should be top of your list. Elvis has sold more recordings than any other world-wide performer – over the past year in the UK alone he has sold almost two million albums, and his global outreach has delivered phenomenal benefits both commercial and cultural to your nation. Internationally he has been, and still is, your country's most famous American, and even in death his home is a major international tourist attraction, second only (we are told) to your White House.

What isn't generally appreciated is that more than any other entertainer Elvis Presley unknowingly encouraged young people across the world to learn the English language, as they painstakingly translated his song lyrics and his movie scripts.

Your country's National Medal of Arts wasn't established until 1983, six years after Elvis died, but I would humbly request that Elvis Presley posthumously receives an award this year. It would be an honour that would be celebrated by his fans not only in the USA, but around the world.

Most respectfully,
ELVIS PRESLEY FAN CLUB
Todd Slaughter

Jack Soden, the CEO of the Graceland division of Elvis Presley Enterprises Inc., agreed it was a valiant proposal but concluded that it was highly unlikely that it would be taken seriously by the White House. I had thought for a long time that Elvis Presley had not been acknowledged by his peers, by the entertainment industry, and by the USA government, for what he had achieved commercially and his generous philanthropy. To that end we empowered Elvis Fans both from our club and around the world to "petition" the President.

It will come as no surprise that Donald didn't drop me a line, but a White House aid responded by saying that their *National Medal of Arts* had been discontinued. No further explanation was added to the communiqué.

On 16th November 2019, the White House Press Office released the following statement. *"Singing legend Elvis Presley was among the seven recipients at US President Donald Trump's first Medal of Freedom ceremony since taking office. The award is the highest honour a sitting president can bestow on a civilian. The White House described Elvis as "an enduring American icon". Among the other six recipients honoured at the White House on Friday were baseball legend Babe Ruth and late Supreme Court Justice Antonin Scalia. NFL hall-of-famers Roger Staubach and Alan Page were the other sporting icons honoured at the ceremony.*

"America is blessed to have the most skill, passion and talent anywhere on Earth," Mr Trump said during his opening remarks. "We are truly a great nation and we are a nation that is doing really, really well right now."

Jack Soden was the designated recipient of Elvis' medal. Fans were shocked that his daughter, Lisa Marie Presley, was conspicuous by her absence from the ceremony.

The Royal Ruler and The Railway DJ is a double autobiography from both sides of the Iron Curtain. This story describes the impact of Communism on the teenagers and musicians in Czechoslovakia, set against the remarkable career of Tony Prince, the DJ who rocked the boat, met Elvis Presley, sang with Paul McCartney and Ringo Starr, toured with the Osmonds and partied with Led Zeppelin. Tony became the only DJ to perform inside the Iron Curtain not long after the Russian invasion of Czechoslovakia which is where the authors first met. This is the story of the daddy of all radio stations and the DJs who entertained an estimated 100 million trans-European listeners every night. Whilst every kid across Europe listened to their transistor radios hidden beneath their pillows in fear of their parents, Jan Sestak listened in the knowledge that the Czechoslovak Secret Police who prowled his land would send him to prison if he were discovered. Their Gestapo predecessors imposed the death sentence on anyone caught listening to western radio stations. There were two incredible sides to the Radio Luxembourg listening experience. Tony's is the first book in the world to reveal what teenage life was like under Communism in the Eastern Bloc and what boundless fun it must have been for the men behind the microphone.

In the spring of 2017 I was invited to the Luxembourg Embassy in London along with a host of celebrities, many who had been former Radio Luxembourg stars, to honour those who had worked for 208 and to launch Tony Prince's joint autobiography. The juxtaposition of two life stories from both sides of the former Iron Curtain was a truly imaginative publication.

Before the presentation started, I was talking with the Queen's jockey Willie Carson, (Her Majesty has won 534 races from 3,205 runs as a racehorse owner and it is thought she has made £7.7million from her hobby during the last 31 years), and BBC News anchor Simon McCoy. Standing in front of us was a "little old lady", who turned around and grabbed my arm as Tony Prince very graciously mentioned me and how we met Elvis. "Oh gosh I must talk to you Todd about Elvis," said the lovely Petula Clark. Willie button-holed Ambassador Engelberg to talk about Prince Phillip whilst Simon plied I Petula with wine as she told us of her meeting, accompanied by Karen Carpenter, with Elvis in his Hilton suite.

After the reception we all piled into the Hard Rock Café as my daughter Jenny joined us, accompanied by three old guys she had met in a local pub who turned out to be the surviving members of the 70s pop group Jigsaw. I had a pint with former Radio 1 DJ Andy Peebles who remarked that we both had something in common. He being the last person to interview John Lennon before he was murdered, and me being the last person to be filmed with Elvis before he died. "Sadly, Todd, we both made history."

Another former Radio Luxembourg DJ, Mark Wesley, has published a trilogy of thrillers featuring the adventures of his fictional character hero James Stack. *Bangk!, Frack!* and *Dead City Exit* are all first rate novels, and big Amazon-selling titles.

The 40th anniversary of Elvis' death attracted a group of over 300 Fan Club members to Memphis to take part in the annual August commemorations. I had earlier contacted our broadcasting friends at Good Morning Britain to see if they might be interested in covering our activities at Graceland. I hadn't heard anything and, because of my medical history, insurers were asking £10,000 to cover my travel insurance. Even £1,000 would have been more than I could have afforded so I chose not to travel. Soon after our group arrived in Memphis, I took a call from Good Morning Britain's entertainment editor, Richard Arnold, inviting me to dinner – dinner at the Peabody on Union Avenue. Our tour operator, Kelvin Ford of Yesterday Once More, arranged for tour escort and former Fan Club branch leader, Linda Haycox, to do the necessary interviews. We had five Fan Club satellite feeds to the UK on GMB from Memphis – more than any other network, anywhere in the world.

In 2018 we decided to leave our dilapidated office premises and move into a new complex on the High Street in Cheadle. Just prior to taking on a new lease I was rushed into the Royal Staffordshire with what felt like an exploding gall-bladder which, after ten days of hospitalisation, was removed.

The remodelling of our new premises was completed in 2019. Sally Molloy and Poppy Beresford, who were employed part time by the Fan Club, were attacking the "northern soul" market and, with our producer, Jon Aldersea, recorded two of his compositions under the performing brand of "Passion and the Veins." I arranged with Radio Caroline to take the girls out to the Ross Revenge at anchor in the Blackwater estuary to film a music video on the decks of the radio ship, to promote the track coinciding with the release of a collector's edition of a vinyl 45. Storm Deirdre was "blowing up a hoolie" which meant that we didn't have to hire a wind machine.

Studio Cheadle, with a recording and broadcasting façade, was opened in the New Year with plans to retail vintage clothing, music, instruments and produce radio material under the direction of Henry Nicholls, with Vicky and the girls managing the Fan Club from the back office. Following a short illness Vicky sadly died on 20th February 2019. With the trauma of her passing and no staff, the Fan Club entered a chaotic period. It was salvaged by Henry who was dealing with not only the grief over the loss of a good friend, but the subsequent understandable absences of her daughter

Sally and best mate Poppy. Both he and I were working 50 hours a week to keep our ship afloat, whilst at the same time mourning the loss of Vicky. Our accounting manager, Glenda Pickering, operating from her home in Derbyshire, had the unenviable task of sorting out the new tax and VAT protocols whilst consecutively having to work through a muddle of documentation and invoices. And then for four months our office had to close due to the Coronavirus pandemic.

Chapter 22 – What Now, What Next, Where To?

Up to half a million Elvis fans visit our social media sites every month. My Radio Caroline Flashback Elvis Hour (8.00pm every Thursday) has doubled its audience. The network management has prioritised their oldies legacy station which is now a standalone service available on line, on digital radio and on your smart speaker. With the soon to be launched fan club ETV YouTube Channel and our website output, we are taking advantage of all the latest technologies. And don't forget that we have our six-times-a-year mailing of the Fan Club members' magazine which is seen by, we estimate, 10,000 readers.

Over the years the Official Elvis Presley Fan Club of Great Britain has achieved more successes than any other affinity support group. During his lifetime we were able to sustain interest for Elvis in a variety of ways, including visits by fans to see him in concert. Our associations with other Elvis clubs across Europe have been successful especially with joint events and projects. Our relationship with Colonel Parker has been unique. Since 1977 our activities have attracted global publicity and our engagement with Elvis Presley Enterprises has enabled their overseas concerts and exhibitions to be viable.

For our fan base there has always been amazing opportunities to attend conventions, members' holidays, concerts and overseas adventures to countries all over Europe, and cities across the USA.

Our future is in the hands of our membership. We receive no financial support from the Presley Estate,

Sony Music or any other businesses that profit from the free publicity that they receive from us. We thank you, and I thank you, for your continued support. Our only source of revenue, to enable us to operate, comes from magazine subscription fees and the sale of Elvis memorabilia. For a free sample magazine write to:

EPFC, PO Box 3456, Cheadle, ST10 9BG
or to subscribe online go to:
www.elvispresleyfanclub.com

MEMORIES

On re-reading this manuscript I see that I have fallen into the trap which "I can't get out of" by name-dropping every single celebrity that I have ever met, but it had to be done. No one ever wanted to meet me because of me, it was because everyone wanted to talk to me about Elvis Presley. It has also helped that I have an unforgettable daft name. I cite a BBC interview between comedian Frank Skinner and Jonathan Ross when Frank said, "I was talking to Todd Slaughter the other day," and Ross' interruption was, "Oh Todd Slaughter – he's the guy that runs the Elvis Presley Fan Club doesn't he?" My silly name immediately leads to a conversation about Elvis and not me. For many years I have been asked to write a book and, although Elvis has consumed my life, this book of words *is* about my life with Elvis dominant throughout – Elvis has been my life.

With a bit of luck, I might live twice as long as Elvis thanks to clever chemistry. The sense of community between Elvis fans and our preservation of his legacy has been exemplary. It saddens me that he didn't live long enough to realise just how much he impacted on our lives, and how his talent influenced his contemporaries.

The success of any star can be measured by the strength and loyalty of their fan club. I believe that Sir Cliff Richard wouldn't have emotionally survived being violated by both the BBC and the Yorkshire Police had it not been for the love and the unquestionable devotion of his wonderful fan base. Cliff brings so much pleasure and joy to his fans that he earns and deserved their support. Although Elvis is only with us now in spirit, his memory and wonderful music will merit our homage forever.

Memories, pressed between the pages of my mind
Memories, sweetened through the ages just like wine
Quiet thought come floating down
And settle softly to the ground
Like golden autumn leaves around my feet
I touched them and they burst apart with sweet memories
Sweet memories

My earliest memories – my mum and dad giving me my teddy bear for Christmas when I was three. Meeting Santa in the Co-op. My first bottle of Coca Cola. Having a packet of cheese crisps. Seeing elephants walk past our house advertising the forthcoming circus. Being told off for eating a whole bar of Ex-Lax thinking it was chocolate. A sip of Port from a cut-glass decanter set – the most valuable thing in our home. Playing with a plastic pair of giraffe-shaped scissors. Owning a tortoise. Being frightened of our budgerigar. Waiting for my dad to come home from work with a bag of sweeties. And the treat of the week – Desperate Dan Pie – pork bones baked in an oven dish covered with a shortcrust pastry lid.

THE FAN CLUB:

www.elvispresleyfanclub.co.uk

Elvis Presley Fan Club, PO Box 3456, Cheadle, Staffordshire, ST10 9BG

FAN CLUB STAFF

Past, present and volunteers : Henry Nicholls, Alice Nicholls, Sam Jones, Glenda Pickering, Lynne Kirk, Jon Aldersea, Ray Hall, Vicky Molloy (dec.), Sally Molloy, Poppy Beresford, Barbara Pendle, Anne E Nixon, Mick Haywood (dec.), Julie Fecitt, Bob Bacon (dec.), Sharon Player, Sharon Daly, Andy Bacon, Ian Bailye, John Huckle (dec.), Anne Knight (dec.), Terry Mailey (dec.), Alan Armes, Gary Barfield, Lorraine Cobb, Tracy Williams, Julie Yeardye, Lizzie Newbrooks (dec.), Jack Newbrooks (dec.), Bob Buffton (dec), Tony Atkinson (dec.), Peter Keegan (dec.), Albert Hand (dec.) and Jean "the Punk". All our local Brand Leaders, together with our DJs Neil Williams and Andy Cordwell (the Nutty Brothers).

MEMORABLES:

Graham Drew, Peter Wilson, Penny Sayer, Tom Lodge, Dave Kaye, Michael Pasternak, Lew Grade, Kenny Everett, Kid Jensen, Earl Richmond, Peter Powell, Ted Beston, Alan Freeman, David Jones, Jill Sadler, David Hamilton, Bill Cotton, Tommy Vance, Paul Rusted, Rose Knox Peebles, Mike Read, Alvin Stardust, Teresa Currie, Albert Hand, Paul Burnett, Paul Sayers, Bill Kenwright, John Kavanagh, Zach Brownhill, Cassie Day, Keith Harris, Les Gray, Frank Worthington, Sten Berglind, John Peel, Hubert Vindevogel, Paul Kaye, Peter Haan, Mario Kombou, Marty Wilde, Ernst Jorgensen, Tom Diskin, Cathy McGowan, Roger Semon, Kim Wilde, Johnny Moran, Freddy Bienstock, Charlie Hodge, Vicky Duncan and Sally Molloy, Joy Shelley, Kelvin Ford, Chris Bowdidge, Sally Heckman, Glenda and Roy Pickering, Lynne Kirk, Henry Nicholls, Jon Aldersea, Sam Jones, Bob and Andy Bacon, Ron Coles, Lorraine Cobb, Shirley Hawkes, Ray Dorset, Alan Trower, Peter Keegan, Tony Atkinson, Dave Kaye, Garry J Foley, Sir Tim Rice, Henrik Knudsen, Barbara Windsor, Dr Susan Ford, Trevor Cajiao, Bernard Roughton, Annette Day, Roger Felice, Guy Fletcher, Dave Fawkes, Pal Granlund, Simon Gray, Ray Hall, Glen D Hardin, Dr Jayan Parameshwar, Jef Hanlon, Richard Arnold, Ernst Jorgensen, George and Goska Jaroszkiewicz, Lex Raaphorst, Anne E Nixon, Alison Quinn, Colonel and Loanne Parker, Colin Paul, Shirley Hawkes Les Reed, Bernard Roughton, Dave Richards, Phil Shakespeare, Janet Wade, Pat Ian and Scott Bailye, and Mark Wesley for his encouraging support!

SPECIAL PEOPLE

Tony and Christine Prince have been dear friends to me and my family for a lifetime. Tony Prince now operates the UK's most innovative radio network - *United DJs Radio* - featuring iconic DJs from all genres of popular music.

There are not enough words of thanks for Joanne, Mike, Josh, Alice and the late Jean for helping me and my son Tom feel at home in Dorset for more than ten years - and a special mention for everyone at the "Bungalhouse" who takes care of Alice.

And finally, I am only able to write this now because of the 26 year old man who agreed to donate his organs for transplantation should he die. I am forever in his debt and appreciative of the thoughtful generosity of his family who agreed to the procedure at a most difficult time.

Royalties from the sale of this book will be donated to the Royal Papworth Hospital Charity.

Printed in Poland
by Amazon Fulfillment
Poland Sp. z o.o., Wrocław

63698142R00157